PICTURE IMPERFECT

Also by Russell Jacoby

PICTURE IMPERFECT

*Utopian Thought
for an Anti-Utopian Age*

Russell Jacoby

COLUMBIA UNIVERSITY PRESS

NEW YORK

Columbia University Press
Publishers Since 1893
New York   Chichester, West Sussex

Copyright © 2005 Columbia University Press
All rights reserved

Library of Congress Cataloging-in-Publication Data
Jacoby, Russell.
   Picture imperfect : Utopian thought for an anti-utopian age / Russell Jacoby.
      p. cm.
   Includes bibliographical references and index.
      ISBN 0–231–12894–0 (cloth : alk. paper)
   1. Utopias. 2. Dystopias. 3. Utopias—Religious aspects.   I. Title.
   HX806.J33   2005
   335'.01—dc22   2004043145

Printed in the United States of America
c 10 9 8 7 6 5 4 3 2 1

For Cristina

Contents

Preface

"OUR MOST IMPORTANT TASK AT THE PRESENT MOMENT IS to build castles in the sky," wrote Lewis Mumford in his 1922 *Story of Utopias*. Four decades later he wondered how, in the wake of World War I, he could have expressed such upbeat sentiments. "I was still living in the hopeful spirit of an earlier age," Mumford explained. He had been writing under the "impetus of the great nineteenth century, with its fund of buoyant idealism and robust social enterprise."[1]

Today only the historically obtuse can believe that to build castles in the sky is urgent. Buoyant idealism has long disappeared. In an age of permanent emergencies, more than ever we have become narrow utilitarians dedicated to fixing, not reinventing, the here and now. Yet the case can be made for writing against the grain of history, for writing under the impetus not of this but of a different period. In an era of intellectual triage, I attend the utopian esprit of another day.

Yet no one can jump over his or her historical shadow. Any study of the utopian spirit must engage its current status. Today most observers judge utopians or their sympathizers as foolhardy dreamers at best and murderous totalitarians at worst. The latter, not the former, charge concerns me. It relies on a reading of the historical record—indeed on a reading of the great "anti-utopian" novels such as *1984*—that is profoundly amiss. It relies on distending the category "utopian" to include any idea for a future society no matter how vicious or exclusionary. Every twentieth-century dictator from Hitler to Pol Pot and every twenty-first-century terrorist gets labeled a utopian. A recent exhibition of utopias in New York and Paris included photographs of an Israeli kibbutz and a Nazi concentration camp, as if each represented a viable utopia.

The utopian tradition may be diffuse, but here it vanishes into nothing and everything. Inasmuch as history saturates utopian thought, no single definition can fix its essence. Nevertheless, over the millennia, certain commitments have marked it consistently. From Greek and Roman ideas of a "golden age" to nineteenth-century fantasies of magical kingdoms, notions of peace, ease, and plenty characterize utopia; often they are linked to universal brotherhood and communal work. In Ovid's "age of gold" the "living creatures trusted one another." Cities did not stand behind "high walls and bridges." Nor did the sound of "clanging swords" break the peace; the earth gave forth "riches as fruit hangs from the tree."[2] Jump forward a few millennia to modern utopian fiction and one finds kindred ideas. In the 1910 *Emerald City*, L. Frank Baum describes the Land of Oz as a place that does not know disease or poverty and where even death was rare: people died only by unfortunate accidents. "There was no poor people . . . because there was no such thing as money. . . . Each person was given freely by his neighbors whatever he required for his use. . . . Every one worked half the time and played half the time." The inhabitants of Oz were "peaceful, kind-hearted, loving and merry."[3]

I contest the notion that Nazi ideologues belong in this company. The Nazi preoccupation with racial purity, war, and nation shares nothing with classical utopian motifs. In his 1930 *Myth of the Twentieth Century*, a founding text of the Nazi Reich, Alfred Rosenberg may dream of a "new human type" and a "new view of life," but Aryan purity and the German fist define this future.

"A people can still pull itself up out of political servitude," he writes, "but never again from racial pollution." For Rosenberg, "black or Jewish bastards" were flooding Germany. They had to be eliminated. "Just when an awakening Germany will reach the stage of carrying out a merciless cleansing with an iron broom and with ruthless discipline is uncertain. But, if anywhere, then in the preaching of remaining pure in race lies the holiest and greatest task."[4] Even before the Nazis seized power, their ideologues came closer to calling for genocide than for utopian peace and brotherhood.

Nor can the more recent spate of global terrorism, often attributed to religious fanatics, be chalked up to utopians. "Like communism," a defense department official informs us, radical Islam "promises a utopia."[5] But what sort of utopia do radical Islamists seek, and what means do they use? Charles Fourier, the great nineteenth-century French utopian, imagined a world of erotic and gustatory pleasure in which even the most modest individuals would enjoy a vast variety of lovers and delicacies. To realize his ideas Fourier wrote books, badgered prospective supporters, and, on one occasion, backed efforts to buy land for a community outside of Paris. Sayyid Qutb, the twentieth-century Egyptian generally considered the intellectual font of the Muslim Brotherhood and radical Islam, would despise Fourier and everything he represented.[6]

Qutb rejects "paganism" in all its forms—liberalism, secularism, sexual openness, and, of course, Judaism. "Most evil theories which try to destroy all values and all that is sacred to mankind are advocated by Jews."[7] Qutb advocated a Jihad that sought "the establishment of Allah . . . and the rule of the divine Shariah [Islamic Law]."[8] While Fourier ridiculed the hypocrisy of the priests and philosophers who denounced (and generally practiced) adultery, and while he proposed to free women from "civilized" subjugation, Qutb specified "severe" punishments for adultery. "For married men and women," he writes in *Social*

Justice in Islam, fornication requires "stoning to death"; for the unmarried it requires "a hundred lashes," which is usually "fatal." Other infractions are treated in the same fashion. The punishment for theft "is fixed at the cutting off of a hand; for a second offense the other hand is cut off, for a third a foot, and then the other foot."[9] Where are the links to utopia?

To be sure, ideas about paradise, equality, and freedom also appear in the writings of radical Islamists like Qutb. Yet a few phrases, or even sentences and paragraphs, do not constitute a utopian vision. The issue is the larger spirit of radical Islam, and this is distant from classical utopias. "You know that paradise is already beautified [for you] and the beautiful angels are calling you after they put on their most beautiful dresses," wrote Mohammad Atta, the lead hijacker in the September 11 attack on the World Trade Center, in his final message to his compatriots. His next sentence instructs them that if they have the "honor" of slaughtering a passenger, they should do so in the name of their parents and proceed by slitting the throat as in the ritual sacrifice of an animal.[10] Compare this to More's Utopia, chronologically five centuries earlier and spiritually ten centuries later, where religious tolerance was practiced and violence detested. More's Utopia included sun worshipers and moon worshipers. "Everyone was free to practice what religion he liked, and try to convert other people to his own faith, provided he did it quietly and politely, by rational argument."

I have no desire to exonerate utopians from each and every crime. I do wish that the broad brush that paints all utopians as terrorists and all terrorists as utopians be exchanged for a more precise tool. It is, for the most part, nationalist, ethnic, and sectarian passions—not utopian ideas—that drive global violence. Where are the utopians in Rwanda, Sudan, Iraq, Northern Island, Sri Lanka, Palestine, and Israel? The struggles in these regions are about power, land, group identity, and religion. Yet "utopian" remains a convenient label for all those inflamed by ideas of nation, religion, and race.

I seek to outline the history of the modern anti-utopian animus. Ironically, anti-utopianism can be traced back to Thomas More, the originator of the term "utopia." With the emergence of Luther and the upheavals of the Reformation, the Catholic More turned against the movement he believed he had helped initiate. The utopian More becomes the anti-utopian More, the bane of so-called heretics. Leading twentieth-century intellectuals such as Karl Popper, Isaiah Berlin, and Hannah Arendt followed in More's footsteps inasmuch as they denounce a doctrine that once attracted them. First drawn to a vaguely utopian Marxism and then repelled by a palpably brutal Stalinism, these "liberal anti-utopians" advanced a critique of a larger totalitarian ideology. Totalitarianism became the catchall for utopianism as well as Marxism, Nazism, and nationalism. Today the liberal anti-utopians are almost universally honored; their ideas have become the conventional wisdom of our day. To the extent that their critique fits totalitarianism or Marxism or its deformations, I have no argument with them. To the extent that their critique blackens all of utopian thought, I object.

The demise of utopian speculation, of course, derives from more than the success of the liberal anti-utopians. In chapter 1, I offer a spectrum of reasons, including the dwindling force of the modern imagination. History affects not only elections and wars but the way we think and imagine. Is it possible that imagination—the source of utopian speculation—has lost its vigor? That a relentless barrage of prefabricated "images" from movies and advertising has shackled its linguistic and factual offspring, "imagination"? Has imagination become unimaginative—or rather practical and realistic? The topic is difficult to circumscribe and my concerns resist proof. I offer only suggestive evidence. I sometimes teach a course on utopianism. The students arrive on the verdant California campus in various colors and sizes but generally with the easy smile and open gaze of those to whom life has been good. I allot time for students to sketch out their own utopias. They come up with laudable ideas—universal health care with choice of doctors; free higher education; clean parks; ecological vehicles—but very little that is out of the ordinary. Their boldest dreams could be realized by a comprehensive welfare state.

To be sure, I hold no brief for building castles in the sky complete with specifications on the size of the sleeping quarters and the hours of meals. The day for those overplanned castles may be over. At least the day may be over when it seemed desirable to diagram the future down to its last door, window, and turret. Yet the spirit of those airy castles remains alive and precious—or so I hope. And herein lies the paradox of this anti-utopian utopian essay. I wish to save the spirit, but not the letter, of utopianism. I am drawing a distinction between two currents of utopian thought: the blue print tradition and the iconoclastic tradition. The blueprint utopians map out the future in inches and minutes. From the eating arrangements to the subjects of conversation the blueprinters—by far the largest group of utopians—gave precise instructions. To overcome age segregation in More's utopia, for example, old and young take seats in alternating groups of four. Supper begins with "a piece of improving literature read out loud. . . . Then the older people start discussing serious problems."

The details have sometimes been inspired. To demonstrate their contempt for precious metal, More's utopians used chamber pots of gold. The inhabitants also wore rustic clothes and failed to understand why they should esteem those with garments of splendid wool. "After all, those fine clothes were once worn by a sheep, and they never turned it into anything better than a sheep." Nevertheless, detailed information about the size, shape, diet, and fashions of the future incurs several risks.

Inevitably, history eclipses or ridicules the most daring plans; it makes them appear either too banal or too idiosyncratic. Worse, such plans often betray more a will for domination than for freedom; they prescribe how free men and women should act and live and talk, as though they could not figure this out for themselves.

I turn instead to the iconoclastic utopians, those who dreamt of a superior society but who declined to give its precise measurements. In the original sense and for the original reasons, they were iconoclasts; they were protesters and breakers of images. Explicitly or implicitly they observed the biblical prohibition on graven images of the deity. "Thou shalt not make unto thee any graven image. . . . Thou shalt not bow down thyself to them, nor serve them" (Exodus 20:4–5). This prohibition, of course, entailed no disrespect of God. On the contrary: it honored Him by refusing to circumscribe Him. In the same way that God could not be depicted for the Jews, the future could not be described for the iconoclastic utopians; it could only be approached through hints and parables. One could "hear" the future, but not see it. Ernst Bloch's 1918 *Spirit of Utopia*, the classic work in this genre, offers no concrete details about the future. He invokes a utopian spirit purely by his reflections on music, poetry, and literature. I survey the roots and contours of such iconoclastic utopianism—iconoclastic inasmuch as it eschews blueprints and utopian inasmuch as it evokes a future "bliss of the fully contented."[11]

The blueprint utopians have attracted the lion's share of attention—both scholarly and popular. They describe utopias in vivid colors; their proposals can be studied and embraced or rejected. From Thomas More to Edward Bellamy, their utopias took the form of stories in which travelers report of their adventures from an unknown future or land. They offered characters, events, and particulars. Bellamy's *Looking Backward*, a classic of blueprint utopianism, commences with a straightforward narrative. "I first saw the light in the city of Boston in the year 1857."

By contrast, the iconoclastic utopians offer little concrete to grab onto; they provide neither tales nor pictures of the morrow. Next to the blueprinters they appear almost as ineffable as they actually are. They vanish into the margins of utopianism. Bloch's *Spirit of Utopia* opens mysteriously. "I am. We are. That is enough. Now we have to begin." In regard to the future the iconoclasts were ascetic, but they were not ascetics. This point must be underlined inasmuch as iconoclasm sometimes suggests a severe and puritanical temper. If anything, it is a longing for luxe and sensuousness that defines the iconoclastic utopian, not a cold purity.

In an image-obsessed society such as our own, I suggest that the traditional blueprint utopianism may be exhausted and the iconoclastic utopianism indispensable. The iconoclastic utopians resist the modern seduction of images. Pictures and graphics are not new, of course, but their ubiquity is. A curtain of images surrounds us from morning till night and from childhood to old age. The word—both written and oral—seems to retreat in the wake of these images. "Everything," writes the theologian Jacques Ellul in his defense of modern iconoclasm, *The Humiliation of the Word*, "is subordinated to visualization, and nothing has meaning outside it." We are living in an "age of extreme visualization."[12]

Even in today's classroom, flashy volumes with eye-popping graphics have replaced wordy old textbooks dotted with gray photos. Multimedia extravaganzas with computer projections and elaborate visuals supplant the old-fashioned lecture. Indeed, "a picture is worth a thousand words," yet it was an advertising man in the 1920s who coined this phrase. He was selling the effectiveness of display advertising in trolleys to his own colleagues. "*Buttersweet is Good to Eat* is a very short phrase," ran his copy, "but it will sell more goods if presented, with an appetizing picture of the product, to many people morning, noon and night, every day in the year than a thousand word advertisement placed before the same number of people."[13] I will not dwell on what it means to live in an "age of extreme visualization." But I believe that in such an age the little noticed iconoclastic utopians are more important than ever.

My goal in this book is first, then, to identify the suspicion of utopia that reigns today and to chart its history. I will consider how some of the most venerable intellectuals of our time, such as Isaiah Berlin, Karl Popper, and Hannah Arendt, shaped a modern anti-utopianism. I also want to separate out two traditions of utopianism—blueprint and iconoclast. I believe the iconoclastic utopians are essential to any effort to escape the spell of the quotidian. That effort is the sine qua non of serious thinking about the future—the prerequisite of *any* thinking. The iconoclastic utopians were both prescient in fathoming the danger of seductive imagery and archaic in abiding biblical injunctions. Like the Jews they mainly were, they did not name or depict God; neither did they inventory the future. I do not pretend that they constitute a compact group, yet from Gustav Landauer to Max Horkheimer, they shared a fundamental orientation. That is all—but that may be enough.

One example here: In 1960 the poet Paul Celan picked up in a Paris bookstore an essay collection on Judaism published in Prague in 1913. Kafka had owned a copy, and several of Kafka's friends such as Max Brod and Hugo Bergmann had contributed pieces. Celan apparently read only one essay with care, Bergmann's "The Sanctification of the Name."[14] Celan, who survived a Nazi labor camp and took his own life at age forty-nine, underlined this sentence from the Talmud: "Whosoever pronounces the Name, loses his share in the world to come."[15]

This sentence encapsulates an axiom of the iconoclastic utopians: their resistance to representing the future. They not only obeyed the taboo on graven images, they teetered on the edge of silence about what could be. If the future defied representation, however, it did not defy hope. The iconoclastic utopians were utopians against the current. They did not surrender to the drumbeat of everyday emergencies. Nor did they paint utopia in glowing colors. They kept their ears open for distant sounds of peace and joy, for a time when, as the prophet Isaiah said, "the lion shall eat straw like the ox" (Isaiah 11:7). We can learn from them.

Los Angeles, California

Acknowledgments

AS IN MY PREVIOUS BOOKS, I KEEP MY ACKNOWLEDGMENTS brief. Several colleagues in the UCLA history department have perused a number of chapters or have responded to my queries. I would like to thank David N. Myers, Gabriel Piterberg, and J. Arch Getty in particular and the participants of the European Colloquium in general for their comments and pointed disagreements. Both Teo Ruiz, chair of the history department, and Scott Waugh, dean of social sciences, have made it possible for me to teach, write, and keep a roof over my head: I am indebted to them. Paul Breines, as usual, gave parts of this book a superb reading. Peter Dimock and Plaegian Alexander, my editors at Columbia backed me and this book from its beginnings. Michael Haskell cooly and expertly piloted the manuscript past various shoals. I also want to pay homage to Paul Piccone, longtime editor of *Telos*, who died as I was completing this work. In his writings and arguments, indeed, in the very texture of his life, Paul incarnated the nonconformist intellectual willing to challenge all academic pieties. I should note that it was Paul (and *Telos*) who brought out in 1978 the first book in English of Gustav Landauer, who figures in my study here. Paul will be missed. Finally, I owe too much to Cristina Nehring, my love as well as a brilliant wordsmith, who brought to this book not only her flawless editorial ear but her passionate spirit and fierce intelligence.

PICTURE IMPERFECT

1. *An Anarchic Breeze*

EVERY GENERALIZATION IS FALSE. WE LIVE IN AN AGE of hope and transformation. We also live in age of resignation, routine, and perhaps alarm. We anticipate the world will get better; we fear it will get worse. We exist amid incredible riches and paralyzing poverty. We conduct our lives in peace and we are surrounded by violence. The wealthy in spacious suburbs worry about keeping their shiny SUVs scratch free. The poor in dusty byways dream of clean water, the refugees in endless civil wars of four walls and a roof. On the outskirts of Johannesburg, the wretched seize land with the idea that "with all the space here, you can make a toilet."[1] Today little can span these realities.

This may, however, speak to both worlds: for both the prosperous and the destitute utopian ideas are as dead as door nails. They are irrelevant for the affluent and immaterial for the hungry— and dangerous for many intellectuals, to boot. To the desperate, utopian ideas seem meaningless; to the successful, they lack urgency or import; to the thinking classes, they lead to a murderous totalitarianism. Yet something must be stated at the outset: the choice we have is not between reasonable proposals and a unreasonable utopianism. Utopian thinking does not undermine or discount real reforms. Indeed, it is almost the opposite: practical reforms depend on utopian dreaming—or at least utopian thinking drives incremental improvements.

Edward Bellamy's 1888 *Looking Backward* not only sketched a future society beyond selfishness and inequality but spurred political groups devoted to practical reform. His best-selling novel might be dismissed as airy speculation of a future America, but this would be misleading. It gave rise to a political association, the Nationalist Clubs, and it accelerated reforms as prosaic as the construction of good sewers. With Bellamy at their head calling for "evolution, not revolution," and "orderly and progressive development," the Nationalist Clubs pushed for reforms in voting, labor, and municipal services.[2] The Bellamyites supported the city of Chicago in extending publicly sponsored electrical service, for instance. Chicago demonstrated that elected municipal authorities could provide electricity "cheaper and better than by private corporations," proclaimed the Club newspaper. "In this 'practical' age men demand fact and not theory." In Chicago they were getting it. In Boston, they were receiving the contrary lesson of private electrical service that was expensive and dangerous.[3]

Nor is *Looking Backward* the exception. History is replete with utopias that spurred reforms and utopians who advanced concrete improvements. Consider the marquis de Condorcet, the eighteenth-century French utopian, who dreamt of "the true perfection of mankind" living in complete equality unsullied by "greed, fear or envy."[4] He also served as the veritable director of the Société des Amis des Noirs (Society of the Friends of Blacks), the first French organization devoted to the abolition of slavery.[5] Condorcet forcefully denounced the scandal of slavery, but far from demanding utopian measures, he proposed a series of moderate reforms leading to black emancipation. He feared the call for immediate freedom would stir too much opposition and checkmate any progress.[6] He authored a founding document of the society that detailed how the group would meet, its yearly costs of membership, and its cautious goals. "Since we intend to concentrate on useful work, we need to repel in advance anyone who attempts to sow suspicion by accusing us of having no fixed aims" or "by presenting us as a dangerous institution."[7]

Or take Enfantin, the nineteenth-century follower of the utopian St. Simon, who looked forward to a future Golden Age. Enfantin possessed more mystical goals than his mentor—and more practical ones. He wanted to link East and West, the female and male principles. He divined how to do this. In 1833 he traveled to Alexandria, Egypt, with a crew of engineers with the idea of building a canal to connect the two realms. It is easy to mock Enfantin's florid language and metaphysical goals, observes Zachary Karabell in his recent history of the Suez canal, but he shared an idiom and sense of destiny with many late-eighteenth-century visionaries, including founders of the United States. Enfantin worked on plans for the canal and assembled work crews to excavate it. After three years of intermittent progress, he quit Egypt, but not before he made his most "avid convert," Ferdinand de Lesseps, who successfully saw through the building of the Suez Canal. [8]

Down-to-earth reforms or feasible social changes coexist with utopianism and are often fed by it. At the beginning of modern utopianism Thomas More described an island community without money or private property. Yet the first section of his 1516 *Utopia* protested injustices of the day; he damned England for its endemic poverty, the theft it gave rise to, and the executions that ensued. Thieves were being hung "all over the place," sometimes "twenty on a single gallows." Why? Because they stole out of hunger. "In this respect you English," comments the reporter from Utopia,

> remind me of incompetent schoolmasters, who prefer caning their pupils to teaching them. Instead of inflicting these horrible punishments, it would be far more to the point to provide everyone with some means of livelihood,

so that nobody's under the frightful necessity of becoming first a thief and then a corpse."[9]

Was this utopianism—this call to provide citizens with "some means of livelihood"? Little sounds more reasonable.

Over a fifty-year period (1805–1855), almost a hundred utopian communities were founded in the United States. Their founders and members did not generally run from but rather toward society; they saw themselves creating and promoting viable models for how people could live better. This was the belief, for instance, of Victor Considerant, the French founder of a Texas community. How will old Europe gain from our community? he asked. He saw his association as "the nucleus of the new society" that will lead to "thousands of analogous organizations." "It is not the desertion of society that is proposed to you, but the solution of the great social problem on which depends the actual salvation of the world."[10]

Or listen to Nathaniel Hawthorne, who fictionalized his brief experience at one utopian community, Brook Farm. "We had left the rusty iron frame-work of society behind us; we have broken through many hindrances . . . we had stept down from the pulpit; we had flung aside the pen; we have shut up the ledger; we had thrown off that sweet, bewitching, enervating indolence." And for what? "It was our purpose—a generous one, certainly, and absurd . . . to give up whatever we had heretofore attained, for the sake of showing mankind the example of a life governed by other than the false and cruel principles on which human society has all along been based."[11]

To be sure, the intention of "showing mankind the example" rarely ended well. The history of utopian communities is largely a history of failure. John Humphrey Noyes, himself a founder of a utopian community (Oneida), marveled that these associations "started so gaily and failed so soon."[12] Yet it wrongs history to ignore failure, as if nothing positive or humane comes out of it. Conversely, victory can testify to the configuration of force or power, rather than to truth or validity. This may seem obvious, but it runs against deep-seated beliefs or prejudices. Success needs no defense; it is its own advertisement. However, the questions tabled by success may be decisive: Success succeeds, but for how long and at what cost? To study only the world's victors keeps thought locked to a narrow reality. Out of defeat emerges ideas, changed people, and new movements.

Even when they failed, utopian communities radically altered people and perceptions. In nineteenth-century America, Hawthorne was but one of the literary and political figures who took away lessons from utopian experiments. Frederick Law Olmsted, for instance, the landscape architect credited with New York's Central Park, visited a New Jersey Fourierist community, the North America Phalanx. He was struck by "the advantages of cooperation" in labor and culture. While he admitted that he was "not a Fourierist for myself," he came away with a belief in making "knowledge, intellectual and moral culture, and esthetic culture more easy—popular." He learned the force of "*democratizing* religion, refinement and information." In such an association, he believed, all people would "live more sensibly, be happier and better."[13]

Today, however, the utopian vision has flagged; it sparks little interest. At best, "utopian" is tossed around as a term of abuse; it suggests that someone is not simply unrealistic but prone to violence. I offer at least three reasons for the fate of utopian thought: the collapse of the communist states beginning in 1989; the widespread belief that nothing distinguishes utopians and totalitarians; and something more difficult to pinpoint, but essential: an incremental impoverishment of what might be called Western imagination.

I can add little to the story of the fall of communism. To many observers, Soviet Marxism and its knockoffs symbolized the utopian project. The failure of Soviet communism entailed the end of utopia. Who can challenge the verdict of history? Of course, over its lifetime Stalinism engendered generations of critics who protested the identification of the Soviet system with human emancipation. But when the Soviet ship went down, it also capsized, willy-nilly, the row boats of dissenters paddling in its wake. It seems unjust that the Victor Serges, Emma Goldmans, Gustav Reglers, and even Leon Trotskys, who fought against authoritarian communism—and suffered the consequences—should share its fate, as if no distinction could be drawn between the accuser and accused. When Soviet communism thrived it silenced critics by its putative success. When it failed, it silenced critics by disappearing. Those who resisted the spell of Soviet success have been unable to escape the pull of its collapse.[14]

This is unfair, but who says the judgment of history is fair? It consists not of an anonymous *Weltgeist* but of countless individuals—writers, scholars, politicians, and ordinary people. Today they more or less agree; utopian thinking is finished. The sixteenth century gave us a new term, "utopia," and the twentieth gave us "dystopia," or negative utopia, the universe of Huxley's *Brave New World* or Orwell's *1984*, where utopia has gone amuck. Perhaps this says it all. The movement from utopia to dystopia ratifies history.

The word "utopia," coined by Thomas More, breathed of possibility, spurred by the recent "discovery" of the New World. "I don't know, Madam," said the narrator in Fontenelle's eighteenth-century *Conversations on the Plurality of Worlds*, "if you grasp the surprise of these Americans" as they encountered the ship-borne explorers. "After that," what is not possible? "I'll bet . . . against all reason, that some day there might be communication between the Earth and the Moon." " 'Really,' said the Marquise, staring at me. 'You are mad.' "[15] This optimism and excitement found its way into utopian visions. Their willingness to learn, reported More's Raphael of the utopians, is the reason they are "so much ahead of us politically and economically."

This news warmed his convivial audience. "In that case, my dear Raphael, for goodness' sake tell us some more about the island in question." They break to dine and return in fine spirits to hear his tale.[16]

Almost five centuries later the world has grown weary. We have come and gone to the moon. In the mid-twentieth century, J. Max Patrick, a coeditor of an anthology of utopian writings, coined the term "dystopia" as the contrary of utopia.[17] He referred to a satirical utopia as the "opposite of *eutopia*, the ideal society: it is a *dystopia*, if it is possible to coin a word."[18] Without doubt, the twentieth-century dystopias look and smell very differently from classic utopias, even those created as recently as the end of the nineteenth century. "My first feeling," reported the voyager as he awakes in William Morris's 1890 utopian *News from Nowhere*, "was a delicious relief caused by the fresh air and pleasant breeze."[19] An opening sentence of Orwell's *1984* reads: "The hallway smelt of boiled cabbage and old rag mats."[20]

Yet a critical problem arises. Is dystopia the opposite of utopia—in the same way that slavery is the opposite of freedom or cold is the opposite of hot—or does dystopia grow out of utopia? The epigram by Nicolas Berdyaev that Huxley used for *Brave New World* puts it well: "We used to pay too little attention to utopias, or even disregarded them altogether, saying with regret that they were impossible of realization." Things have changed. "Now, indeed, they seem to be able to be brought about far more easily that we supposed, and we are actually faced by an agonizing problem of quite another kind: how can we prevent their final realization?"[21] For Berdyaev it is utopias themselves that are the threat.

Few would claim that freedom leads to slavery or that frigid water will boil, but many do argue that utopia leads to dystopia—or that little distinguishes the two in the first place. The blurred border between utopia and dystopia compresses the historical judgment. Dystopia does not relate to utopia as dyslexia does to reading or dyspepsia to digestion. The other "dys-" words, derived from a Greek root meaning diseased or faulty, are disturbed forms of something healthy or desirable, but dystopia is judged less as an impaired than as a developed utopia. Dystopias are commonly viewed not as the opposite of utopias but as their logical fulfillment. No one suggests that dyslexia signifies we should renounce reading, but many believe dystopias invalidate utopias.

Why? The short answer has to do with the blood bath of communism—Stalinism, Maoism, Pol Pot, and the rest—and alludes, again, to the great twentieth-century dystopian novels that apprehend that experience. Fair enough—or is it? This judgment raises questions about the popular, not the scholarly, reading of texts. From *Brave New World* or *1984*, generations of high school and college students learn the lesson that utopias in general, and communism in particular, are not only doomed, but destructive. Yet the twentieth-century dystopic novels were not emphatically anti-utopian—and certainly its authors were not. Years after *Brave New World*, Huxley wrote *Island*, a novel rarely assigned to students but that praises a utopian society based loosely on Buddhism and cooperative living. "We're not interested in turning out good party members; we're only interested in turning out good human beings," the island guide informs the visitor, who finds the utopians both happy and healthy.[22]

Nor was Huxley anticommunist or antisocialist. Like H. G. Wells, another utopian, he was obsessed by the promise and threat of science.[23] The visitor to *Island* asks, who owns everything? "Are you capitalists or state socialists?" "Neither," comes the reply. "We're co-operators."[24] In his 1958 reconsiderations of *Brave New World*, twenty-seven years after he wrote it, Huxley approved the redistribution of property. It is, he wrote, "a political axiom" that "power follows property." Now "the means of production are fast becoming the monopolistic property of Big Business and Big Government. Therefore, if you believe in democracy, make arrangements to distribute property as widely as possible."[25] Are these the comments of a dystopic thinker? Today they sound utopian.

While Huxley does allude to Soviet communism in *Brave New World*, which features a character named Lenina, neither communism nor Nazism much bothered him. "*Brave New World* was written in 1931," he recalled later, "before the rise of Hitler . . . and when the Russian tyrant had not yet got into stride."[26] The fetish of youth, the dangers of consumerism, the manipulations of the human psyche: these worried him, especially as he observed them in America of the 1920s.[27] After all, the American auto manufacturer Henry Ford, who pioneered mass production, pervaded *Brave New World*. The leaders were called Fords; the "T" (from the Model T automobile) was a sacred sign; dates were marked "A.F." (After Ford); Ford's Day was celebrated; and a slogan attributed to Ford ("History is bunk.") is honored. Huxley feared a technological and Americanized future. The dystopia of *Brave New World* is less a rejection of utopian paths than a rejection of mass marketing and standardization.

Orwell's *1984* targets Soviet communism much more directly. Yet even this book, and certainly its author, cannot be simply classified as anti-utopian. Orwell retained a belief in a socialist future.[28] "Every line of serious work that I have written since 1936," he declared, "has been written, directly or indirectly, *against* totalitarianism and for democratic Socialism. "[29] He protested that *Animal Farm* and *1984* were being read as anti-utopian or antisocialist tracts. He had intended to highlight destructive tendencies surfacing in the Soviet Union, England, and Nazi Germany—not reconcile people with the status quo. In the preface to the Ukrainian edition of *Animal Farm*, Orwell explained that many in England retained illusions about the Soviet Union. "Indeed," he wrote, "nothing has contributed so much to the corruption of the original idea of Socialism as the belief that Russia is a Socialist country and that every act of its rulers must be excused, if not imitated." Orwell believed "that the destruction of the Soviet myth was essential if we wanted a revival of the Socialist movement."[30]

At the end of his abbreviated life the misinterpretations of *1984* increasingly agitated Orwell—to the point that he dictated a press release to his publisher to clarify his intentions.[31] He saw a danger "in the structure imposed on Socialist and on Liberal capitalist communities by the necessity to prepare for total war." He feared the "totalitarian outlook" and worried that the capitalist and communist superstates would line up against each other. Obviously, the Anglo-American "block" would not be called communist, but something like a "hundred per cent Americanism."[32] In response to an inquiry from an American union member, he wrote that *1984* "is NOT intended as an attack on Socialism or on the British Labour Party (of which I am a supporter) but as a show-up of the perversions to which a centralized economy is liable and which have already been partly realized in Communism and Fascism."[33]

Indeed, to read *1984* as a straightforward attack on utopia or socialism takes some doing. Many elements bespeak capitalist Britain, not communist Russia. The "proles," or the workers, live in dingy suburbs and pass their time—apart from labor—in gambling, films, and football; they play darts and watch films "oozing with sex." They also read trashy newspapers filled with crime stories, astrology, and sports. None of this rang true of the Soviet working class. Isaac Deutscher, an acquaintance of Orwell, noted, "Orwell knew well that newspapers of this sort did not exist in Stalinist Russia, and that the faults of the Stalinist press were of an altogether different kind."[34]

Moreover, at the intellectual climax of the book, when O'Brien, representing the Party, interrogates Winston, not communism but a system that has left far behind even a pretence of justice or emancipation is exposed. O'Brien, who punishes Winston for incorrect answers, demands to know, what is the "motive" of the Party? "Why should we want power?" Winston thought he knew. "The Party did not seek power for its own ends, but only for the good of the majority," who were too weak and incapable to govern themselves.

This was the wrong answer, however; it demonstrated that Winston still imagined the Party retained a progressive commitment to happiness or freedom. O'Brien corrected Winston. The Party seeks power for its own end, simply to wield power. "The object of power is power." Why? To cause suffering. "Do you begin to see, then, what kind of world we are creating?" asks O'Brien. "It is the exact opposite of the stupid hedonistic Utopias that the old reformers imagined." The Party aims for "a world of fear and treachery and torment. . . . If you want a picture of the future, imagine a boot stamping on a human face—forever."[35] *1984* implicitly defends the "stupid hedonistic Utopias" that "old reformers" like Orwell continue to believe in.

Before *1984* stood Yevgeny Zamyatin's dystopic novel *We*, which Orwell had read, reviewed, and, to some degree, imitated.[36] Written in the early 1920s, *We* prompted Zamyatin's exile from the Soviet Union. With its "One State," an omniscient "Benefactor," the "Bureau of Guardians," a "Table of Hours" that regulates all activities including sex, and a story of love and subversion, the book anticipated many elements of *1984*. Zamyatin intended *We* as a savage attack on Soviet communism—and it was read that way. "Everything here is untrue," wrote a Soviet apologist. "Communism does not strive to subjugate and keep society under the heel of a single state." This guardian of orthodoxy cautioned that Zamyatin was following "a very dangerous and inglorious path"—not quite as dangerous as this critic, who disappeared in Stalin's purges.[37]

It takes nothing away from the book to note that Zamyatin's concerns went beyond Soviet communism. He rejected not revolution or transformation but the idea that history had stopped. The new revolutionaries forgot that each revolution must be succeeded by another. "My dear," asks the subversive comrade of her irresolute lover, who is a state mathematician, "Name me a final number . . . the ultimate, the largest." "That's preposterous!," he replies. "How can there be a final number?" Her point exactly. "Then how can there be a final revolution? There is no final one; revolutions are infinite."[38] On this turned Zamyatin's objections to utopias: they ended history and change. "Utopia is always static," he wrote in an essay on H. G. Wells.[39]

The love of routine and repetition upset Zamyatin, who had spent several years in England. Prior to *We* he satirized an English obsession with mechanical precision and timetables.[40] The Vicar in his short story "The Islanders" schedules his eating, walking, repenting, alms giving—and love making with his wife. When she sits on his lap in an unprescribed moment, he upbraids her. "My dear," intones the Vicar, "you remember . . . life must become an harmonious machine and with mechanical inevitability lead us to the desired goal. . . . If the functioning of albeit a small wheel is disturbed. . . . Well, but you understand."[41]

Orwell understood. He had been searching for a copy of *We* for some years and finally located a French translation. He recognized that the book was more than an anticommunist tract. In 1922 Zamyatin could hardly be charging the Soviet system with creating a boring life, Orwell argued. Rather, Zamyatin targeted "not any particular country but the implied aims of industrial civilization. It is in effect a study of the Machine."[42]

The briefest inquiry reveals that the key dystopic books of the twentieth century were not anti-utopian; they did not deride utopian ventures as much as they mocked authoritarian communism or a technological future. They did not link utopia and dystopia; they damned contemporary society by projecting into the future its worst features. Herein lies the difference between utopia and dystopia. Utopias seek to emancipate by envisioning a world based on new, neglected, or spurned ideas; dystopias seek to frighten by accentuating contemporary trends that threaten freedom.

The common wisdom that utopias inexorably lead to dystopias not only derives from texts, it appeals to history to make its case. New words help make the argument. Like "dystopia," the term "genocide" belongs to the twentieth century. Inevitably these new terms seem related; they seem to address kindred experiences. Raphael Lemkin, a Polish-Jewish refugee, coined "genocide" in 1944 "to denote an old practice in its modern development"—the annihilation of a national or ethnic group. He believed the Nazi practices occasioned a new word.[43] While Lemkin worked tirelessly to spread the news about genocide—with few rewards[44]—he did not associate it with either utopia or dystopia.[45]

Yet scholarly and conventional opinion today consistently links genocide and utopia and bills the blood bath of the twentieth century to "utopians" such as Stalin, Hitler, and Mao. From Hannah Arendt's 1951 *Origins of Totalitarianism* to Martin Malia's 1994 *Soviet Tragedy*—its last chapter is titled "The Perverse Logic of Utopia"—scholars have thrown communism, Nazism, and utopia into one tub. Prestigious savants like Isaiah Berlin and Karl Popper have persuasively argued that utopia leads to totalitarianism and mass murder. "We must beware of Utopia," wrote Ralf Dahrendorf. "Whoever sets out to implement Utopian plans will in the first instance have to wipe clean the canvas, on which the real world is painted. This is a brutal process of destruction;" it leads to hell on earth.[46]

To question this approach requires asking what utopias are actually about—and why, for instance, Nazism should not be deemed a utopian enterprise. Even the vaguest description of utopia as a society inspired by notions of happiness, fraternity, and plenty would apparently exclude Nazism with its notion of Ayrans dominating inferiors in a Thousand Year Reich. What connects Thomas More's *Utopia* and Hitler's *Mein Kampf?* Virtually nothing.[47]

More, a saint in the Catholic Church, offered a vision of a world where "everyone gets a fair share, so there are never any poor men or beggars. Nobody owns anything, but everyone is rich—for what greater wealth can there be than cheerfulness, peace of mind, and freedom from anxiety?" He dreamt of a place where man can "live joyfully and peacefully." War was despised "as an activity fit only for beasts," and tolerance extended to various religions. The leader of Utopia called it "arrogant folly" to enforce religious conformity by way of "threats or violence." If "fighting and rioting" decide religious controversies, the best men will succumb to the worst "like grain choked out of a field by thorns and briars." [48]

Hitler dreamt of a Reich resurrected on the basis of a "great, unifying idea of struggle," anti-Semitism. He believed that the gassing of "twelve or fifteen thousand" Jews would have changed the outcome of World War One. He called for a race war to protect the bloodline since "all the human culture, all the results of art, science and technology . . . are almost exclusively the creative product of the Aryan." The "mightiest counterpart to the Aryan is represented by the Jew," who poisons and corrupts the pure Nordic blood. The "contamination of our blood . . . is carried out systematically by the Jew today . . . these black parasites of the nation defile our inexperienced young blond girls and thereby destroy something which can no longer be replaced."[49] In 1939 Hitler threatened to eliminate Jews from Europe. "If international finance Jewry . . . succeeds in precipitating the nations into a world war, the result will not be . . . the victory of Jewry, but the annihilation of the Jewish race in Europe."[50] This does not sound like Thomas More.

Careful scholars, such as Jost Hermand in *Old Dreams of a New Reich: Volkish Utopias and National Socialism*, have explored utopian writings that preceded and accompanied Nazism.

Yet the term "utopian" in his study takes on a peculiar cast, which he half acknowledges by frequently putting it in quotes, as if having the words "Nazi" and "utopia" in one sentence violate sense, which it does. He cited an example of a pre-Nazi "utopian" novel from 1913 that sketches a future ice age that eliminates inferior peoples and opens the way for a more powerful Germanic race, "tall in stature, blond, blue-eyed." In the new Germany, "totally absent are the racial vermin, the small in stature, the squat, the stocky, the black-haired. . . . The Ice Age exterminated them. . . . All that remained was the Germanic people, who, liberated from all Celtic, Mediterranean, and Oriental parasites, could now breathe free."[51] The themes of racial superiority studded with violence and mysticism permeated "utopian" fiction throughout the Third Reich, but that literature contained little of the brotherhood and harmony that marked classical utopias.

Hans Mommsen, a distinguished historian of Germany, titled an essay "The Realization of the Utopian: The 'Final Solution of the Jewish Question' in the 'Third Reich.' " Did the annihilation of the Jews really fulfill a utopian vision? Mommsen barely says. He is as explicit as the following: "The utopian dream of exterminating the Jews could become reality only in the half-light of unclear orders and ideological fanaticism."[52] Yet this "dream" does not partake of a utopianism that from Hesiod to Bellamy imagined a world at peace. The fact that Mommsen used the term "utopian" sparingly or misleadingly seems to have struck his translators. They translated this essay, "Die Realisierung des Utopischen," into "The Realization of the Unthinkable."[53]

Yet numerous observers continue to tack together utopianism, totalitarianism, and Nazism.[54] This is the wisdom of our age. A well-visited and -reviewed exhibit on utopia, subtitled "The Search for the Ideal Society in the Western World," held in New York and Paris, included Nazi items and paraphernalia such as anti-Semitic posters and Hitler's *Mein Kampf*. The exhibit displayed photos of a Nazi concentration camp and an Israeli kibbutz, as if both presented comparable faces of utopianism. Apparently, genocide and humanism both illustrate "the search for the ideal society." In an essay, "Utopia and Totalitarianism," from the exhibit's catalog, a French scholar admits that "utopias do not all forecast totalitarian regimes to the same degree." Yet the "differences" between them shrink before the similarities. "Precisely because of their utopian aims," he writes, they are all "harbingers of totalitarianism."[55] This is inexact, but typical. Does Fourier's notion of lavish dinners—"more exquisite than the best kings can obtain"—foreshadow totalitarianism?[56] Historical precision surrenders to a liberal anti- utopian animus.

A recent book by the historian Eric D. Weitz, titled, *A Century of Genocide: Utopias of Race and Nation* seconds this approach. He argues that utopias undergird twentieth-century genocidal regimes. Taking up Stalin's Soviet Union of the 1930s, Hitler's Germany of the 1940s, the Khmer Rouge of 1970s Cambodia, and the Miloševic's Serbia of the 1990s, Weitz writes that "all articulated powerful visions of the future. Each of them promised to create utopia in the here and now."[57] To discover utopianism in all his cases, however, Weitz stretches the term to incoherence. What was utopian in Miloševic's violent efforts to create a greater Serbia? Weitz identifies a belligerent Serbian nationalism "imbued with a sense of aggrievement" and a Serbian hatred for Muslims, but where is the utopianism in this? He tosses about and finally offers that "every so often" "glowing" images of the future appeared in the rhetoric of Serb nationalists. For instance, a Serbian bishop declared that Serbia "had become the largest state in heaven." Aggressive Serbian nationalism hardly confirms a utopian-genocide linkage.

He also scrambles to find a utopian note in Nazism. Anti-Semitic, racist, xenophobic, nationalist, authoritarian, but utopian? Weitz emphasizes the mystical, agrarian, and communitarian features of Nazism that might at first glance seem utopian. He tells us that the Nazis promoted whole-grain breads and "greater consumption of fresh fruits and vegetables," as if this demonstrated a nefarious utopianism. Indeed, he informs us that "whole-grain bread was called the 'final solution' to the bread question." He might as well dub the current movement for healthy school lunches utopian and genocidal. The Nazis did champion a "new" man and woman, but it was less the utopianism of this concept than its racism that proved lethal. The Nazi case does not establishes a utopian-genocidal tie.[58]

In classifying Nazism as a utopian venture, scholars ratify the anti-utopian bias. They clinch the case against utopianism. The casualty list for utopian enterprises lengthens and any lingering sympathy for it vanishes. Utopians stand condemned by the blood they have shed. Yet where is the evidence? The question Hegel asked still hangs over us, "But even regarding History as the slaughter-bench at which the happiness of peoples, the wisdom of States, and the virtue of individuals have been victimized—the question involuntarily arises—to what principle, to what final aim these enormous sacrifices have been offered"[59] Can we say today that utopians are responsible? Do mass deaths largely derive from crazed, or indeed sane, utopians?

To assess this argument requires entering the morgue of history, not only to count the corpses but to determine the cause of death. More than a strong constitution and medical skills are required. Politics saturates the task. From the numbers of deaths (and their causes) in the New World after the European "discovery" to those killed in twentieth-century Rwanda, experts and partisans squabble. How many and why? A temptation to come up with larger and larger numbers—as if numbers themselves clinch an argument—overwhelms many inquiries. To attribute mass deaths to utopian striving is standard.

In the 1930s scholarly opinion estimated the population of the Western Hemisphere at the time of Columbus's arrival at about

8 million. Fifty years later many scholars posit 150 million inhabitants. But as David Henige notes in his *Numbers from Nowhere*, between 1930 and 1980 "there was no change in the evidence at all." The "High Counters, "as he calls them, "find numbers, believe them, multiply them."[60] However, the numbers form only the subtext of the debate; the cause and responsibility for the American Indian depopulation constitute the real issue. With larger numbers comes more blame.

The classic account here is David Stannard's 1992 *American Holocaust*, which examines the devastation of Native Americans after Columbus. Stannard provided many figures and much evidence, but it is the numbers that primarily to bolster his case. "The destruction of the Indians of the Americas," writes Stannard "was, far and away, the most massive act of genocide in the history of the world." He estimates one hundred million dead—over at least a century and leveled mainly by disease.[61] Yet Stannard does not look for any utopian mission among the slaughterers—for good reason. If anything, the Native Americans appeared the utopians, living communally in peace and ease. As Peter Martyr stated in his sixteenth-century account of the New World peoples.

> The land belongs to everybody, just as does the sun or the water. They know no difference between *meum* and *tuum*, that source of all evils. It requires so little to satisfy them, that in that vast region there is always more land to cultivate than is needed. It is indeed a golden age, neither ditches, nor hedges, nor wall to enclose their domains; they live in gardens open to all. . . . Their conduct is naturally equitable.[62]

The Native Americans, wrote Hoxie Neal Fairchild is his classic study of the Noble Savage, were frequently "represented as a virtuous and mild people, beautiful, and with a certain intelligence, living together in nakedness and innocence, sharing their property in common."[63]

No one presented the Spaniards (or the English) in these terms. Familiar and pedestrian goals fired them. "The Spaniards' mammoth destruction of whole societies generally was a by-product of conquest and native enslavement, a genocidal means to an economic end," writes Stannard.[64] He could have cited the sixteenth-century denunciation *The Devastation of the Indies*, by the Spanish priest Bartolomé de las Casas, who put it concisely. "The reason for killing and destroying such an infinite number of souls," wrote Las Casas in 1552, "is that the Christians have an ultimate aim, which is to acquire gold, and to swell themselves with riches in a very brief time. . . . It should be kept in mind that their insatiable greed and ambition, the greatest ever seen in the world, is the cause of their villainies."[65] Las Casas, writing just several decades after More's *Utopia*, found no hint of utopianism in these mass deaths.

To be sure, assessing the intentions of the slaughterers and estimating the numbers killed in any century is a dark business, and few have essayed it. The opening sentence of Gil Eliott's neglected *Twentieth Century Book of the Dead* reads: "The number of man-made deaths in the twentieth century is about one hundred million." The major terrains of violence he considers—the book was published in 1972—include World War I, China (mainly the Sino-Japanese war), the Russian Civil War, the Soviet state, the Jews of Europe, and World War II.[66] Only a portion of these deaths, about one-fifth or one-quarter, could be chalked up to utopians, even loosely conceived.

One might counterpose to Eliott a recent book by French scholars, *The Black Book of Communism*. Stéphane Courtois, its main editor, comes up with the same figure as Eliott—but just for those killed by communists in the twentieth century, which is also the number that Stannard computes for Native American deaths. "The intransigent facts demonstrate that Communist regimes have victimized approximately 100 million people in contrast to the approximately 25 million victims of the Nazis," writes Courtois, although he is vague as to how he derived his figures. For Courtois, the numbers infer a "similarity" between Nazism and Communism and justify extending the term "genocide" to the communist system. He identifies utopianism as a root cause. "The real motivation for the terror," writes Courtois in his conclusion, "becomes apparent: it stemmed from Leninist ideology and the utopian will."[67]

Those who refer to Nazi and Stalinist totalitarianism as the death knell of utopia might give more attention to World War I, a bloodletting that directly spurred the Russian Revolution and, indirectly, Nazism. Scholars have never found a shred of utopianism either in the events leading to its outbreak or its four years of hostilities. World War I, writes Enzo Traverso in his *Origins of Nazi Violence*, was "the founding act" of twentieth-century violence. It introduced the world to "the bombing of towns, the internment of nationals of enemy countries and the deportation and forced labor of civilians." It marked "a new threshold in the escalation of violence."[68] "Bolshevism and Fascism are the children of World War I," stated the historian François Furet. If that is so, then what do we know of the parents? Unfortunately very little. World War I "remains one of the most enigmatic events of modern history." It is almost beyond recall or sense, noted Furet. "It is very difficult for us to imagine the nationalist passions that led the peoples of Europe to kill each other for four full years."[69] Yet isn't this often the pedestrian story of modern violence? Not utopianism, but plain old nationalism? Even though he tried to classify as "utopian" the movement for a greater Serbia, Weitz in his *Century of Genocide* admits it was mainly driven by the "desperate efforts of an old elite" that mobilized people by nationalism.[70]

A recent effort to survey war deaths over three centuries concludes that "the most frequent objectives" were "territory or independence." In other words, nationalism spurred these conflicts, although the twentieth century showed a sharp increase in "civil wars."[71] For the period from the end of World War II to the end of the twentieth century, perhaps the most comprehensive accounting of war deaths has been assembled by Milton Leitenberg of the Center for International and Security Studies at the University of Maryland. To assess only the conflicts that caused the greatest loss of life—above 500,000—communist "utopians" certainly held their own, mainly in Asia, where many millions of deaths are ascribed to the Pol Pot regime in Cambodia (1975– 1978), perhaps 2 million; and many more are attributed to Chinese policies of land-reform (1949–1954), 4.5 million; their suppression of counterrevolutionaries (1949–1954), 3 million; and the cultural revolution (1965–1975), 2.1 million.[72]

Numbers like these are impossible to apprehend. But the morgue of history allows no easy exit. To get to the door requires a walk through cavernous rooms to count the corpses and inspect the death certificates. For instance, the Chinese Civil War (1946–1950), which preceded these blood baths, cost the country 6.2 million lives. To step back a bit further—before 1945—total deaths in the Sino-Japanese war, which began with the invasion of China by Japan and ended with Japan's defeat by the United States, reached 10 million.[73] Or, to remain in Asia for the post–World War II years, we find 1.5 million deaths in the civil war in Bangladesh (1971); almost a million in the partition of India (1946–1948); and perhaps another million in Indonesia, largely communist party (PKI) members or sympathizers, following the unsuccessful coup of 1965. A CIA study, not usually guilty of hyperbole, concluded, "in terms of the numbers killed, the anti-PKI massacres in Indonesia rank as one of the worst mass murders of the twentieth century." (The study added that unlike Nazi genocide or Stalin's purges, these deaths have gone virtually unnoticed.)[74] Or to look at some numbers from sub-

Saharan Africa: we find a series of civil wars, ethnic conflicts, and independence struggles, each with tolls of about a million or more in the post–World War II years: Angola, Ethiopia, Mozambique, Nigeria (two million in the 1967–1970 civil war), Rwanda, Sudan, Uganda.

What can be gleaned from this melancholy listing? Perhaps nothing. Or this: the human community has much more reason to fear those with an ethnic, religious, or nationalist agenda than it has to fear those with utopian designs. Indeed, this jumps out more forcefully in scanning contemporary lethal conflicts. "The last decade of the twentieth century," writes Samantha Powers "was one of the most deadly in the grimmest century on record."[75] She is referring to Rwanda, but internecine hatreds marked virtually all recent conflicts: the Ethiopia-Eritrean War, Sudan, Algeria, Sri Lanka, Kosovo, Bangladesh, Kashmir, Afghanistan, Congo.[76] The toll in a few of these—the Congo and the Sudan—reach into the millions. But where are the utopians?

In *We Wish to Inform You That Tomorrow We Will Be Killed with Our Families*, Philip Gourevitch tells of meetings that preceded the Rwandan genocide in which hatreds were fanned and payoffs promised. Local leaders "described Tutsis as devils— horns, hoofs, tails and all—and gave the order to kill them. . . . The local authorities consistently profited from the massacres, seizing slain Tutsis' land and possessions . . . and the civilian killers, too, were usually rewarded."[77] This seems a far cry from utopianism. In an increasingly rational and scientific world, primal attachments of blood, clan, and religion enflame global slaughter. This is not exactly ignored; on the other hand, neither is it given the equal gravity with the misdeeds of utopians.

Imagination nourishes utopianism. Zamyatin intuited that imagination, far from leading to a totalitarian society, threatens it.

The authorities in the One State of his *We* discover a medical operation to surgically remove the subversive imagination. "Rejoice!" proclaims the *One State Gazette*, science can now overcome imagination, the "last barricade on our way to happiness." Imagination has been a "worm" that gnaws at people, causing widespread unhappiness. "The latest discovery of State Science is the location of the center of imagination—a miserable little nodule in the brain. . . . Triple-X ray-cautery of this nodule—and you are cured of imagination—Forever." You become perfect and anxiety free. "Hurry!" command the authorities. Line up and get the "Great Operation."[78]

If imagination sustains utopian thinking, what sustains imagination? As a historical problem, not a psychological or philosophical one, this is rarely pursued.[79] Hundreds of books and articles consider imagination in literature, myth, cognition, perception, understanding, and philosophy, but skirt its history. Eva Brann's encyclopedic *The World of Imagination* covers imagination from Plato to Bergson; she follows it through cognitive psychology and visual perception and surveys it in logic, poetry, and religion. She even takes up imagination and utopia. Yet in all her 800 pages she does not even allude to imagination as a historical entity, as something that shifts over the decades or centuries.[80] The issue here is not so much its role in thinking, remembering, or learning but its social and historical configurations. How does the shape of imagination change over time? Does it evolve or weaken? Was "the imagination" the same in 1800, 1950, and 2000?

To ask is not to answer. It seems reasonable to assume that the woof and warp of imagination register historical changes. However, to get at the specifics of imagination requires a series of conjectures. Imagination probably depends on childhood— and conversely, childhood depends on imagination. To be sure, this was a notion cherished by romantics like Rousseau and Wordsworth, who idolized the child as a creature of imagination and spontaneity.[81] Yet nowadays a facile historicism about the "construction" or "invention" of childhood (or family or anything) often ends in a more facile relativism, suggesting that what is invented or constructed cannot be sturdy or desirable. However, buildings are constructed; they also stand up and, sometimes, dazzle. To put it differently: The romantics might have idolized childhood as the domain of imagination; this does not invalidate imagination. Nor does the fact that the "romantic child" was "narrowly confined to an elite" render it spurious.[82] What is restricted to a few is not for that reason illegitimate; it may be the reverse. Literacy was once limited to an elite, but who would argue that it should remain so?

If childhood nourishes imagination, what nourishes childhood? Much historical work has explored the shifting dimensions, indeed, almost the discovery, of childhood. The classic study, Philippe Airès's *Centuries of Childhood*, published over forty years ago, argued that childhood itself belongs to the modern period.[83] Employing pictorial evidence, statistics on child morality, and the custom of sending children off for service or work, he concluded that childhood went unrecognized till the sixteenth and seventeenth centuries; until then children were seen as miniature adults. While this idea has proved resonant, historians have challenged most, if not all of it. "Airès's views were mistaken," writes Nicholas Orme in his recent *Medieval Children*, "not simply in detail but in substance. It is time to lay them to rest."[84] The danger, however, is switching them around and finding that nothing has changed. The historian Keith Thomas has concluded that the continuity of childhood far surpasses any changes in it. "Since the development of the child's mind and body is essentially a biological constant, it is not surprising that there should be great similarities between the ways of children in early modern England and their ways today."[85]

This seems clearly to exaggerate the continuities. At least in the modern period, a series of factors have shaped, if not revolutionized, childhood. Family size, mortality, child-rearing practices, labor, schooling, and play assume major roles.[86] None of these permit easy generalizations as to how they have changed in the last two centuries. Some elements can be more easily documented than others. The establishment of compulsory education and restrictions on child labor can be tracked, for instance, and indeed were often linked. The first French child-labor legislation of 1841 required children to attend school in order to be employed (and limited the work day to eight hours for children between ages of eight and twelve!).[87] These laws did not always exist and became more comprehensive over the years. Eventually, they kept more children out of the workforce or shortened the workday and created a prolonged reserve for learning, growing, and playing.[88] At the same time "the decline in family size from an average of six children in the 1860s to three in the 1900s and two in the 1920s" and a rising standard of living may have allowed increased care and attention to each child.[89]

With what consequence for imagination? Things can sometimes be best glimpsed in their decline. As the waters ebb, the old depth lines catch the eye. A "fall of childhood" literature has emerged that posits a thinning of the emotional and psychic space that enveloped the growing child. A protective zone—always delicate—succumbs to marketing forces. "The modern make-up of society," wrote Max Horkheimer in the 1940s, "sees to it that the utopian dreams of childhood are cut short in earliest youth."[90] If this happens, then the "classical" notion and the reality of childhood turn out to be not only fragile but obsolete, arising in the late eighteenth century and being eclipsed in the late twentieth century. But does it happen? The "decline" literature itself may be situated historically as a product, as one critic put it, of a "peculiarly contemporary malaise . . . of panic and nostalgia."[91]

Yet this same critic, David Buckingham, admits the contours of leisure have shifted for children in the last decades. Not only have merchandisers targeted children, but due to increased affluence and anxiety about external dangers, "the principle location of children's leisure has moved from public spaces (such as the street) to private spaces (the bedroom)." Playing outside has been "steadily displaced by domestic entertainment (particularly via television and computers) and—especially among more affluent classes—by supervised leisure activities such as organized sports, music lessons and so forth."[92] This tallies with Neil Postman's observation in *Disappearance of Childhood* of an erosion of games that children play by themselves. "Except for the inner city, where games are still under the control of the youths who play them, the games of American youth have become increasingly official, mock-professional, and extremely serious."[93]

In a fifty-year period, the time children spend before television screens and computers has jumped from zero to at least three or four hours daily.[94] During the same stretch, the advertising budget of toy makers has escalated from zero to billions. Advertisers target children, who have become a major market. This has brought about what Juliet B. Schor has called the "reshaping" or "commodification" of childhood.[95] In 1955 a major toy manufacturer with $50 million in sales spent a few hundred dollars on advertising to children.[96] Today, the television-advertising budget alone directed to children is about a billion dollars. "The average American child watches more than thirty thousand commercials a year, or roughly 82 a day."[97]

Can it be doubted that those hours and those advertisements affect children? Is it possible that unstructured playtime that gives space to imagination has diminished? While boredom has hardly disappeared, "boredom" as a dreamy Sunday afternoon with nothing to do may be short-circuited by channel surfing and computer games. "Boredom is the dream bird that hatches the egg of experience," wrote Walter Benjamin in 1936. And he added, "his nesting places—the activities that are intimately associated with boredom—are already extinct in the cities and are declining in the country as well."[98]

Does boredom, an unstructured zone of inactivity and purposelessness, allow imagination to develop? And is boredom itself a product of time and place? "Boredom does have a history," writes the historian Peter Burke, "in the sense that the occasions of boredom and also what might be called the 'boredom threshold' are subject to change over time." He finds that boredom was fairly common among the intellectual elite in early modern Europe; in their villas and life the elite sought to pass the time to escape from tedium.[99] Of course it is possible to go back to the Greeks, Roman, and early Christians. Acedia, or sloth, is as old as the Greeks, although it is not until the early Christian Fathers that it becomes a major concern. Sloth threatened pious souls, especially monks, but also marked a stage in spiritual growth. To attain oneness with God, it might be necessary to risk acedia. In *Foundations of Coenobitic Life*, acedia ranks as the sixth of eight temptations.[100] As sloth, tedium, or ennui, boredom has a long history.[101]

Like many historical inquiries, the disputes turns on the accents placed on continuity and discontinuity. How new is boredom, or how different is modern boredom? The term itself may be instructive. "The word 'boredom' dates from the nineteenth century," writes Patricia Spacks in her book on boredom. "The verb 'to bore' as a psychological term comes from the mid-eighteenth century."[102] Etiquette manuals regularly counseled how to avoid being a "bore," although their advice frequently went unheeded. "Only eleven o'clock, is it?" recounted Mrs. Humphry Ward in her account of a mid-nineteenth-century country dinner party. "I thought it was at least one—that Lady Broadlands is such a stupid, proud fool, and he *such* a bore."[103]

Yet what might be an elite phenomenon and a personal failing undergoes two changes after World War II, argues the historian Peter Stearns. "Being bored began to be much more important than doing the boring." To claim "boredom" was a legitimate complaint. Second, the arena of boredom shifts to children. "I'm bored," as expressed by a child, is not a fact but an accusation; it means "entertain me." Stearns adduces various parental columns and books that address the danger of boredom among children. "Quite simply, boredom increasingly mutated, after the late 1940s, from being an attribute of personality . . . to being an inflicted state that demanded correction by others. . . . Children were easily bored," and the fault lay with parents and society.[104]

While Stearns does not cite it, he could have referred to a 1957 best seller to bolster his case. The title itself, *"Where Did You Go?" "Out" "What Did You Do?" "Nothing,"* expressed a new anxiety about boredom—or more exactly a protest against it. Robert Paul Smith, its author, tells about what he did as a kid—and what his children and their friends do. As a kid he didn't know the word "bored": "We never thought that a day was anything but a whole lot of nothing interrupted occasionally by something." Much of his book describes those somethings. "We sat in boxes. . . . We stood on boards over excavations. . . . We looked at things like knives and immies and pig nuts and grasshoppers and clouds and dogs and people. We skipped and hopped and jumped. Not going anywhere—just skipping and hopping and jumping and galloping." What he means is that "we did a lot of nothing. . . . But now, for some reason, we're ashamed of it." Now if a grownup sees a child doing "nothing," we "want to know what's the matter."[105] As Smith explained elsewhere, "I think it is a dirty shame society won't let kids alone. Children should learn they don't have to be doing something every minute. It's fine just doing nothing."[106]

When did "doing nothing" become unacceptable to parents, and perhaps to children as well? Why the shift? New parental anxieties about delinquency and school failure; suburbanization that insulated children from other children; smaller families that meant fewer sibling available—and those around were closer in age and more rivalrous; more mothers working: into this vacuum stepped manufactured products: comics, movies, television, toys. They answered a need, and they were needed. Parents felt an imperative to keep their children busy. "The need to keep children entertained," writes Stearns, "and, often, to buy things or services in order to do so is a fruit not only of growing marketing aimed at children but also of growing parental commitment to the provision of fun."[107]

Of course, the vast enlargement of the toy market is part of the story. Toys are obviously not new, but their incessant selling to children is. "The most obvious impact of toy-marketing," writes Steven Kline in *Out of the Garden*, "is that it makes children want more toys."[108] Indeed, "the children's market is huge," over $200 billion in 1997 in the United States, both in direct purchases and family purchases influenced by children.[109] Such purchases pervade play and fantasy. Toys and video games, made by adults, replace toys and street games, made by children. "We are seeing something new," observes John Holt. The old games of house and hide-and-seek succumb to games patterned on television superheroes. Now children "have most of their daydreams made for them."[110] Or, as Gary Cross put it in his history of toys, *Kid's Stuff*, "Captain Action replaced Hopalong Cassidy. Barbie bested Betsy Wetsy. . . . New playthings embodied dreams of growing up fast to a glamorous world of consumption or a heroic realm of power and control."[111]

Is this really true? The classic study by Iona and Peter Opie, *Children's Games in Street and Playground*, finds little change. Their book, which is subtitled "Chasing, Catching, Seeking, Hunting, Racing, Duelling, Exerting, Daring, Guessing, Acting, Pretending," details with great gusto a host of children's games still played in streets and parks; the authors scoff at the notion of decline. "The belief that traditional games are dying out is itself traditional." They note that children's street games take place in the sides and corners of towns, where adults barely see them. As we age, "we no longer have eyes for the games, and not noticing them suppose them to have vanished."[112] Rather like Jane Jacobs in *Life and Death of Great American Cities*, they believe that unplanned spaces in cities support games and play, now and in the future.

Yet even the Opies note those spaces are changing, and more children live by schedules and play in teams or in school. Something disappears when games require coaches, uniforms, and equipment. Parks departments now advertise for "Play Leaders." The Opies wonder if manicured lawns and renovated parks undermine playing. The authorities "invade" parks and organize play areas. "The center of our own home town possessed, miraculously, until two years ago, a small dark wood," a natural habitat for playing children. No longer, or no longer in the same way: "Now the trees have been cut down, the ground leveled, a stream canalized, and the area flooded with asphalt."[113] Moreover, their study was completed decades ago, in the England and Scotland of the 1960s. Even the sanguine Opies doubt that children's games persist unchanged.[114]

If unstructured childhood sustains imagination, and imagination sustains utopian thinking, then the eclipse of the first entails the weakening of the last—utopian thinking. To be sure, historical causes cannot be neatly marshaled, as if A causes B that causes C. Moreover, the subject at hand—the vitality of imagination—cannot be simply circumscribed or dissected. Despite these uncertainties, it seems likely that the colonization of children's space and time undermines an unfettered imagination. Children have more to do, more done for them, and less inclination—and perhaps fewer resources—for utopian dreaming.

Robert Paul Smith's book begins as he turns to a bunch of kids, none of whom "seemed to know what to do for the next fifteen minutes." "I said to them, 'How about a game of mumbly-peg?' And can you believe that not one of these little siblings knew spank the baby from Johnny jump the fence?" Nor do they play "immies" (marbles), nor stoop ball. When they play baseball it is "in something called The Little League and have a covey of overseeing grownups hanging around and bothering them and putting catcher's masks on them and making it so bloody important." When we played we just played with kids on the block with no interfering adults. "Kids, as far as I can tell, don't do things like that any more."[115]

The great scholar of Jewish mysticism, Gershom Scholem, once wrote that Jewish messianism can be described "as a kind of anarchic breeze."[116] He alludes to the "profound truth" that "a well-ordered house is a dangerous thing." In that house, "a window is open through which the winds blow in, and it is not quite certain just what they bring in with them." He added that it is "easy to understand the reticence and misgivings" of traditional housekeepers.[117]

At least in part, this book hopes to constitute an "anarchic breeze" in the house of utopia. In the utopian tradition, virtually all attention is focused on what may be called the "blueprint" school of utopianism. From Thomas More to B. F. Skinner, the blueprint utopians have detailed what the future will look like; they have set it out; they have elaborated it; they have demarcated it. Sometimes these particulars have been inspired, sometimes pedantic, sometimes mad. "The people dress in undershirts of white linen over which they wear a suit combining jacket and trousers in one piece," wrote Tommaso Campanella of his seventeenth-century "City of the Sun." "This has no folds, but there are splits on the side and beneath, which are closed with buttons. The trouser part reaches to the heels, which are covered with heavy socks and shoes." Four times a year, when the sun enters Cancer, Capricorn, Aires, and Libra, "the Keeper of the Wardrobe" distributes new outfits.[118]

Such details can bestow on utopian speculation a certain weight and plausibility. This is how people shall work or dine or play, they suggest. It is feasible, they imply. The utopian blue-printers give the size of rooms, the number of seats at tables, the exact hours at which to arise and retire. Yet the strength of the blueprinters is also their weakness. The plans betray, and some-times celebrate, a certain authoritarianism. They say: this is the way people *must* dress; this is the hour they *must* eat. In his reconsideration of his *Story of Utopias*, Lewis Mumford mulled over the fact that where he had been looking for fresh ideas in the history of utopias, he stumbled upon far too many dictatori-al schemes: "These rigid virtues," he wrote, "these frozen insti-tutions, these static and self-limiting ideals did not attract me."[119]

To be sure, these unattractive features, Mumford explained, do not constitute the whole of utopias. If so, he would have "dropped [his] investigation" immediately. Beyond the authori-tarian rules, he found a largesse of spirit and imagination woe-fully lacking in contemporary society. "Utopian thinking . . . then, was the opposite of one-sidedness, partisanship, partiality, provinciality, specialism."[120] This is true—but not true enough. The blueprints not only appear repressive, they also rapidly be-come dated. Even with the best of wills, the blueprinters tether the future to the past. In outfitting utopia, they order from the catalog of their day. With their schedules and seating arrange-ments, their utopias stand condemned not by their capaciousness but by their narrowness, not by their extravagance but their poverty. History soon eclipses them.

The blueprint tradition constitutes only a part, albeit the main part, of utopianism. Less noticed and less easily defined are the anti-blueprint utopians, who could be called the iconoclastic utopians. Rather than elaborate the future in precise detail, they longed, waited, or worked for utopia but did not visualize it. The iconoclastic utopians tapped ideas traditionally associated with utopia—harmony, leisure, peace, and pleasure—but rather than spelling out what could be, they kept, as it were, their ears open toward it. Ears and eyes are apposite, for insofar as they did not visualize the future, they listened for it. They did not privilege the eye, but the ear. Many of these thinkers were Jews, and explicitly or implicitly, they obeyed the commandment prohibiting graven images. God, the absolute and the future defied visual representation. Like the future, God could be heard but not seen. "Hear, O Israel!" begin the Jewish prayers.

The iconoclastic utopians were also Jews drenched in German romanticism. If they were against images of the future, they sought hints of it in music, poetry, and mystical moments. "In the years before 1914," recalls Hans Kohn, who is linked with several of the iconoclastic utopians, "German intellectuals rediscovered romanticism and mysticism."[121] Iconoclastic utopianism drew upon not only Jewish sources but the romantic idiom of fin de siècle Germany. Ideas of "*Geist*," "society," "experience," "unity," and "life" permeated the romanticism of the early twentieth century; the romantics specialized in spiritual transcendence. The "Neue Gemeinschaft" (New Society) group, for instance, founded by Heinrich and Julius Hart, sought to overcome "the spirit of disunion, of duality."[122] Jewish utopian thinkers borrowed this romantic idiom and gave it a sharper edge; they translated a largely mystical and individualist tongue into a political language. They fashioned a utopianism committed to the future but reserved about it. Against the dominant tradition of blueprints, they offered an imageless utopianism laced with passion and spirit.

Iconoclastic utopianism did not entail a puritanical severity. On exactly this issue it frequently differed with conventional utopianism and socialism infused with notions of purity and obedience. Heine may best capture this sensuous utopianism in his presentation of German thought to the French. "Don't be angry with us," he beseeched the French, "you virtuous Republicans."

> We are fighting not for the human rights of the people, but for the divine rights of mankind. In this and in many other things we differ from the men of the Revolution. We do not want to be sansculottes, nor simple citizens, nor venal presidents; we want to found a democracy of gods, equal in majesty, in sanctity, and in bliss. You demand simple dress, austere morals, and unspiced pleasures, but we demand nectar, ambrosia, crimson robes, costly perfumes, luxury and splendor, the dancing of laughing nymphs, music and comedies.[123]

What Adorno wrote about Heine could be said of any of the iconoclastic utopians. "In contrast to socialism he held fast to the idea of uncurtailed happiness in the image of a just society, an idea quickly enough disposed of in favor of slogans like 'Anyone who doesn't work won't eat.' "[124] The renunciation of images of the future protected the idea of the end of renunciation.

The classic book of the Jewish iconoclasts is Ernst Bloch's *The Spirit of Utopia* from 1918. Bloch called it a work of "revolutionary Romanticism" or "revolutionary gnosis."[125] The book explores inwardness, music, and soul. Not a sentence addresses the size of the sleeping quarters. Yet "elective affinities"— Goethe's term, employed by Michael Löwy in his *Redemption and Utopia*—can be found among a series of central European Jewish thinkers and writers—from Martin Buber and Gustav Landauer to Walter Benjamin and T. W. Adorno, and perhaps Kafka.[126] These were iconoclastic utopians without precise maps, yet utopians nonetheless. Scholem highlighted their utopianism—and, indeed, he was a close friend of Benjamin. For Jews, said Scholem, redemption was never a purely inward event.

> After all, that restitution of all things to their proper place which is Redemption reconstructs a whole which knows nothing of such separation between inwardness and outwardness. The Utopian element of messianism which reigns so supreme in Jewish tradition concerned itself with the whole and nothing but this whole.

Scholem found this utopianism alive and well in Bloch, Benjamin, Adorno, and Herbert Marcuse, "whose acknowledged or unacknowledged ties to their Jewish heritage are evident."[127]

While the prohibition on graven images has spurred innumerable commentators, no one has argued that the refusal to visualize the deity diminishes him. On the contrary: this refusal was conceived as an act of piety. For the fiercely monotheistic Jews, the prohibition on graven images, and the corresponding reluctance to write the name of God, did not belittle but honored God. It suggested the vast gap between God and humankind. God, said the twelfth-century Jewish philosopher Maimonides, could not be described positively; every positive attribute limits the deity. He can only be approached indirectly—"by negation." "For whatever we utter with the intention of extolling and of praising Him, contains something that cannot be applied to God, and includes derogatory expressions; it is therefore more becoming to be silent, and to be content with intellectual reflection."[128] For the same reason God could not be painted or portrayed; visual details define and confine.

An Ariadne thread runs from this negative theology of the twelfth century to the iconoclastic or negative utopians of the twentieth. The refusal to describe God transmutes into the refusal to describe utopia, which can only be depicted in negative terms. Yet like the resistance to naming God, the reluctance to depict utopia does not diminish but exalts it. It bespeaks the gap between now and then. It refuses to reduce the unknown future to the well-known present, the hope to its cause.

"The gate to justice is learning," wrote Benjamin in his essay on Kafka. "And yet Kafka does not dare attach to this learning the promises which tradition has attached to the study of the Torah. His assistants are sextons who have lost their house of prayer; his students are pupils who have lost their Holy Writ."[129] Benjamin understood the "negative inversion" of Jewish categories in Kafka, according to Scholem: "The teaching no longer conveys a positive message, but offers only an absolutely Utopian—and there as yet undefinable—promise of a post-contemporary world."[130] Michael Löwy, who sought to tease out the Jewish and anarchist dimensions of Kafka, titled his chapter on him " 'Theologia negativa and Utopia negativa.' "[131]

"Utopia negativa" is not exactly a rallying cry. Yet the positive utopian tradition of blueprints for the communal kitchens of the future has atrophied. It has suffered too many reversals; it has been eclipsed by too much history; and its imaginative sources have been drained. In an age of triumphalism and self-promotion, to advertise the future only adds to the clutter. Another utopian blueprint looks like just another billboard or video. The future, perhaps, can be heard, not envisioned. The iconoclastic utopians knew this. They approached it as they approached the absolute—with open hearts and ears.

2. On Anti-Utopianism

More or Less

WHAT FUELS THE ANIMUS AGAINST UTOPIA? THE IMAGES of plenty and ease that constituted classical utopian visions hardly seem to justify contempt or fear. Early literary texts of the Greeks do not promote violence and mayhem. It is difficult to envision these writings inspiring murderous totalitarians.[1] They generally praise peace and damn violence. Hesiod, the eighth-century-B.C. poet usually credited with the first description of utopia, wrote in *Works and Days* of the "golden" men who lived like gods, "carefree in their hearts, shielded from pain and misery."[2] Old age did not exist, and with "limbs of unsagging vigor," this golden race "enjoyed the delights of feasts." "Every good thing was theirs." They "knew no constraint and lived in peace and abundance as lords of their land."

It did not last. Hesiod's is a story of decline. The golden men vanished from the earth and with them, peace and the good life. "The gods of Olympus" formed a second race—"a much worse one"—now of silver. These men, after they reached adolescence, lived only for a short while and succumbed to foolishness. "They could not refrain from reckless violence against one another and did not want to worship the gods." An angry Zeus buried them and made a third race of bronze, which also turned violent. Zeus made a fourth race, and then a fifth race of iron, which includes the age of Hesiod himself. "Neither day nor

night will give them rest as they waste away with toil and pain."
It is a period of suffering and ingratitude. "There will be no af-
fection between guest and host and no love between friends or
brothers as in the past." The lawbreakers "will sack one another's cities." Evildoers will triumph. "Might will make right and
shame will vanish."[3]

Could it be plainer? Not utopia, but its collapse is associated
with violence. Nor does Hesiod foster an ethereal fantasy often
linked with utopias. On the contrary, he encourages practical
tasks and duties. *Works and Days* is largely directed at Hesiod's
brother, whom he considered slothful and unjust. The poem calls
for hard work and a righteous life. "Let there be order and measure in your work / until your barns are filled with season's har-
vest. / Riches and flocks of sheep go to those who work." It is
filled with advice on how to build and when to plow. "Remember!
That is the right time for lumbering. / Cut a three-foot log for
your mortar and three-cubit pestle." Hesiod's utopianism sounds
no more dreamy than do the maxims of Benjamin Franklin.

> Do not postpone for tomorrow or the day after tomorrow;
> barns are not filled by those who postpone
> and waste time in aimlessness. Work prospers with care;
> he who postpones wrestles with ruin.[4]

Most scholars see the poem enjoining a decent and disciplined
life. Its "central thesis," writes one classicist, is that "injustice
arises from trying to win livelihood and wealth without working
for them."[5]

To be sure, even in their Greek incarnation literary utopias
did not simply call for citizens to lead a righteous life. Inasmuch
as they envisioned another world, the Greek utopias implicitly
criticized the state of society.[6] How much and to what end? This
is a basic conundrum of the utopian tradition. To what extent
are utopian dreams an attack on the here-and-now, the pedes-

trian, nonutopian reality, and to what extent are they imaginations of a future? Scholars continue to argue whether Aristophanes' play *The Birds* is a hard dig at Athenian society or a light musing about the future?[7]

Two Athenians leave their home ("We can't get away from Athens fast enough") complaining of its litigious population. "We're looking for a less strenuous residence, a City where we can pass our lives in peace." They seek a "carefree place."[8] With two birds as guides they search for Tereus, himself transformed into a hoopoe (an Old World woodland bird) by Zeus. When they find Tereus, they ask where they can find an easy city "where a man can loaf and stretch and lie down in peace." Tereus suggests various Greek cities, which the visitors peremptorily reject, before they turn and ask, "what is life like here among you Birds?" "Not bad," answers the hoopoe. "No money, of course." "There go most of your problems right away," proclaims one Athenian. "As for food," adds the hoopoe, "we have poppy seed and myrtle, white sesame, mint." This information excites the travelers. "It is a non-stop honeymoon!" They come up with a plan: they will join the birds and set up a new society, which they dub "Cloud-cuckoo-land," perhaps the only phrase from Aristophanes adopted into modern English.

Aristophanes paints Cloud-cuckoo-land in broad strokes. As the classicist Victor Ehrenberg writes, the wandering Athenians wish to establish a place where "food and love" reign supreme.[9] To this end, they reject numerous new arrivals who want to join but who would strangle the new utopia with the old terrestrial problems: a beggar priest, an oracle-monger, a lawyer, an opportunist poet. "In honor of Cloud-cuckoo-land, that Great City, / I have composed the following lyric items. . . . Long have I meditated on this city," begins the poet. "Impossible," replies a founder. "Why, only a minute ago I was dedicating the place, giving it a name!" They pack off the poet. So too the decree vendor, who arrives to hawk various laws. "I am a dealer in the latest decrees. Satisfaction guaranteed." He is dispatched. As is the lawyer asking for some "wings." Why? He would fly about looking for trade with a "belly full of lawsuits for ballast." While the utopianism in *The Birds* remains vague, it would be difficult to construe it as implicitly or explicitly advocating violence—or even "totalitarian" control. Indeed, one hopeful settler is a mathematician, who arrives with a plan "to subdivide the air into square acres." He is advised to depart and "subdivide somewhere else."

Like many utopias, Cloud-cuckoo-land inhabits ambiguous territory; it spoofs both the society it has left behind and the effort to create something entirely new. The chorus proclaims "Here Love and Wisdom dwell / And through the streets the Graces go / And Peace contrives her spell." But how seriously can this be taken? Is this a light-hearted comedy or a pointed political sally? Does it ridicule an airy utopia or terrestrial imperialism, inasmuch as Athens had just dispatched an expedition to subdue Syracuse, which Aristophanes presumably opposed?[10] "*Birds* should not be read as an escapist fantasy," writes A. M. Bowie. The play seeks to deflate Athenian arrogance and militarism.[11] Undoubtedly, a polemical or political ethos colors *The Birds*, a sentiment it shares with other plays by Aristophanes such as the antiwar play *Lysistrata*. Yet Aristophanes leavens its earnestness with comedy and jokes, a recurring tactic in utopian literature. The parody bespeaks seriousness.[12]

Lighthearted utopianism remains alive and well several centuries later in Lucian, the Greek satirist, whose writings are sometimes considered to have inaugurated the genre of utopian science fiction. Lucian put his cards on the table in *The True History*: "I have no intention of telling the truth. . . . I am writing about things entirely outside my experience. . . . Do not believe a word I say." Lucian travels to the moon and back and even stumbles across Aristophanes' Cloud-cuckoo-land. " 'So Aristophanes was telling the truth after all,' I said to myself."

On earth, he and his fellow travelers come to the Island of the Blest, infused with a "wonderful perfume." Birds sing and a pleasant breeze wafts through the trees. Nobody grows old. "Instead of four seasons they have only one . . . spring." A delightful party permanently takes place. "Guests recline at their ease on beds of flowers, and are waited on by the winds." Sexual relations are free and easy. "They see nothing indecent in sexual intercourse, whether heterosexual or homosexual." (Lucian adds: "The only exception was Socrates, who was always swearing his relations with young men were purely Platonic.") Good spirits are much facilitated by the waters of laughter and pleasure. "The first thing a guest does when he gets there is take a sip from each of these springs, and from then on he never stops laughing and having a wonderful time."[13]

Jesting utopianism with a serious message still flourished a millennium and half later in More and Rabelais, both aficionados of Lucian. Along with Erasmus, More translated several of Lucian's dialogues. As More's biographer comments, "Lucian would seem an unlikely interest for two Christians, since he was bawdy, sometimes obscene, always skeptical of supernatural religion."[14] Yet his irony, his boldness, and perhaps his utopianism appealed to Erasmus and More. Erasmus's *Praise of Folly*, first published in 1511, was dedicated to More and punned on the Greek noun *moria* ("folly") associated with his name; it also defended the Lucian-like approach to humor Erasmus and More shared.[15] Erasmus wrote (to More) in his letter-introduction to *Praise of Folly* that "trifling may lead to something more serious."

> Jokes can be handled in such a way that any reader who is not altogether lacking in discernment can scent something far more rewarding in them than in the crabbed and specious arguments of some people we know—when, for example, one of them endlessly sings the praises of rhetoric or philosophy in a botched-up oration, another eulogizes a

prince. . . . Nothing is more entertaining than treating trivialities in such a way as to make it clear you are doing anything but trifle with them.[16]

This spirit informs More's *Utopia*, published in 1516, from the title, itself a joke (*utopia* = no place) to the characters. The main figure reporting about utopia is called—in a more literal English translation—Raphael "Nonsenso."[17] The original text included a page with the "utopian alphabet" and a specimen of (bad) utopian poetry written by the Poet Laureate, "Mr. Windbag." In his letter-introduction, More winks that he has heard of a "very pious theologian" who desperately wants the pope to send him to Utopia as its bishop. Before departing from his utopian island Raphael gives the inhabitants Greek works including Aristophanes and Lucian, "whom they find delightfully entertaining."[18] One recent study concludes that Lucian's *True History* was the "inspiration" for More's *Utopia*.[19] T. S. Dorsch, the classicist and translator, wrote, "I should place *Utopia* next to my copy of the works of Lucian."[20] Rhetorical lightness does not undermine More's seriousness—or Aristophanes'.

All this is equally true of another utopian sketch that appeared only fifteen years after More's *Utopia* by another admirer of Lucian, and the name of its author has become synonymous with satire and comedy: François Rabelais. Like More, Rabelais had translated Lucian; unlike More, in the words of his biographer, he "aspired to become the French Lucian."[21] To emphasize a link to More, in *Gargantua and Pantagruel* Rabelais named Gargantua's kingdom "Utopia."[22] In a series of famous chapters ending book 1, Gargantua builds the Abbey of Thélème to reward Friar John for his help in battle. The friar declines to direct an existing religious community; instead, he requests Gargantua to found a new "religious order in exactly contrary ways to all others."

The request pleases Gargantua who proceeds with gusto.

"Because ordinarily monks and nuns make three vows, that is of chastity, poverty, and obedience, it was decreed that there anyone could be regularly married, could become rich, and could live at liberty." He also dispensed with a tiresome schedule. Gargantua believes that "the greatest waste of time he knew was the counting of hours—what good does it do? —and the greatest nonsense in the world was to regulate one's life by the sound of a bell." Inasmuch as in religious communities "everything is encompassed, limited, and regulated by hours," in the Abbey of Thélème, "it was decreed that there be no clock or dial at all." This was a religious institution with a difference. For the residents:

> All their life was regulated not by laws, statues, or rules, but according to their free will and pleasure. They rose from bed when they pleased, and drank, ate, worked and slept when the fancy seized them. Nobody woke them; nobody compelled them either to eat or drink or do anything else whatever. So it was that Gargantua had established it. In their rules there was only one clause:
> DO WHAT YOU WILL.[23]

Yet the lightness and good cheer that generally enveloped utopianism dissipated. This can be stated more exactly and almost paradoxically. The announcement of "utopia" by Thomas More corresponds to its denouncement by Thomas More. Utopianism and modern anti-utopianism converge in More. The vast secondary literature on More covers all aspects of his life, yet most of it focuses on *Utopia* and, to a lesser extent, on his execution in 1535 after his refusal to countenance the succession of Anne Boleyn as queen of England. More entered royal service in 1518 and advanced to "theological councillor" and, in 1529, to Henry VIII's lord chancellor. However, he declined to accept Henry's machinations to shift the Church's supreme authority in England from the pope to himself as king. Through this maneuver Henry sought to legalize his divorce and remarriage—a series of acts that precipitated the English reformation.

For his unbending resistance to the king and his wide learning, history has been kind to More; he has generally been viewed as a great and principled humanist. The Catholic Church sainted him. The 1960 Broadway play (later turned into a movie) *A Man for All Seasons* painted More in the warmest of colors. "I do none harm," he states in the play. "I say none harm, I think none harm, and if this be not enough to keep a man alive, in good faith I long not to live."[24]

Yet More did do harm. In the service of the Crown he hunted and pursued Protestants and heretics. Historians and biographers have long known and argued over this, but it has barely intruded upon public consciousness—and has remained neglected when it did. A seven-hundred-page collection of "essential articles" on More barely mentions him as the scourge of heretics and Protestants.[25] Of course, for those interested in utopianism, More is simply the author of *Utopia*. J. H. Hexter's classic study concerns itself with reconstructing More's environment and mind as he was writing *Utopia* in the summer of 1515 and the fall of 1516—with one brief consideration of 1518, when More entered royal service.[26]

However, for those considering the larger events of the day—and the vagaries of utopia—More's reputation as a noble and sensitive humanist seems questionable. He pursued until death William Tyndale, the Protestant theologian whose English translation of the Old and New Testaments formed the basis of the King James Bible. The literary critic George Steiner has judged that Tyndale not only endowed the English Bible with a rare eloquence but that he "molded the governing forms of English style." Of the 287 words in the Sermon on the Mount in the Kings James Version, 242 are from Tyndale: "No man can serve two masters. For either he shall hate the one and love the other."[27] This is Tyndale, the man More persecuted tirelessly.

Brian Moynahan's recent account of More and Tyndale, subtitled " A Story of Martyrdom and Betrayal" closes bitterly. Like Steiner he reminds us that the King James Bible is largely based on Tyndale's work, but Tyndale is forgotten. On the other hand,

> Posterity has treated him [More] well. His general revelry in the stake and fire [for heretics], and his individual and obsessive hatred of William Tyndale, are largely forgotten. He progressed smoothly from beatification . . . to canonization. . . . He is plentifully honored in the names of schools, colleges, housing estates, and streets, by statues and monuments. . . . Paul II did him the ultimate honor on 31 October 2000 proclaiming him to be the patron saint of politicians.

Moynahan adds that this papal act is "at the very least, bizarre. Politicians persecute opponents readily enough without having More dangled in front of them as a role model."[28]

J. H. Hexter's study opens by musing on More's "mysterious" intention in writing *Utopia*, but the mystery thickens when one views the whole of More's career. After *Utopia* a new side of More surfaces: unyielding, ill humored, intolerant. The utopian More gave rise to the anti-utopian More. In *Utopia* the king laid down the rule that "every man might cultivate the religion of his choice, and might proselytize for it, provided he did so quietly, modestly, and rationally and without bitterness towards others." The king believed it was "errant folly for anyone to enforce conformity with his own beliefs by means of threats or violence," which would only lead to "fighting and rioting." "So he left the whole matter open, allowing each individual to choose what he would believe."[29]

After More entered into service to the crown, however, he did not "leave matters open" but fought with a heavy hand what he considered sedition and heresy. In the epitaph he wrote for himself, he proudly owned that he was a "molester of thieves, murderers, and heretics."[30] This formulation troubled even his admirers. When his monument was restored in the nineteenth century, "heretics" vanished from the epitaph. More now fought only "thieves and murderers."[31] Controversy continues as to whether More, while lord chancellor, personally oversaw the execution of six Protestants. An older account states emphatically, "the facts in this controversy seem clear: More did establish full toleration of all religions in Utopia . . . and he did, later, not only approve but also bring about the execution of heretics."[32]

What is beyond dispute is that More fought with increasing vigor and malice what he considered Lutheranism and sedition, censoring books and imprisoning their purveyors. As John Guy summarizes in his recent biography: in his first year as lord chancellor, More secured decrees and proclamations to proscribe over a hundred books. He arranged the arrest of those dealing in this literature, and when they were

> brought before More in Star Chambers, he applied the full severity of the law in the punishments which he handed down. The booksellers were fined and imprisoned. Their stocks of heretical literature were publicly burned. Lastly, they themselves were forced to perform public penance: being paraded on market days through the streets of London on horseback, sitting back-to-front, their coats 'pinned thick' with the proscribed books, while they were pelted with rotten fruits.[33]

More wrote a series of tracts attacking Luther and supporting the "burning of heretics" as something "lawful, necessary, and well done." [34] He relentlessly cursed, maligned, and insulted

Luther and his supporters. While violent and earthy language marked all English polemics of his day, More's deserves special mention. A prose sample of England's leading humanist:

> [Luther] has nothing in his mouth but privies, filth and dung, with which he plays the buffoon. . . . If he will swallow down his filth and lick up the dung with which he has so foully defiled his tongue and his pen . . . to carry nothing in his mouth but bilge-water, sewers, privies, filth and dung . . . We will take timely counsel, whether we wish . . . to leave this mad friarlet and privy-minded rascal with his ragings and ravings, with his filth and dung, shitting and beshitted.[35]

In one of these tracts he came close to disavowing *Utopia*. He replied to a charge that seeds of Lutheranism might be found in the book of his good friend Erasmus's *In Praise of Folly*. More denied it, but went on to say that "in these days" men "by their own default misconstrue and take harm of the very Scripture of God." If someone "would now translate *Moria* into English, or some works either that I have myself written ere this," probably referring to *Utopia*, More would take these books and "burn them both with my own hands."[36]

What turned the author of *Utopia* into a censor and persecutor? John Guy's measured conclusion is that the "the schizophrenia created by More's dual role as author of *Utopia* and inquisitor in heresy cases will never be dispelled."[37] Richard Marius, an editor of the complete works of More, offers a harsher assessment still. More, he writes in his biography, pursued heretics without "any flash of mercy or tolerance."

> More believed that they should be exterminated, and while he was in office he did everything in his power to bring that extermination to pass. That he did not succeed in be-

coming England's Torquemada [the Spanish Inquisitor] was a consequence of the king's quarrel with the pope and not a result of any quality of mercy that stirred through More's own heart.[38]

The biographer Jasper Ridley concludes the darkest judgement of all in *The Statesman and the Fanatic*. He calls More a totalitarian and mass murderer, the equal of any twentieth-century Stalinist or Nazi. He was a brilliant intellectual "whose principles and flawless logic" and repressed hatred "would have turned him into a fanatic determined to crush what he considers to be the forces of evil." One can imagine More, Ridley concludes, "after writing books about socialism and planning [his *Utopia*], becoming more and more obsessed with the menace of the enemy who was assaulting civilization, and reaching the point where he justified by specious arguments, the liquidation of millions of human beings as regrettable but necessary." For Ridley, people like Thomas More threaten the world.[39]

Ridley's conclusion cannot be sustained; he uses twentieth-century categories to damn More. Nevertheless, Ridley's argument deserves attention inasmuch as it exemplifies the anti-utopian ideology as it has taken shape in the last half century. He highlights the light-hearted utopian turning into the heavy-handed anti-utopian. Indeed, with More, or through More, we can see the emergence of modern anti-utopianism. Ridley links too neatly utopianism and totalitarianism, but something does happen to More that is worth considering. More's anti-utopian sentiment does not simply emerge out of the mystery or paradoxes of his character.

The world changed after More wrote *Utopia*. Lutheranism, Anabaptism, and the peasant wars swept through Europe. The utopianism that once seemed to More innocuous now struck him as dangerous speculation. "The past centuries have not seen anything more monstrous than the Anabaptists," wrote More in

1528.[40] As C. S. Lewis put it, "the times altered; and things that would once have seemed to him permissible or even salutary audacities came to seem to him dangerous." In *Utopia* More half seriously, half playfully defended a kind of communism. After the Reformation upsurges he attacked the communism of the Anabaptists as a horrible heresy—and defended private riches.[41]

As More responded to these religious and political threats of the sixteenth-century Reformation, he turned against his own past; perhaps for the first time, a virulent anti-utopianism surfaced in history. In two ways More anticipated the future. His own anti-utopianism, fed by a sense of betrayed utopian hopes, would prove typical, perhaps exemplified in the 1950 collection *The God That Failed* by disillusioned former communists such as Arthur Koestler and Ignazio Silone. In addition, twentieth-century accounts of totalitarianism would ratify More's vendetta. The classic work here is Norman Cohn's *The Pursuit of the Millennium*, published in 1957 and subtitled "Revolutionary Messianism in Medieval and Reformation Europe and Its Bearing on Modern Totalitarian Movements."

Cohn linked medieval and Reformation millenarianism with both Nazism and communism. This messianism sought to establish through a miraculous event or "final" struggle a world "inhabited by a humanity at once perfectly good and perfectly happy." For Cohn millennium movements not only issued into violence but prefigured modern totalitarianism. "The more carefully one compares the outbreaks of militant social chiliasm during the later Middle Ages with modern totalitarian movements the more remarkable the similarities appear." Both share a "form of politics" that Cohn dubs "subterranean revolutionary eschatology." Both operate with "phantasies" of a final struggle in which "the world will be renewed and history brought to its consummation."[42]

Cohn's book closes with a discussion of Thomas Müntzer and the militant Anabaptism that disturbed Thomas More. For

Marxists from Friederic Engels to Karl Kautsky and Ernst Bloch, Müntzer has long been a hero, a mystical revolutionary championing the common people.[43] Conversely, for critics of Marx, Müntzer prefigures everything deplorable about utopianism. "If one compares these two old Testament types" of Müntzer and Marx, writes Abraham Friesen in *Reformation and Utopia*, "one finds the greatest similarities in their thought. The point of departure for both is an eschatological one: the hoped-for Kingdom of God on earth, that is the communist classless society."[44] While nothing directly links Müntzer and More, Müntzer emerged from a world defined by Luther on one side and Erasmus on the other.[45] More was battling what he saw as his own illegitimate offspring—utopianism gone amuck.

Cohn's *Pursuit of the Millennium* (1957) belongs to a series of writings that appeared in the wake of World War II and defined contemporary anti-utopianism. In a dozen years a liberal anti-utopian consensus took shape that has not only endured but has gained strength with each passing decade. Its major writings include Karl Popper's *The Open Society and Its Enemies* (1945), J. L. Talmon's *The Origins of Totalitarian Democracy* (1951), Hannah Arendt's *Origins of Totalitarianism* (1951), and several essays of Isaiah Berlin from the 1950s. Together, these texts make a compelling and inclusive case about the dangers of utopian thought. Popper begins with Plato; Cohn with the Middle Ages; Talmon with the eighteenth-century Enlightenment; Arendt with the French Revolution. Not only do their intellectual approaches complement each other, but their biographies share a great deal. For starters they roughly belonged to the generation born before or during World War I: Popper (1902–1994); Arendt (1906–1975); Berlin (1909–1997); Cohn (1915–); Talmon (1916–1980). Second, they were all Jewish or of Jewish descent. Third, except for Cohn, they fled or left their countries of origin. Fourth, except for Cohn, they came from the left.[46]

To be sure, these features do not automatically produce anti-utopianism. Yet they determined anti-utopian thought in several ways. The facts of the authors' lives bestowed upon anti-utopianism an indisputable gravitas. The criticism of utopia seemed as considerable as its eminent exponents. People such as Hannah Arendt and Isaiah Berlin appeared to the Anglo-American universe as emissaries from another world; they were veterans, and sometimes refugees, of wars, upheavals, and lethal governments.[47] They tapped experiences unavailable to Americans. They spoke English with old world accents. To denizens of Berkeley Hannah Arendt incarnated the central European revolutionary. "Rosa Luxemburg has come again," remarked one student, after hearing Arendt lecture.[48]

The experiences of war and flight saturate their writings. They spoke for a generation that had witnessed everything. "We no longer hope for an eventual restoration of the old world order with all its traditions," wrote Arendt in the opening to *Origins of Totalitarianism*. "Two world wars in one generation, separated by an uninterrupted chain of local wars and revolutions, followed by no peace treaty for the vanquished and no respite for the victor" means that the "essential structure of all civilizations is at the breaking point."[49] Their analyses borrowed an aura of profundity from their lives. These sages knew of what they wrote, what Arendt called "the truly radical nature of Evil."

Their biographical similarities also colored anti-utopianism in specific ways. By dint of their age and political inclinations they had been attracted to communism before confronting fascism. The Russian Revolution, the European revolutionary upheavals after World War I, and Marxism in the 1920s stamped their work. Disenchantment with communism marked their lives but preceded the full threat of fascism of the 1930s. This meant they sought understanding of what happened to Marxism before turning to fascism; the latter was viewed through the lens of the former. Eventually they saw Marxism and fascism as related phenomena, different versions of totalitarianism. Inasmuch as a utopianism informed Marxism (despite the anti-utopian pronouncements of Marx and Engels), the theory of totalitarianism, which they developed, underlined the poisonousness of utopianism. Presented by refugee scholars of great repute and allure, it carried the day. Their liberal criticism became the conventional wisdom of our time; it damned utopianism as the scourge of history.

This trajectory is exemplified by Karl Popper, who was the first and probably the most important figure of this group to elaborate a forceful anti-utopianism. In *The Poverty of Historicism* and *The Open Society and Its Enemies*, which date from 1944 and 1945, Popper presented a full-scale criticism of utopian thought that has continued to resonate. He dedicated *The Poverty of Historicism* to the "memory of the countless men and women of all creeds or nations or races who fell victims to the fascist and communist belief in Inexorable Laws of Historical Destiny." While "belief in Inexorable Laws of Historical Destiny" might seem distant from utopianism, for Popper they were synonymous.

Popper, who was born in Vienna in 1902, believed Jews were treated reasonably well in prewar Austria, but anti-Semitism did cause his parents to convert to Lutheranism—"to become assimilated."[50] He belonged to a network of family and friends dense with gifted artists, musicians, and scientists. He was related, for example, both to Bruno Walter, the conductor, and Josef Breuer, the doctor who collaborated with Freud.[51] Intellectually inclined, he gravitated, like many of his acquaintances, toward politics and psychology. He was twelve when World War I began; he was sixteen when it ended in upheaval and revolution. The Austro-Hungarian monarchy, a vast, unwieldy collection of territories and peoples, became, among other things, the Austrian Republic. "The war years, and their aftermath," he recalled, "were in every respect decisive for my intellectual development."[52] In a "historical note" to *The Poverty of Historicism*, Popper wrote that its thesis "goes back to the winter of 1919–20."

For a moment a red revolution flickered and attracted the young Popper, who joined the ranks of the far left. In the Spring of 1919 Popper participated in a demonstration organized by communists to free comrades held in the central police station. Shooting broke out, and several young workers were killed. "I was horrified and shocked by the brutality of the police," Popper recalled, "but also by myself. For I felt that as a Marxist I bore part of the responsibility for the tragedy—at least in principle." He questioned whether the "scientific" Marxist creed promising "to bring about a better world" was based on real knowledge about society. "The whole experience . . . produced in me a life-long revulsion of feeling."[53]

Popper remained emphatically leftist, however,[54] and so much in the romantic thrall of the proletariat that for several years he tried turning himself into a manual worker—first a road builder and then a cabinetmaker. He eventually drifted into social work, teaching, and philosophy. His ideas on the deficiencies of Marxism continued to develop, but he kept them under wraps for political reasons: he did not want to weaken the Marxists, who formed the backbone of the opposition to fascist authoritarianism. However, the situation in central Europe deteriorated. Even before 1933, when the Nazis came to power in Germany, Popper sensed that the days of Austrian democracy were numbered, and with it the days of Jews. By the mid-1930s Popper actively sought to leave Austria. In 1937 he sailed for New Zealand to accept an offer of lectureship at Canterbury University College—none too soon. In 1938 Hitler marched through the cheering streets of Vienna. With the demise of

Austria, Popper believed he no longer needed to "hold back" his criticism of the socialists. He set out to elaborate his ideas in *The Poverty of Historicism* and *The Open Society and Its Enemies*.

The Poverty of Historicism puns on Marx's *The Poverty of Philosophy*, itself a spoof of Proudhon's *The Philosophy of Poverty*. While Popper's language is frequently idiosyncratic, if not misleading—this was only the second work he wrote in English—his anti-utopian convictions stand out. Popper identifies as overlapping failings historicism, historical prophecy, and utopianism. He frequently uses formulations like "Utopianism and historicism agree." For Popper, historicism posits laws and rhythms of history; it seeks to know the future and, sometimes, to intervene to control or quicken "impending social developments." Marxism "excellently represents the historicist position," a position that spells out the rise and fall of capitalism and calls for the proletariat to speed its demise.[55]

To drive his point home on the dangers of utopianism, Popper draws parallels between nonhistoricist (and nonutopian) and "historicist" (and utopian) ideas and two different approaches to social reform. The nonhistoricist perspective employs what Popper calls "piecemeal engineering." Factual limitations impress the piecemeal engineer, who like any good scientist focuses on parts, not the whole. He or she believes in "small adjustments and re-adjustments" and proceeds "step by step, carefully comparing the results expected with the results achieved." The piecemeal reformer "tinkers" but does not pursue a "method of re-designing it [society] as a whole." On the other hand, the historicist, "holistic," or "Utopian engineer" aims at "remodeling the 'whole of society' in accordance with a definite plan or blueprint." Yet the whole, Popper believes, "cannot be made the object of scientific study" or "control or reconstruction." This eludes the utopians who plan to "reconstruct our society 'as a whole' " and thereby succumb to the "totalitarian intuition."[56]

Popper expanded these ideas in the two volumes of *The Open Society and Its Enemies*, which is devoted to understanding totalitarianism and the fight against it. He remarked that his book was conceived in March 1938, "the day I received the news of the invasion of Austria" by the Nazis. Yet the book is mainly devoted not to Nazism but to Marxism and utopianism. Popper observes an elective affinity between democracy and piecemeal engineering, on one side, and totalitarianism and utopian engineering, on the other. The former examines specific institutions and their functions and asks questions about appropriate means for given ends, such as "is this institution well designed and organized to serve" these goals? He provides an example: insurance.

The social engineer does not care whether the insurance industry originated to serve private profit or the public good. However, he may "offer a criticism of certain institutions of insurances, showing, perhaps, how to increase their profits, or . . . to increase the benefits they render to the public." In other words, the social engineer examines means, not ends, and judges whether something is tailored to its goals. The utopian, on the other hand, considers origins, ends, and "true roles" of insurance. He or she will evaluate whether "its mission is to serve the common weal." The utopian takes the standpoint of history and assesses the intention of the founders and its contemporary significance. [57]

The piecemeal engineer is as committed to social betterment as the utopian, but he uses tools that are more practical and less violent. For the engineer, perfection is not attainable. While every generation has a right to happiness, instead of seeking "the greatest ultimate good" the down-to-earth engineer diminishes the great evils afflicting mankind. For Popper, "this difference is far from being merely verbal. . . . It is the difference between a reasonable method of improving the lot of man, and a method which . . . may easily lead to an intolerable increase in human suffering." Moreover, the existence of specific injustices can be agreed upon, unlike "the establishment of some ideal."

> It is infinitely more difficult to reason about an ideal society. Social life is so complicated that few men, or none at all, could judge a blueprint for social engineering on the grand scale; whether it be practicable. . . . As opposed to this, blueprints for piecemeal engineering are comparatively simple. They are blueprints for single institutions, for health and unemployed insurance, for instance, or arbitration courts, or anti-depression budgeting or educational reform. If they go wrong, the damage is not very great, and a re-adjustment not very difficult. . . . It is easier to reach a reasonable agreement about existing evils . . . than . . . about an ideal good.

The utopian blueprinters aim to realize a far-reaching ideal, and this leads to a dictatorship. They want to transform society, "leaving no stone unturned." It is the "sweep" of utopianism—its "desire to build a world which is not only a little better and more rational than ours, but which is free from all its ugliness: not a crazy quilt, an old garment badly patched, but an entirely new gown, a really beautiful new world"—that makes it so dangerous.[58]

Popper formulated these ideas sharply in a 1947 lecture, "Utopia and Violence." In title and sentiment the talk anticipated Arendt's "Ideology and Terror" in her (revised) *Origins of Totalitarianism.* Popper called himself a rationalist, but for this Austrian philosopher we can judge an action rationally "only relative to some given ends." Utopianism, however, comes up with new ends or "a more or less clear and detailed description or blueprint of our ideal state." We know these ends "from the dreams of our poets and prophets." They cannot be rationally discussed but "only proclaimed from the housetops." Inasmuch as these ends resist proof, the utopian must use violence to bring them about. The scientist behaves more carefully. "No amount of physics will tell a scientist that it is the right thing for him to construct a plough, or an airplane, or an atomic bomb. Ends must be adopted by him, or given to him."

Yet even Popper admitted that this is almost too simple. Did it mean one must never have ideals or goals but just accept assignments or the status quo? Not exactly. He writes that one must know how to distinguish between "admissible plans for social reform and inadmissible Utopian blueprints." He has some advice: avoid large and distant goals. "Work for the elimination of concrete evils rather than for the realization of abstracts goods. . . . In more practical terms: fight for the elimination of poverty by direct means—for example, by making sure that everybody has a minimal income. Or fight against epidemics and disease by erecting hospitals and schools of medicine. . . . But . . . do not allow your dreams of a beautiful world to lure you away from the claims of men who suffer here and now." Much could be achieved "if only we could give up dreaming about distant ideals and fighting over our Utopians blueprints for a new world and a new man."[59]

Popper's reasonable argument has echoed down the intellectual corridors of history; each decade it gains more recruits. In the immediate future it would be supplemented by "end of ideology" thinkers such as Raymond Aron in France and Daniel Bell in the United States. Other refugee thinkers would confirm and collaborate Popper's positions. They would expand the category of utopians to include all those with a plan, and they would charge utopians with violence. Implicitly or explicitly, "utopians" meant "Marxists." That much, perhaps most, of twentieth-century mass violence had little to do with utopians barely intruded upon the argument. Were the principal actors of

World War I utopians? Were Adolph Eichmann and the Nazis? On this Arendt would change gears, but liberal wisdom, including her own, would not be affected.

Jacob Talmon left Poland in 1934 as a young man to study at the Hebrew University in Palestine. He continued his studies in France, fleeing Paris for London as the Nazis arrived in 1940.[60] He recalled researching "the Jacobin terrorist dictatorship" as the Soviet Union staged the Moscow Trials in 1937 and 1938. The similarities between the Jacobin and Stalinist repression struck him. "The parallel seemed to suggest the existence of some unfathomable and inescapable law which causes revolutionary salvationist schemes to evolve into reigns of terror, and the promise of a perfect direct democracy to assume in practice the form of totalitarian dictatorship."[61]

Talmon's chef-d'oeuvre, his three-volume study entitled *The Origins of Totalitarian Democracy*, *Political Messianism*, and *The Myth of the Nation and the Vision of Revolution*, written over thirty years (1951 to 1980), traced the history of this "salvationist" ethos. He almost exclusively examined radical, socialist, and Marxist movements from the French Revolution to the Russian. He explained that many historians might be tempted to dismiss the "Messianic ideologies" as the expression of lunatics with "long-winded and utterly unreadable treatises or obscure ephemeral journals," who conduct "bizarre experiments in communal living and Utopian communes." This would be a mistake, he believes: these leftist ideas haunt the world.[62]

In *The Origins of Totalitarian Democracy* Talmon distinguishes what he called "liberal democracy" and "totalitarian Messianic democracy." In terms echoing Popper, he writes that liberal democracy employs "trial and error" and "pragmatic contrivances," and messianic democracy posits a "preordained, harmonious and perfect scheme of things." Inasmuch as an "absolute ideal" drives the totalitarian faith, it ignores, coerces, or intimidates men. "Political Messianism is bound to replace empirical thinking and free criticism with reasoning by definition, based in *a priori* collective concepts which must be accepted whatever the evidence of the senses."[63] Or, as he wrote elsewhere, "the tragic paradox of Utopianism" is that instead of leading to freedom "it brought totalitarian coercion."[64]

Talmon's first volume took up the French Revolution and its aftermath; the second volume explored socialists, Marx, and some virulent conservatives up till 1848. He reaffirmed his basic thesis: "No period before or after has experienced so luxurious a flowering of Utopian schemes." Now he preferred the term "political Messianism" to cover all the "rivers and rivulets into which the Revolutionary Messianic flood broke in the early nineteenth century." They all shared "the totalitarian-democratic expectations of some pre-ordained, all-embracing" social order that would issue into "real freedom of men."[65] Yet Talmon was too much the honest historian to force the material into his categories. In this volume, and increasingly the next, his information overwhelms his argument, which continues to retreat.[66] He tries to be comprehensive, but everything does not fit. Do the reactionary romantics like de Maistre, who, at best, idolized irrationality, force, and authority, confirm the idea of "political Messianism" or revolutionary utopianism? Talmon summarizes de Maistre but hardly links him to his own argument.

The third volume, *The Myth of the Nation and the Vision of Revolution* further revises Talmon's thesis. The main theme of modern history, which he had earlier posited as the contest between liberal and totalitarian democracies, now becomes the struggle between totalitarian democracy, as expressed in Bolshevism, and nationalism, as expressed in "Fascism-Nazism." Was Nazism some sort of utopianism? This is not clear, for, like Popper before him, Talmon concentrates on socialism, Marxism, and Bolshevism. In this 600-page volume only a dozen pages take up Nazism. As with Popper, the imbalance in coverage suggests the imbalance in the theory, which almost exclusively focuses on the formation and malformations of Marxism.

In his conclusion Talmon seeks to affirm his argument. He asks forthrightly, what is the relationship between these two totalitarianisms, Bolshevism and Nazism? "If their origins and development were wholly disparate, why the striking similarities in patterns of thought and modes of operating?" Talmon weakly concludes that a "salvationist" ethos marked each: both claimed the truth; both adhered to a "Manichean view of history." Yet the "ultimate differences between messianic totalitarian democracy and Nazi-Fascist totalitarianism" should not be ignored, he admits. Even if the differences "make little difference in practice," the Marxist tradition claimed the French Revolution with its vision of universal brotherhood. The Nazi-Fascists "defiantly and uncompromisingly rejected that vision."[67]

Talmon's *Origins of Totalitarian Democracy* had "vast influence among historians," but the larger impact of his work has been limited, and probably has declined since the 1980s, especially compared to that of Isaiah Berlin and Hannah Arendt.[68] Perhaps because he modulated his original thesis as his studies proceeded and respected his findings more than his categories, a militant anti-utopianism finds little support in his work. Only one book by Talmon remains in print, for example, but scores of Arendt's books are available—and over a hundred works about her contributions are on the shelves. She is "the most discussed figure in recent political theory dissertations," trumpets an admirer.[69] Prizes, stamps, streets, and even a rail connection (between Karlsruhe and Hannover) have been named after her. "Hannah Arendt," concludes Walter Laqueur, "has been more successful than any other German philosopher, living or dead."[70] Isaiah Berlin hardly trails; in fact, he may lead with over sixty volumes of editions, anthologies, and collections in print—virtually everything that Berlin ever wrote or introduced.

In a sign of the times, the enthusiasm for Berlin has extended to encompass even his juvenilia. Oxford University Press recently published a Berlin collection containing a story by the preadolescent sage with learned commentary about its meaning. "While we certainly would do badly to read conceptual opinions into the minds of this twelve-year-old author," qualifies Ian Harris before taking the leap, "the piece reveals the disposition which finds expression in Berlin's mature work." In particular, Harris detects a link between the "cosy little home" in Master Berlin's story and the concept of "negative freedom" in Professor Berlin's theory.

The plot thickens, however. Berlin's literary executor reports that the story won a "hamper of tuck" (an anglicism for sweets) in a children's literary competition—at least according to the mature Berlin. However, this claim has not yet been confirmed by scholarly investigation. "Frustratingly," confesses Berlin's indefatigable editor, Henry Hardy, the 1922 "Tuck Hamper Competition" of *The Boy's Herald* does not list Berlin as a prizewinner. Hardy ponders the delicate situation. Could Berlin have claimed an award he did not receive? Hardy examines other prize submissions. Inasmuch as the other winners are "merely humorous anecdotes" and are much briefer than Berlin's, "perhaps" the judges awarded the youth "an *ex gratia* hamper for an impressive contribution in the wrong genre."[71] The matter awaits further study.

Berlin was born in Riga, Latvia, in 1909 to an affluent Jewish lumber-merchant family that moved to Petrograd in 1915. After the October Revolution his father continued to do business with the Soviets, but he "hated" them from the beginning.[72] Distaste for the Bolsheviks, Russian anti-Semitism, and Berlin's senior's Anglophilia led the family to emigrate to England in 1921, when

Berlin was eleven. He explained later that his youthful experience of the Russian Revolution—in particular his witnessing of a Tsarist policeman being dragged off to be lynched—cured him forever of any sympathy for communism.[73] He attended Oxford, and—except for several years during the war when he served the British foreign office as a press-attaché and as first secretary in New York, Washington, and Moscow—he stayed at Oxford in various capacities for the rest of his life.

While Popper was known as cantankerous and lived in "legendary seclusion" in the rural outskirts of London,[74] Berlin was engaging, social, and famously available at Oxford, where he gave innumerable interviews. Popper broke with almost all his students and colleagues and believed himself underappreciated; Berlin took pride in maintaining relations even with his critics and believed his own contribution inflated. Undoubtedly, Berlin's impact hails partly from his charm, demeanor, and social skills.

His work reflects his winning personal traits; his style is conversational, readable—and diffuse. His sentences meander on. "When men, as occasionally happens," begins the title essay in *The Sense of Reality*,

> develop a distaste for the age in which they live, and love and admire some past period with such uncritical devotion that it is clear that, if they had their choice, they would wish to be alive then and not now—and when, as the next step, they seek to introduce into their lives certain of the habits and practices of the idealized past, and criticize the present for falling short of, and for degeneration from, this past—we tend to accuse them of nostalgic "escapism," romantic antiquarianism, lack of realism; we dismiss their efforts as attempts to "turn the clock back", to "ignore the forces of history" or "fly in the face of the facts", at best touching and childish and pathetic.[75]

With the single exception of a small book on Karl Marx, which was written as an introductory text, Berlin wrote essays, and these essays derived almost exclusively from commissioned projects and invited lectures. Berlin was well aware of the limitations of his work. He never pursued a book-length argument, and he revised and softened the pronouncements of even his most famous essays. One tough-minded critic compared the original "four essays" on liberty, published in periodicals, with those in the book and found significant revisions. In adding only a word or deleting a sentence, Berlin sometimes altered a decisive point. He had closed his classic 1950 "Political Ideas in the Twentieth Century" by stating that the political problems "are *eo facto* not the central questions of human life. They are not, and never have been, the fundamental issues which embody the changing outlook and the most intense preoccupation of their time and generation."[76] In the book version, Berlin inserted "only" before "central questions," dropped the second sentence and added a couple of murky lines. Political problems now "are *eo facto* not the *only* central questions of human life" (emphasis added). The notion that they are "never" central has been revoked. Between 1950 and 1969 political issues become fundamental.

Moreover, as Anthony Arblaster, who compared the versions, notes, Berlin frequently made almost random substitutions in his learned lists that established historical lineages of ideas. In the book version, Thomas Hobbes replaces Thomas Aquinas; "Christian Socialists" replace "Bonapartists"; Schopenhauer replaces Tolstoy; Chekhov replaces Marx; de Maistre replaces Machiavelli. Arblaster comments: "The frequency of these changes undermines confidence in Berlin's judgement in selecting the names. Reviewers have often written admiringly about Berlin's 'vast erudition,' 'pyrotechnical brilliance.' . . . Perhaps too many readers have been so blinded by the extraordinary range of references that they have not been able to see clearly enough to consider whether Berlin's grand generalizations really do apply to all the thinkers he links with them."[77]

"Political Ideas in the Twentieth Century" also includes Berlin's signature reference: a quotation from Kant about the "crooked timber of humanity," which appears throughout his essays and as the title of a collection.[78] For Berlin the phrase virtually encapsulates his ideas on pluralism and his distaste for planned utopias. The conclusion to "Political Ideas in the Twentieth Century" is pure Berlin in its rejection of utopian planning and its embrace of messy pluralism. We are ensnared in a dilemma of freedom or government welfare:

> The way out must therefore lie in some logically untidy, flexible, and even ambiguous compromise: every situation calls for its own specific policy, since out of the crooked timber of humanity, as Kant once remarked, no straight thing was ever made. What the age calls for is not (as we are often told) more faith or stronger leadership or more rational organization. Rather it is the opposite—less Messianic ardor, more enlightened skepticism, more toleration of idiosyncrasies, more frequent *ad hoc* and ephemeral arrangements.[79]

While it may be foolhardy to argue with these laudable sentiments, Berlin enlists Kant for his own purposes. As Perry Anderson has observed, "Here, we are given to understand, is a signal expression of that rejection of all perfectionist utopias" by pluralism. Yet Anderson suggests that Berlin, who cites Kant on this score at least eight times in his main essays, distorts his meaning.[80] For one thing, the citation comes from Kant's most utopian writing, his "Idea for a Universal History." In their compendious survey of Western utopianism, Frank and Fritzie Manuel find in this essay "an emotional quality" rarely evident in anything else he wrote. "It represents Kant's utopia and his belief, sometimes a bit faltering, that mankind was getting there, a German version of the dream of reason."[81]

In this little work Kant broaches the possibility of a universal history in which humanity advances toward utopia. As its original 1784 editor stated, "One of Professor Kant's cherished ideas is that the ultimate end of the human race is the attainment of the most perfect civil constitution." He added that Kant points out "the extent to which humanity has at different times approached or distanced itself from this end, as well as what is still to be done to attain it."[82] Moreover, the way that Kant develops this idea of mankind progressing toward perfection is almost the opposite of Berlin's. Kant argues that natural antagonisms force individuals to leave isolation and unfold their talents in society, thereby attaining culture, happiness ("as far as it is possible on earth"), and freedom. Mankind needs a social order to become free. In other words, society that might appear repressive actually provides security and education that permit an individual to prosper. It is not so much that out of the crooked timber of humanity nothing straight can be made, but that to grow straight and true humanity needs a good social order.

> It is just as with trees in the forest, which need each other, for in seeking to take the air and sunlight from each other, each obtains a beautiful, straight shape, while those that grow in freedom and separate from one another branch out randomly, and are stunted, bent, and twisted [*krüppelig, schief, und krumm*].

Kant adds that "all the culture and art" of mankind are a product of this discipline; they are the fruit of a social order.[83]

Isaiah Berlin once remarked that he was like a taxicab; hailed, he went in any direction. But this is an overstatement, perhaps a misstatement. Berlin returned again and again to basic themes of pluralism. His much-cited essays from the 1950s hammered away at the virtues of pluralism and the dangers of utopianism. That was his taxi stand. His categories sought to distinguish a dangerous idea of utopian freedom from a benign pluralistic freedom. In "Two Concepts of Liberty," "negative" freedom entails a domain of noninterference. "The wider the area of non-interference the wider my freedom."[84] The problem resides with "positive" freedom, "not freedom from, but freedom to—to lead one prescribed form of life." It fuels many of the "nationalist, communist, authoritarian, and totalitarian creeds of our day." In other words, "negative" freedom constitutes pluralism and "positive" freedom dictatorships.[85]

In earlier formulations (in a series of lectures from 1952), Berlin distinguished two notions of liberty, but here he identified them as Anglo-French and German. "The principal preoccupation of many Western European thinkers was to guard the liberty of the individual against encroachment. . . . What they meant by liberty was non-interference—a fundamentally negative concept." English and French reformers, even revolutionaries, sought to create "a certain vacuum" around the individual, providing a space where one can fulfill one's wishes. "One should not criticize these wishes. Each man's ends are his own; the business of the State is to prevent collisions." Next to this idea, there is "another notion of freedom, which blossomed among the Germans."

Berlin finds the other idea first developed by Fichte, where freedom signifies submission to the collectivity or nation. "What of that individual freedom . . . which the British and the French writers defended?" Fichte and those who follow him dissolve the Anglo-French notion into the community, whose greatest force is the leader who molds the nation into "a single organic whole." Here we have two notions of liberty, "the liberal and authoritarian, open and closed."[86] In the later formulation Berlin gave up the national linkage, but renamed as negative and positive, he saw the two kinds of freedom as unfolding in "divergent" directions. "These are not two different interpretations of a single concept [of liberty], but two profoundly divergent and irreconcilable attitudes to the ends of life"[87]

Both as an argument and a piece of intellectual history, Berlin's treatment of liberty leaves much to be desired. One need look no further than Matthew Arnold's *Culture and Anarchy* to find a position that derails Berlin's. Arnold can hardly be categorized as an adherent of a closed society, yet this liberal thinker enunciated a cogent criticism of what Berlin calls "negative" freedom. Indeed, he entitled one chapter of *Culture and Anarchy* "Doing as One Likes." "Our prevalent notion," he wrote, "is that it is a most happy and important thing for a man merely to be able to do as he likes. On what he is to do when he is thus free to do as he likes, we do not lay so much stress."[88]

Arnold wrote elsewhere "Freedom, like Industry, is a very good horse to ride;—but to ride somewhere." The Englishman who shouts "We are free! we are free!" thinks it is "the highest pitch of development and civilization" when his letters are carried between Islington and Camberwell twelve times a day; and trains run between them four times an hour. "He thinks it is nothing that the trains only carry him from an illiberal, dismal life at Islington to an illiberal, dismal life at Camberwell; and the letters only tell him that such is the life there."[89] For Arnold the relentless English emphasis on "doing as one likes"— in Berlin's terms, celebrating negative freedom—constitutes a failure to look at the ends of freedom and the wider society.

As with many of Berlin's arguments, the lineages established and the details furnished hardly matter. The point, rather, is that Berlin ratifies an inherent and irreducible pluralism that gives the lie to any utopian theorizing—perhaps to any theorizing. His insistence on the pluralism of values, the individuality of freedom, and the fraud of total solutions is Berlin's greatest strength, but also his greatest weakness. "There have always been people who have wanted to be secure in some tight establishment . . . in some rigid system," said Berlin in his 1952 lecture on Hegel. "But that is not what we call liberty." Liberty lies in "the ability to choose as you wish to choose, because you wish to choose, uncoerced, unbullied, not swallowed up in some vast system."[90]

Twenty-five years later in "The Decline of the Utopian Ideas in the West," and thirty-five years later in "The Pursuit of the Ideal," Berlin rephrases these ideas, ratifying them with quotes by Kant on the "crooked timber of humanity." "Side by side" with the collision of values, "there persists the age-old dream" that will provide "the final solution to all human ills." But this is an illusion because "ultimate values may be incompatible with one another"; moreover, the illusion is lethal, giving "a wide licence to inflict suffering on other men" for the sake of utopia.[91] The notion of a "perfect whole" or "the ultimate system" is "incoherent" and "unattainable." "The search for perfection does seem to me a recipe for bloodshed." Instead of seeking perfection, we must realize that the "collision of values" is the essence of "what we are." We are "doomed to choose, and every choice may entail an irreparable loss."[92]

These truths teeter on the edge of truisms. They retain a conceptual bite by virtue of context. Verities are worth trumpeting where they are unknown or challenged. But Berlin's propositions are not. His ideas on pluralism and the dangers of utopianism partake of the basic Anglo-American mental household. We should be wary of "drastic action, in personal life or in public policy," he writes, since they may lead to unanticipated suffering. Instead of fighting for a "new and nobler society" we must engage in "utilitarian solutions" and "trade-offs." "The best that can be done, as a general rule, is to maintain a precarious equilibrium that will prevent the occurrence of desperate situations."[93] Stefan Collini remarks on the "collective self-congratulation" in Berlin's rehearsal of the necessity of partial answers. If Berlin had addressed this argument to some real opponents in the 1950s, say to Marxist historians like Christopher Hill or Eric Hobsbawm, observes Collini, "it would be easier to see that it was genuinely cutting wood." Offered, however, to the readers of *The New York Review of Books* in the 1980s it has the "reassuringness of a bedtime story."[94]

It is not simply that Berlin preached to the converted; he also muffled his context and argument. He admitted that his "Two Concepts of Liberty" was "deliberately" anti-Marxist. "I was maddened by all the Marxist cheating which went on, all the things that were said about 'true liberty,' [the] Stalinist and communist patter about 'true freedom.'"[95] Yet he never approached his targets closely. He discussed the dangers of utopianism and totalitarianism; he took up Marxism; he appraised past intellectual luminaries; but he stayed safely insulated from his contemporaries.

It is striking, even astonishing, that this much-honored, much-celebrated liberal political philosopher never risked a single sustained encounter with another twentieth-century thinker. He felt at home among eighteenth- and nineteenth-century writers, most of them Russian, but kept his distance from those of his own century. He must be the only twentieth-century intellectual esteemed for his engagement with the world who successfully avoided engagement with authors of his time.[96] Weber or Freud, Husserl or Heidegger, Camus or Sartre, Benjamin or Adorno: they pass unmentioned by Berlin—or barely mentioned. In typical Berlinian manner, he preempts criticism by humility. "I am told that Heidegger undermined traditional epistemology," he remarks in a footnote, "but since I do not understand his language or views, I am in no position to comment."[97]

Nor does Berlin's biography offer a contrasting picture to his philosophical cautiousness. In political and intellectual worlds alike, Berlin played it safe. Drawing on his personal contact with Berlin and Michael Ignatieff's biography, Christopher Hitchens

suggests that Berlin "sometimes felt or saw the need to be courageous, but usually—oh dear—at just the same moment that he
remembered an urgent appointment elsewhere."[98] His few interventions do not burnish his image as a righteous liberal. He privately helped blackball the Marxist historian Isaac Deutscher,
while publicly claiming he did not; he criticized T. S. Eliot for
anti-Semitism and diplomatically withdrew the criticism.
Ignatieff notes that Berlin sensed that his own politeness "shad-
ed into obsequiousness." On the major issues of the day he either said nothing or vaguely endorsed the establishment.
Hitchens summarizes: "In every instance given by Ignatieff, or
known to me, from the Cold War through Algeria to Suez to
Vietnam, Berlin strove to find a high 'liberal' justification either
for the status quo or for the immediate needs of the conservative
authorities."[99]

If these comments can be chalked up as leftist gripes, virtually the same charges have emerged from the opposite shore.
Tapping, like Hitchins, into his own experience and Ignatieff's
biography, the neoconservative Norman Podhoretz finds Berlin
guilty of "spinelessness." Berlin praised one of Podhoretz's he-
roes, Chaim Weizmann, for believing that one must not remain
neutral or uncommitted toward the great issues of the day; it is
an absolute duty, come what may, to take stands. Yet, Podhoretz
notes, "time after time, it was precisely this 'absolute duty' that
Berlin failed to discharge." His only criticism of Israel came on
his death bed, when he implored the Israelis to accept a com-
promise and territorial partition with the Palestinians—a position, Podhoretz notes, that put Berlin "solidly in line with the
opinion being voiced by practically everyone else."[100] Berlin
privately lamented the actions of student radicals in the 1960s
but publicly said nothing. "Where was Berlin?" asks Podhoretz.
"He was nowhere to be seen. . . . So much for his willingness to
stand . . . unflinchingly for his convictions." Podhoretz offers
other examples of Berlin's disappearing act and concludes that

this "great equivocator" was "fearful" of taking any political stand that "might jeopardize his ever-growing intellectual and social prestige"[101]

Berlin's waffling contrasts sharply with the political forthrightness of the liberal hero from whom he borrowed his ideas about the two forms of liberty. Benjamin Constant, the Swiss-French nineteenth-century liberal publicist, distinguished ancient and modern forms of liberty. For Constant, commerce and private interactions constituted modern liberty. "To be happy," he wrote in 1814, anticipating Berlin, "men need only to be left in perfect independence in all that concerns their occupations, their undertakings, their sphere of activity, their fantasies."[102] The ancients had sought their freedom in the public domain, not in their home or individual activities. The moderns reverse this; they focus on the private sphere. "Our freedom must consist of peaceful enjoyment and private independence."[103]

Constant wrote with eloquence and force about liberty. He was also far ahead of Berlin—as well as very different from him. Constant believed in the "perfectibility" of mankind or a movement towards equality,[104] which would earn him a totalitarian label from Berlin. The Oxford philosopher derived "negative" or modern liberty from a "conception of freedom . . . scarcely older than the Renaissance or the Reformation." It is "comparatively modern. There seems to be scarcely any discussion of individual liberty as a conscious political ideal . . . in the ancient world." For Berlin this conception defines freedom: "The desire not to be impinged upon, to be left to oneself, has been a mark of high civilization." [105]

Constant, more rooted in material life than Berlin, derived the modern idea from new social conditions, not from a new "conception." In his lecture "The Liberty of the Ancients Compared with That of the Moderns," he enumerates the markedly distinct situation of ancient cities and modern states. In ancient Greece liberty entailed public participation in city government; citizens gathered to discuss and vote. This is no longer possible—nor desirable. Simply the size of modern Britain or the United States forbids direct participation. Second, the abolition of slavery eliminates the "leisure" indispensable for active citizens. "Without the slave population of Athens, 20,000 Athenians could never have spent every day at the public square in discussion." Third, the onset of commerce—read capitalism—redirects man's activities from public meetings to private business. Now each man is preoccupied with "his speculations, his enterprises, the pleasures he obtains or hopes for." Commerce leaves no time for "the constant exercise of political rights, the daily discussion of the affairs of state . . . the disagreements, confabulations." It inspires a "vivid love of individual independence" and a distaste for government interventions.[106] Today "free men must exercise all professions, provide for all the needs of society."

Yet the rub for Constant, as it must be for any serious political thinker, was the nature of public liberty and how it structured "negative" or private freedoms. He recognized that the strength of modern liberty could be its weakness: an indifference to the larger society—and perhaps an indifference to public despotism. "The danger of modern liberty is that, absorbed in the enjoyment of our private independence, and in the pursuit of our particular interests, we should surrender our right to share in political power too easily."[107] This was not simply a moral point—although it was that as well. As an exile in Göttingen from Napoleon's rule, news reached him that the French army had set Moscow aflame. He wrote a friend,

I cannot be but greatly moved when reflecting on the sum of evil spreading across the land. Apart from those who are directly affected, this event is of some importance. But here, everyone is so wrapped up in study and science that I cannot find one soul . . . to talk about it. A city of 500,000 can be blown up without one professor in Göttingen lifting his eyes from his book.[108]

Private liberty depended on public liberties and their protection by a benign government. In his lecture on ancient and modern liberty, Constant seeks to "combine the two together." He closed on a very Arnoldian tone; he called upon legislators to seek "the moral education of the citizens." Nor were these empty words for Constant; he was a political animal, sometimes an elected deputy and an activist journalist. As a deputy Constant denounced slavery and press censorship;[109] his pursuit of a miscarriage of justice has been compared to Voltaire's intervention in the Calas affair.[110] "Those who accept Isaiah Berlin's portrait of privacy-addicted Constant," wrote Stephen Holmes in his book on Constant, "cannot explain why he devoted the last fifteen years of his life to public service"—not to "cozy town meeting communalism," but to "radical, reformist activism."[111]

Hannah Arendt stood at the opposite pole from Isaiah Berlin in several respects; she was as immoderate as he was cautious. Where he distrusted abstractions, she reveled in them. Her works were often long and ambitious, his short and modest. Just their titles suggest a very different reach. He wrote essays such as "A Note on Vico's Concept of Knowledge;" she wrote books with titles such as *The Human Condition*. I propose, she writes in the prologue, "a reconsideration of the human condition from the vantage point of our new experiences and our most recent fears."[112] Her final work, *The Life of the Mind*, explored nothing less than Western philosophical thought from Plato to Nietzsche. Before her death she had completed "Thinking" and "Willing," published in two volumes, but not the third section on "Judging."[113]

She was, in fact, a master of judgment, as exemplified in

Eichmann in Jerusalem, her account of the Adolph Eichmann trial in Israel. Where Berlin waffled, Arendt took stands. The *New Yorker* magazine published the piece that became her most famous work and continues to provoke the most controversy— as much by its harshness as its argument. "It is that heartless, frequently sneering and malicious tone . . . to which I take exception," declared Gershom Scholem, dean of Jewish studies, in a letter that marked a break with her.[114]

Arendt was born in 1906 in Königsberg, the capital of East Prussia and the home of Immanuel Kant, to a family of reform Jews. Pursuing her university studies in the mid-1920s she fell under the personal and intellectual sway of Martin Heidegger— a relationship that for better or worse decisively colored her work.[115] She put an epigram from Heidegger in the first volume of her last book, *The Life of the Mind*, and wanted to dedicate *The Human Condition* to him.[116] If Heidegger and German romanticism served as one pole of her orientation, Zionism—or issues of Jewish identity—served as the other.

Her first book (after her thesis) was a biography of Rahel Varnhagen, an eighteenth-century Berlin *salonnière*. Her book opened with a deathbed quote from Varnhagen. "The thing which all my life seemed to me the greatest shame, which was the misery and misfortune of my life—having been born a Jewess—this I should on no account now wish to have missed."[117] With the rise of Hitler, Arendt helped Jews flee Germany and then escaped herself to Prague and Paris, where she worked for Jewish refugee organizations. In 1941, after the fall of France, Arendt made her way it to New York, where she began to make a living as a writer and teacher.

In his letter to Arendt, Scholem disdainfully accused her of sharing attitudes about Judaism typical of German leftist intellectuals. Arendt corrected him about her past. "I am not one of the 'intellectuals who come from the German Left.' You could not have known this, since we did not know each other when we were young."[118] What did Arendt mean? Both her parents were socialists—and as testimony to the depths of their commitment, they had become so when the socialist party was still illegal in Germany. Her family was personally and intellectually close to the Vogelsteins, who were leading Social Democrats.[119] Her mother supported the firebrand Rosa Luxemburg and brought the young Hannah to a demonstration in behalf of the ill-fated revolutionary upsurge spearheaded by the Polish-Jewish agitator. "As they ran through the streets," Elisabeth Young-Bruhl, Arendt's biographer, records, "Martha Arendt shouted to her daughter, 'You must pay attention, this is a historical moment!'"[120]

Whatever their differences in approach and style, Arendt like Berlin, Popper, and the other liberal anti-utopians, paid most attention to Marxism, although this is less evident in the book that made her reputation, *Origins of Totalitarianism*. To be sure, *Origins* is a difficult work to follow or summarize. Virtually all commentators note its ungainliness; its sections seem unconnected to an overall argument. In does not help matters that Arendt has a penchant for windy prose and vague abstraction, which she abandoned in *Eichmann in Jerusalem*. She frequently employs Heideggerian idioms with unhappy results. "Totalitarian domination . . . bases itself on loneliness, on the experience of not belonging to the world at all, which is among the most radical and desperate experiences of man." She makes points that only seem profound. "Ideologies are never interested in the miracle of being." And she regularly uses arguments that highlight her learning but go nowhere. Her learned discussion of the origins of "ideology" ranges over the Latin root word *logoi* and the meaning of "idea" in Plato and Kant but says nothing of its real history in Destutt de Tracy, Marxism, and the sociology of knowledge.[121]

Origins provides both a history of anti-Semitism, racism, and imperialism, and a phenomenology of the totalitarian experience of concentration camps and terrorism. For Arendt totalitarianism signifies something radically novel in history—terror for the sake of terror and an effort to transform human nature. Yet when Arendt leaves her murky idiom ("Here, there are neither political nor historical nor simply moral standards but, at the most, the realization that something seems to be involved in modern politics that actually should never be involved in politics as we used to understand it, namely all or nothing—all, and this is an undetermined infinity of forms of human living-together or nothing"), she offers up something familiar as the driving force of totalitarianism: ideology. "The aggressiveness of totalitarianism springs not from the lust for power . . . nor for profit, but only for ideological reasons: to make the world consistent, to prove that its respective supersense has been right."[122]

Though the starting point is very different, Arendt ends up very close to Popper; she sharply contrasts a deadly "ideology" and something she simply calls "common sense." It is this distinction that puts her in the circle of Popper, Berlin, and the other anti-utopians. To be sure, unlike Popper she exempts virtually all of Western philosophy from the sin of totalitarianism. "Nazism owes nothing to any part of the Western tradition, be it German or not, Catholic or Protestant, Christian, Greek or Roman. . . . Nazism is actually the breakdown of all German and European traditions, the good as well as the bad."[123] Arendt does not conjure up a totalitarian Plato or Hegel; here she appears at the opposite of Popper. This is no small difference. Yet when she sought to generalize about the motor of totalitarianism, she targeted the familiar "ideology," a cousin of utopia. "Ideology" serves as the linchpin for her analysis of totalitarianism, and "ideology" is to Arendt what "historicism" is to Popper—a logical, closed system that posits the laws of history and that issues into mass murder.

With its iron logic and utopian vision, "ideology" produces totalitarianism, she wrote in her original conclusion to *Origins*:

While the totalitarian regimes are thus resolutely and cynically emptying the world of the only thing that makes sense to the utilitarian expectations of common sense, they impose upon it at the same time a kind of supersense which the ideologies actually always meant when they pretended to have found the key to history or the solution to the riddles of the universe. Over and above the senselessness of totalitarian society is enthroned the ridiculous supersense of its ideological superstition. . . . Common sense trained in utilitarian thinking is helpless against this ideological supersense, since totalitarian regimes establish a functioning world of no-sense.[124]

The first chapter of *Origins* is titled "Antisemitism as an Outrage to Common Sense." While Arendt might seem an unlikely defender of common sense, she regularly underscored the opposition of a deadly ideology and a reasonable utilitarianism. Her final chapter of the revised *Origins*, "Ideology and Terror," argues that ideology fueled totalitarianism. Ideologies claim "total explanations"; they are "independent of all experience"; and they are "absolutely logical. . . . You can't say A without saying B and C and so on, down to the end of the murderous alphabet."[125]

To be sure, the hodgepodge of German fascist ideas hardly seemed a paradigm of logic, and Arendt presents her case about the terrorist rigor of ideology with no examples from Nazism. Like Popper and Berlin, she articulates an argument that hardly applies to Nazism; like them, she directs her heavy conceptual artillery predominantly at Marxism. In a close study of *Origins*, Roy T. Tsao notes that while Arendt spends many pages on Nazism, she bases her central argument on Stalinism. Apparently she changed her mind while writing the book—indeed, after handing in most of the manuscript. Originally she planned to examine solely Nazism; later she decided to take up totalitarianism in the final part, but that concluding section bore little relationship to the preceding discourses on anti-Semitism and imperialism.[126] Much of what she writes about totalitarianism could only be applied to Stalinism—her references to "selflessness" in the movement and confessions at show trials clearly refer to the Soviet experience. Popper called it historicism; Arendt called it ideology. Ideology "promises to explain all historical happenings, the total explanation of the past, the total knowledge of the present, and reliable prediction of the future."[127]

But this is not the whole of the matter. The absolute novelty of the totalitarian system impressed Arendt. She called its unprecedented mix of ideology and state terror "absolute evil," an entity alien to Western philosophy. "It is inherent in our entire philosophical tradition that we cannot conceive of a 'radical evil.' . . . We actually have nothing to fall back on in order to understand a phenomenon that . . . breaks down all standards we know."[128] What is "absolute evil?" Arendt can not be precise. We may say that "radical evil has emerged in connection with a system in which all men have become equally superfluous."

Karl Jaspers, Arendt's philosophical friend, questioned this formulation, and she tried to explain it to him: "Evil has proved to be more radical than expected." The Western tradition can only understand sinful and selfish motives. "Yet we know that the greatest evils or radical evil has nothing to do anymore with such humanly understandable, sinful motives." Radical evil renders human beings "superfluous."[129] Arendt's thinking remains obscure here. Did she think that "the manipulators of this system believe in their own superfluousness as much as in that of others" and that they are "all the more dangerous" because they do not care if they live or die? Does this fit Hitler and other leading Nazis? Stalin and the Bolsheviks?

The problem however, is not only Arendt's frequent vagueness or woolly terminology. Rather, it is the extent to which she tacitly withdrew her influential totalitarian theory when she covered the Eichmann trial ten years later. It testifies to her intellectual openness that she recast her thinking about the nature of evil when she confronted Eichmann, but it throws the argument of *Origins* into doubt. Scholem observed that Arendt had previously identified "radical evil" as characterizing totalitarianism. "At that time," he wrote mockingly to her, "you had not yet made your discovery, apparently, that evil is banal." The subtitle of her Eichmann book read "A Report on the Banality of Evil." Arendt admitted the shift. "You are quite right: I changed my mind and do no longer speak of 'radical evil.' " She explained that "it is indeed my opinion now that evil is never 'radical,' that it is only extreme, and that it possesses neither depth nor any demonic dimension."[130]

This was not a diplomatic statement on Arendt's part. She mentioned her altered outlook to various people. She wrote to her friend Mary McCarthy that the Eichmann book stands partly "in conflict" with the totalitarianism study. The notion of the "banality of evil" opposes that of "radical evil." Moreover, she told McCarthy, she had exaggerated the impact of ideology in the earlier book. "One sees that Eichmann was much less influenced by ideology than I assumed in the book on totalitarianism. The impact of ideology upon the individual may have been overrated by me."[131]

Arendt framed her uncompleted *Life of the Mind* as exploring this problem. She explained that she had come to Eichmann's trial drenched in a Satanic notion of evil. "However, what I was confronted with was utterly different. . . . I was struck by a manifest shallowness in the doer that made it impossible to trace the incontestable evil of his deeds to any deeper level of roots or motives." The doer, she wrote in the introduction to *The Life of the Mind*, was "quite ordinary, commonplace, and neither demonic nor monstrous. There was no sign in him of firm ideological convictions or of specific evil motives."[132]

With these observations, the pillars of her totalitarianism theory buckle. In the continuing controversy sparked by *Eichmann in Jerusalem*, few noticed how her argument contradicted *Origins*. Reviewers had other fish to fry. More recent and scholarly explorations note a shift of position but rarely pursue the issue. The Arendt experts generally see the later book as embellishing or filling-out the former. "*Eichmann in Jerusalem* must be regarded therefore as a partial sequel to *The Origins of Totalitarianism*," writes one scholar.[133] "Does the concept of radical evil that Arendt analyzes in *The Origins of Totalitarianism* 'contradict' (as Scholem claimed) Arendt's notion of the banality of evil?" asks Richard J. Bernstein. Answer: "No!"[134] "Banality," writes Margaret Canovan, was really "a more accurate way" of describing what she had said about totalitarianism.[135] As Dana R. Villa, one of the best Arendt scholars puts it, "commentators have tried to diminish the force" of Arendt's " 'change of mind,' arguing, for example, that the notion of 'radical evil' is compatible with that of the 'banality of evil,' or that, under totalitarianism, radical evil becomes banal."[136]

One chapter of the Eichmann book is called "Duties of a Law-Abiding Citizen." The conclusion seems difficult to avoid. The lesson she drew from the Eichmann case on the "banality of evil" directly contradicts the central idea of *Origins*: demonic evil driven by ideology. Eichmann represented bureaucratic evil beyond ideology. Perhaps the Eichmann book can be seen as a rejoinder to her baroque language and Heideggerian philosophizing of *Origins*. When she approached the concrete reality, she discovered how wrong she had been. Ernst Gellner put it this way: "After she had given a kind of account of totalitarianism [in *Origins*] which was half Kafka's *The Trial* and half Wagner, the ordinariness of Eichmann was bound to strike and puzzle her."[137]

The issue, here, however is less the shift in Arendt's position and more how it affected her earlier anti-utopian ideas. In letters and in the preface to *Life of the Mind*, Arendt admitted she surrendered the notion of "radical" evil. Yet she never openly stated or considered how her change of mind revoked her earlier theory of totalitarianism. For countless readers the message of *Origins*, which targets an evil utopian ideology, repealed as it is by *Eichmann in Jerusalem*, retains its validity.

The anti-utopian ethos has swept all intellectual quarters. Utopia has lost its ties with alluring visions of harmony and has turned into a threat. Conventional and scholarly wisdom associates utopian ideas with violence and dictatorship. The historical validity of this linkage, however, is dubious. Already with More, though, utopianism spawned an angry anti-utopianism. This may be prototypical. The newly converted are haunted by their own sins; they seek to slay their past selves. "The final battle would be between the Communists and the ex-Communists," wrote Richard Crossman in his introduction to *The God That Failed*.[138] The utopian More becomes the anti-utopian More. The Marxist Popper becomes the anti-Marxist Popper. Of course, more than psychology is at work. Beginning in the sixteenth century and increasingly in later centuries, utopian thought inspired individuals to revamp the real world—and provoked others to block this effort. Anti-utopianism is not simply a psychological rejoinder, but a political reply to the political project of realizing utopia.

The record of utopian-inspired politics, including socialism and communism, is decidedly mixed. Yet it would be a gross distortion to attribute twentieth century violence mainly to utopians. Unfortunately, this attribution has become an enduring legacy of liberal anti-utopians from Popper to Berlin. Using a notion of totalitarianism that blurs the distinction between Nazism and Stalinism, they identify utopianism—also labeled "historicism," "positive liberty," and "ideology"—as the source of modern totalitarianism. To the degree that this is accurate, it addresses

Stalinism and authoritarian communism but not Nazism, fascism, murderous nationalism, lethal racism, and religious sectarianism—the stuff that increasingly provokes modern bloodletting.

The imbalance of this liberal critique derives partly from biography. Marxism attracted these scholars in a way that Nazism could not. For a few years, Popper considered himself a communist. Both of Arendt's husbands had been Marxists; and her arguments about totalitarianism bear the imprint of the second, Heinrich Blücher (to whom she dedicates *Origins of Totalitarianism*), a former member of the German Communist Party.[139] Moreover, Marxism was a worthy target for these critics simply because of its intellectual heft and legitimacy. The "enemy" of the open society for Popper is Marxist totalitarianism. He barely mentions Nazism. Ditto for Talmon and Berlin. Could Popper have written two volumes attacking Nazi philosophy as he did Platonic-Hegelian logic? Probably not, since an articulate Nazi philosophy barely existed. This does not mean he and his colleagues were unconcerned with virulent nationalism or fascism: not at all, but their theories hardly addressed these subjects. Large sections of *The Origins of Totalitarianism*, for example, take up anti-Semitism and Nazism. Yet these topics do not figure into Arendt's theory of totalitarianism, where she limits her comments to a sometime utopian "ideology" with little application to Nazism.

The point here is not to defend Marxism; it is to defend utopianism—or its iconoclastic version. Marxism does not exhaust utopianism, and to damn Marxism is not necessarily to damn utopian thought. The point is also to expose the confusion, or the intellectual sleight of hand, by which utopia is banished in the name of violence that can be far more justly attributed to bureaucrats, nationalists, and religious sectarians than to dreamers.

3. To Shake the World off Its Hinges

AT DAYBREAK OF SEPTEMBER 15, 1825, THE INHABITANTS of the frontier village of Buffalo were startled out of their slumber by a loud detonation booming from the front of the Court House and reverberating across the Lake." So began "Embarkation for Utopia," a chapter in a 1936 biography of Mordecai Noah, a nineteenth-century American Jewish journalist and politician; it describes his effort to found a utopian community called Ararat on Grand Island in the Niagara River.[1] "I cannot be insensible to the many difficulties which may present themselves," stated Noah in his speech that day to the assembled throng. "The attempt may be pronounced visionary and impracticable—the reluctance of some to countenance the effort—the timidity of others, and the apprehensions of all may be arrayed against an enterprise extraordinary and interesting."[2]

Noah saw Ararat as a refuge for persecuted Jews of the world, but the skeptics were right. Ararat still surfaces occasionally in Jewish fiction, most recently in Ben Katchor's *The Jew of New York*, but apart from the booming cannon, the parade, and the pronouncements, little happened. The German Jewish scholar Leopold Zunz, who supported the project from afar, remarked that the plan yielded only a costly postage bill for himself.[3] A three-hundred-pound corner stone of the community remains today—nothing else. Even Noah's own commitment seemed limited in retrospect. As a character in Katchor's novel aptly notes, Noah kept "a return ticket to his [New York city] apartment."[4]

Noah's ideas for Ararat, considered the first American Jewish utopian project, were sketchy at best;[5] he sought to assemble the ostracized Jews of the world into an agrarian community.[6] As a recent account puts it, "typical Enlightenment reforms," which encouraged literary and mechanical arts, informed Noah's project.[7] His ideas also elicited protest from Jewish worthies whom he had appointed (unasked) as honorary sponsors of his community. When the chief rabbi of Paris (Abraham de Cologna) learned of his position as sponsor, he protested Noah's personal and textual legitimacy. He instructed Noah that "God alone knows the epoch of the Israelite restoration, that he alone will make it known to the whole universe by signs entirely unequivocal, and that every attempt on our part to reassemble with any politico-national design is forbidden."[8] Practically and religiously, Noah's "embarkation" for utopia went nowhere.

Noah moved on to other endeavors, but the rabbi's admonition highlighted a peculiarity of Jewish history: its dearth of well-developed utopias. To be sure, this absence seems contradicted by a familiar truth; from Marx to Rosa Luxemburg and from Trotsky to Abbie Hofman Jews have gravitated to leftist thought and practice. "Jews have unquestionably been a pioneering element" and a "ferment and a catalyst within modern socialist and revolutionary movements," writes Robert S. Wistrich in *Revolutionary Jews*.[9] Beginning at the beginning of Jewish history, the nineteenth-century French historian Ernest Renan called the Jewish prophets "impetuous publicists" and "fanatics of social justice," the sort "that we call today socialists and anarchists."[10]

Yet, devotion to justice or far-reaching reform is not the same as a detailed utopian vision; they may coincide or overlap, but they need not and often do not. Marx exemplifies this orientation—a utopian temper that shuns depicting the future. Not many will doubt his commitment to revolution, but in his entire oeuvre the descriptions of a postrevolutionary or utopian society consist of a few passing sentences. He would stick to "actual facts," he remarked, rather than write "recipes for the cookshops of the future," as the utopians wanted him to do.[11] Noah's venture itself barely bucks this disposition inasmuch as his projected settlement was more a gesture than a developed blueprint.

The issue is not the absence of utopian hope or longings but the absence of detailed descriptions or plans about the future among Jews. The Jewish tradition gave rise to what might be called an iconoclastic utopianism—an anti-utopian utopianism that resisted blueprints. This iconoclastic utopianism was "antiutopian" to the extent that it refused to map out the future; it was utopian in its commitment to a very different future of harmony and happiness. The iconoclastic utopians inclined toward the future, but unlike the blueprint utopians, they abstained from depicting it. To put this differently, while Jewish history is replete with reformers, revolutionaries, and visionaries, it includes almost no equivalent to Thomas More, Charles Fourier, or Edward Bellamy, who demarcated the exact dimensions of utopia. Rather, it gave rise to iconoclastic utopians drenched in romantic and mystical longing for the future.

An obvious exception to the dearth of Jewish blueprint utopians might be Theodor Herzl. To be sure, even as he depicted a future he generally fled from utopian pronouncements. His founding text for Zionism, *The Jewish State* (1896) sought to avoid a utopian taint. "I must, in the first place" he wrote in the preface, "guard my scheme from being treated as Utopian by superficial critics who might commit this error of judgment if I did not warn them." He claimed that "I should also, in all probability, have obtained literary success more easily if I had set forth my plan in the irresponsible guise" of a romantic utopia. He distinguished his plan from that of Theodor Hertzka's utopian *Freiland* with its "numerous cogged wheels fitting into each other."[12]

Unlike Hertzka, Herzl dispensed with many details because

his was a practical, not utopian vision. "I shall not be lavish in artistically elaborated description of my project, for fear of incurring the suspicion of painting a Utopia." He emphatically believes "in the practical outcome" of his scheme, although he has not "discovered the shape it may ultimately take." He provides some details of what his "new State" will look like; he tells us the working day will be seven hours and the worker's quarters will be composed of "detached houses in little gardens." Yet Herzl is at pains to distance himself from utopianism. "My remarks on workmen's dwellings, and on unskilled laborers and their mode of life, are no more Utopian than the rest of my scheme." Everything he describes is already in practice "only on an utterly small scale, neither noticed nor understood."[13]

Nevertheless for several reasons Herzl cannot be easily detached from blueprint utopianism. Not only does *The Jewish State* include details of the future, but within a half-dozen years, Herzl himself tried his hand at a fully described utopia, *Altneuland* (Old-New Land), published in 1902. In his diaries he explained that as his efforts to gain support for his Jewish state stumbled, he put more and more energy into his fictitious utopia. "My hopes for practical success have now disintegrated," and I am "industriously working" on *Altneuland*. "The novel is my life."[14]

Altneuland tells the tale of Freidrich Loewenberg, a café denizen in fin de siècle Vienna, who belonged to the overeducated and underemployed Jewish "proletariat." Rebuffed in life and love, Loewenberg responds to a personal advertisement in the daily press: "Wanted, cultured and despairing young man willing to try last experiment with life. Write N.O. Body c/o this paper." "Nobody" turns out to be a wealthy German-American, seeking a companion for his private island in the Pacific where he plans to spend the rest of his life in quiet seclusion. On the way to the island by a private yacht, the pair embark on a whim for a visit to Palestine, which they find shabby and disagreeable.

They proceed to their island retreat, but after twenty quiet years curiosity drives them to revisit Europe. They return via the Suez canal and stumble upon a transformed Palestine. This has become prosperous and clean, a new Jewish country under the leadership of a cooperative New Society, "an association of citizens who are trying to find their happiness in work and cultural activities." The society created is neither capitalist nor communist. "With us," lectures their guide "the individual is neither ground small between the millstones of capitalism, nor beheaded by the leveling-down-process of socialism." Education is free; women's emancipation is complete; religion is private.

Altneuland paints a picture of cooperative society that has united Jews and others in an attractive country. Was it a utopia? David, the guide, instructs the visitors that past utopians constructed "socialist dreams" in the sky—"cloud-cuckoo-land." Even Bellamy offered a "castle in the air." "In his cloud land everybody can eat from the common dish. . . . Wolf and lamb graze together. All very fine—but that would mean that wolves were not wolves any longer, and human beings not human." But the new Palestine did not depend on a transformed people or new machinery but existing human power. "Where did it come from? Why, from the immense pressure exercised upon us [the Jews] from all sides, from persecution, from suffering . . . A whole people found itself united—reunited."

> And we created the new society not because we were better than others; no, only because we were simple people with the simple human needs—air and light, health and honor, freedom to make our living and security to enjoy what we had made. And having to build, naturally we chose the model of 1900 and not that of 1800 or 1600 or of any ancient period.[15]

Altneuland can be situated within a handful of Jewish blueprint utopias that appeared around the time of Bellamy's 1888

Looking Backward. "Jewish literature did not include utopias proper until the late nineteenth century," writes Miriam Eliav-Feldon, who surveys the few that have appeared.[16] For instance, Max Osterberg-Verakoff's *Das Reiche Judäa im Jahr 6000* (1893) and H. Pereira Mendes's *Looking Ahead: Twentieth-Century Happenings* (1899), both evidently inspired by Bellamy, painted in broad strokes the founding of a new Palestine. Osterberg-Verakoff's book includes a discussion and criticism of Bellamy as too utopian, and he recommends as superior August Bebel's down-to-earth book *The Woman*. People liked Bellamy's tract, his guide tells the visitor, because adults remain children and enjoy fairy tales. Equality between individuals can be achieved, but not a fool's paradise (*"Schlaraffenland"*). "It is not good if mankind sets goals that are unreachable. Reasonable people guard themselves from such mad exaggerations."[17]

Looking Ahead may also exemplify the small subset of Jewish blueprint utopias, but it provides almost no details on the new Jewish Palestine. The book takes up the political machinations leading to the founding of Palestine but gives the barest information on the nature of life, government, or economy. "Roads were made, villages were rebuilt. . . . The activity of the Palestine cabinet exceeded all expectations": this is as far as Pereira Mendes goes—which is almost too far. After several paragraphs of bare pronouncements, he stops. "But why continue?" he asks. In its asceticism toward the future, Peieria Mendes remains within the main tradition of Jewish utopianism. The book closes, "no need to speak of what we all taste to-day—universal peace, universal brotherhood, universal happiness."[18] A slightly earlier Jewish utopia, Edmund Eisler's *Zukunftsbild* (1882) begins with the author's nightmare of an anti-Semitic mob threatening his family and does offer details of a future Palestine. Eisler gives extracts from some hundreds of laws such as law 201, "Hebrew is the language of the state," or law 651, "all citizens are equal before the law."[19]

Altneuland can be grouped with this and other late-nineteenth-century blueprint Jewish utopias that bear the stamp of Bellamy; indeed, it may be indistinguishable from other Bellamy-inspired sketches.[20] For both contemporary and recent critics, this proves a telling criticism of *Altneuland*: Herzl's "New Society" lacked anything specifically Jewish. A resident of the "New Society" explains to a visitor:

> The so-called intellectuals of twenty years ago had object-
> ed to Zionism on the grounds of its being, as they said,
> based on outmoded ideas. The whole conception of a
> Jewish national revival has been depicted as . . . a sort of
> millennial nightmare. . . . This was far from being so. The
> New Society was the last to favor obscurantism. . . .
> Questions of faith were definitely excluded from all influ-
> ence in public affairs. Whether you prayed in a synagogue,
> a church or a mosque, in a museum or at a philharmonic
> concert—it was one to the New Society. How you sought
> to get in touch with the Eternal was your own affair.[21]

Secular, technological, cosmopolitan, its inhabitants speaking Western European languages, *Altneuland* seemed less Jewish than French or German. "You must be tired from your trip," counsels the guide. "Now you must rest. And in the evening, if you like, we can go to the opera, or to one of the theaters— German, French, English, Italian, Spanish."[22]

The criticism that *Altneuland* lacked a Jewish identity has been advanced by those on the opposite ends of the political-intellectual spectrum. A Palestinian academic, Muhammad Ali Khalidi, has recently argued that "the non-Jewish character" of *Altneuland*, which includes even the utopian community's name, "The New Society," can only be explained by Herzl's desire to gain support from European Christians. "To put it more bluntly, Herzl's intention is to describe a model society that would cause gentile Europeans to conceive of the Jewish state as a testing ground for various experimental schemes in which they themselves had been interested as of the late eighteenth century and which, if successful, could then be implemented in Europe"[23]

Ironically, Ali Khalidi follows the contemporary Jewish criticism of Herzl by Ahad Ha'am, who emerged from Russian Hasidism to become the leading exponent of "cultural" Zionism. Ahad Ha'am, the pen name of Asher Ginzburg, tangled with Herzl, whom he considered too technological and instrumental. Ahad Ha'am represented a Zionism professedly more spiritual and "Eastern" than that of Herzl's Zionism, which was anchored in "Western" Europe. Herzl wanted a new state for the Jews, but Ahad Ha'am wanted more: he sought a community of Jews with a state, not "a state of Germans or Frenchmen of the Jewish race." The "political" Zionists seek prosperity, tranquility, and a refuge from anti-Semitism. The "cultural" Zionists considered this insufficient. Even when Jews attain "comfortable economic positions" and full equality, the issue of Judaism will not be resolved; this requires a renewal of culture and spirit.[24]

In a slashing review of *Altneuland* in 1903, Ahad Ha'am protested that Herzl's political Zionism and his "utopia" lacked anything especially Jewish—even the lingua franca appeared to be German. The language, learning, and technology all suggested Western Europe. Herzl broached a plan that depended on engineering and joint-stock companies, but not on Jewish learning and culture. It could be adopted by any nation-building group, for instance, blacks who were returning to Africa.[25] Or, as Ahad Ha'am put it more crudely, Herzl's *Altneuland* exemplified spiritual servitude, "an extended bow before the goyim." He accused Herzl and his supporters of "kneeling and bowing" before Christian eminences.[26]

Histories of Zionism typically present the conflict of Herzl and Ahad Ha'am as a major dividing line. *Altneuland*, its savage review by Ahad Ha'am, and the brutal rejoinder by Herzl's confederate Max Nordau marked two visions of Zionism, one focused on state building and the other on cultural renaissance.[27] "Herzl envisaged a modern, technologically advanced and enlightened state inhabited by Jews, not a specifically Jewish state," writes Walter Laqueur in his history of Zionism. "Ahad Ha'am looked in vain for some specific Jewish qualities in Herzl's vision."[28] Conversely, Herzl, who commissioned Nordau to respond, saw Ahad Ha'am representing a ghetto and East European Judaism. "In fact, *Altneuland* is a piece of Europe in Asia." We want "the Jewish people, like any other educated people, to develop within a Western culture, not within a wild barbarian Asia [*in einem kulturfeindlichen, wilden Asiatentum*], as Ahad Ha'am apparently wants." Nordeau dismissed Ahad Ha'am as no Zionist; he was just a "protesting rabbi [*Protestrabbiner*]."[29]

The story of Zionism cannot be neatly separated into two categories, either Herzl's political or Ahad Ha'am's cultural variants;[30] the charge or label of "utopian" would show up in various quarters.[31] Yet a specifically Jewish utopianism may reside less in Herzl's blueprint than in Ahad Ha'am's iconoclasm. "True," writes his recent biographer, "Ahad Ha'am wrote no utopia; in fact, it is the elaboration of anti-utopia . . . that best suited his temperament." Yet, continues Steven J. Zipperstein, he retained a "vision of a future society."[32]

Is it possible that Herzl's explicit utopia represented a blueprint utopianism that was not specifically Jewish—and that another and more distinctive Jewish iconoclastic utopianism existed outside or against it? Biography may come to the rescue and unravel the tangled knot of Jewish utopianism; it may help us follow the threads of the iconoclastic utopianism that bypass Herzl and run from Ahad Ha'am's cultural Judaism to Martin Buber and a series of fin de siècle and Weimar figures.

The philosopher Martin Buber became known as a leading Zionist, as well as a philosopher and interpreter of Hasidism. Buber, some twenty years younger than Herzl and Ahad Ha'am, knew them both but viewed the latter as his teacher. Inasmuch as Ahad Ha'am wrote in Hebrew, which few read in Germany, Buber became Ahad Ha'am's German translator and representative. He called Ahad Ha'am a man with a "golden scale in his mouth," who weighs honestly the claims of "ideas and reality."[33] In the fallout over *Altneuland*, Buber defended Ahad Ha'am from Herzl's counterattack. Like Ahad Ha'am, Buber stood for a spiritual revival of Judaism, not simply for the founding a new state.[34]

While Buber appreciated much about Herzl's drive and accomplishments, he considered him only partially a Jew. "There was nothing fundamentally Jewish in Theodor Herzl," Buber wrote on the occasion of Herzl's death. Herzl was "a Western Jew without Jewish tradition, without Jewish childhood impressions, without Jewish education. . . . He grew up in a non-Jewish environment . . . he entered Judaism not because of Judaism but because of a crystallizing manliness. He was a whole man , but he was not a whole Jew."[35] This explained Herzl's vision of a secular Palestine that lacked Jewish culture and religiosity. Buber recalled meeting Herzl in the Zionist Central Bureau office in Vienna, where a map of Palestine adorned the wall. Herzl tapped on the map and ardently spoke of future industrial projects: factories, ports, new towns. As his finger came to the Jordan River, Herzl proclaimed the plan to build a vast dam—bigger than any in America. "How much horsepower has Niagara? Eight million? We shall have ten million!"[36] Buber was horrified.

For Buber, close to Ahad Ha'am, this missed the heart of the matter. In a series of addresses in 1909 that elicited much attention, Buber accentuated the inner religiosity of Judaism that required renewal; he drew upon his research on Hasidism to lecture a Prague Zionist group about the mystical and millennial dimension that must infuse a Jewish renaissance. The historian Hans Kohn, then a student in Prague, recalled Buber's impact. "In those days before 1914, Buber was a young man, in his early thirties, hardly ten years older than we. We, rightly, looked up to him." As Kohn put it, "Nineteenth-century Jewish scholarship . . . had interpreted Judaism as a rational religion and had paid little attention to its mystical undercurrents. . . . Buber revealed the existence, outside of 'official' Judaism, of a subterranean Judaism and its manifestation in the pietistic-mystical sect of Hasidism."[37]

The Prague group included people such as Franz Kafka and his friend Max Brod, who had been stirred by Buber to become a Zionist.[38] Gershom Scholem, a generation younger than Buber, recorded the impact of those talks. "I am among those who in their youth," he recollected, "when these speeches appeared, was deeply moved by them."[39] Buber called for a renewal that went beyond the usual "rationalization of faith, simplification of dogma, modification of the ritual law." He appealed to "the spirit of prophetic Judaism" that shows up in Ahad Ha'am. While Buber hardly dismissed the hope of establishing Judaism in Palestine, for him it did not suffice. A Palestinian colony can "promote scholarly work" and "even become a social model." Yet "it cannot beget the only things from which I expect the absolute to emerge—return and transformation, a change in all elements of life."[40]

Buber may be more important for his web of connections and concerns than he is for his own writing. He kept alive, personally and intellectually, an iconoclastic utopianism, primarily through his life-long commitment to his friend Gustav Landauer. To be sure, Buber's works often veered into aestheticism and lax romanticism. A recent and skeptical assessment charges that Buber offered up "Hasidism as the mirror-image of Western society." He responded to the prevailing cliches of Jews as deracinated and materialistic with a picture of Jews as rooted, spiritual, and emotionally intense.[41] Scholem himself objected to Buber's Judaism. In a critical appreciation after his death, Scholem extended his "gratitude" for Buber's contribution but avowed that he often found it "thoroughly opaque, questionable, or unacceptable." He not only made a dig at Buber's Jewish observances—in his thirty years in Israel, "nobody ever saw [Buber] in a synagogue"—but claimed that Buber interpreted Hasidism in an oversimplified and unhistorical manner. "Hasidism's 'love affair' with the world turns out to be Buber's love affair with the world."[42]

Nevertheless, from the time he met Landauer in 1899 to *Paths in Utopia* five decades later, Buber championed an iconoclastic utopianism. He took the German romanticism of the day, which was aswirl with mystical ideas of community and spirit, and recast it in social terms. Buber moved from "mysticism" to "social thought," to follow Paul Mendes-Flohr's study of him.[43] This was the same trajectory as Landauer. If the iconoclastic utopians such as Buber and Landauer were spiritual, unlike the German romantics they were also political in their worldly hopes for the future and Jewish in their resistance to depicting it.

An anarchist utopian, Landauer had made a name for himself in prewar Germany as a writer, translator, and lecturer. Buber met the slightly older Landauer in the "New Society" circle, a loose collection of artists and writers with vague communitarian and romantic goals.[44] The meeting marked a turning point for Buber. In publications and letters throughout his life Buber remained loyal to Landauer and to Landauer's utopian esprit—a loyalty that was returned inasmuch as Landauer named Buber executor of his estate.[45]

Buber's utopian spiritualism can be found in his earliest encounters with the "New Society" group, at which the twenty-two-year-old Buber gave a talk in 1900 on the "old and new society." In that lecture he announced that the new society diverged from the dead economic and religious structure of the past. The "new" taps the sources of life; it is "an expression of the overflowing yearning for the whole of life [*überströmender Sehnsucht nach dem ganzen Leben*]." Only when a vibrant life sets aside "dead convention" and the "joyful rhythms" overcome old rules will the new society emerge. The future society places itself on completely "different grounds" than did the past. The new society does not "wish" to be the revolution. "It *is* the revolution."[46]

In a later address dedicated to Landauer, "The Holy Way," published at the end of World War I, typical Buber themes surface: an accent on community, human relationships, and inner religiosity—and a distrust of purely political and technological approaches. Buber raised a warning to "those who are exclusively political-minded." The new "Jewish Commonwealth" in Palestine "must not become just another of the numberless small states that are devoid of spiritual substance, a place like any other in today's Western world where spirit and people are separated, with both languishing." It must not become a place "where possessing replaces being, and mutual exploitation replaces mutual help."[47]

Buber's utopianism can be followed forward to his *Paths in Utopia*, published at the end of World War II, which surveyed major utopian figures. In order to save a socialism that has "strayed" into a blind alley, "the catchword 'Utopia' must be cracked open" and reexamined. What did Buber find in that nut? Few particulars. He discovered something he called "real fellowship." Both industrialized society and Marxist socialism suppress the encounter of human being with human being. He objected to the purely technological utopia. "Utopia . . . has become wholly technical. . . . Utopias which revel in technical fantasias mostly find foothold nowadays only in the feeble species of novels. . . . Those . . . which undertake to deliver a blueprint of the perfect social structure, turn into systems." Rather, Buber prized the molecular dimension of human interaction. He favored a "rebirth of the commune" or community where human rapport was cultivated. "I sometimes think that every touch of helpful neighbourliness in the apartment-house" and "every wave of warmer comradeship" means "an addition" to the world community.[48]

In *Paths in Utopia* Buber discussed the village commune and kibbutz in Israel, which he dubbed not a success but "an experiment that did not fail" or a "signal non-failure." Yet these settlements did not constitute utopian communities according to Buber. They responded "not to a doctrine but . . . to the needs, the stress, the demands of a situation." Their "ideal motive remained loose and pliable." For Buber, this was praise; the kibbutz residents exemplified utopians without blueprints. "They had as their goal the creation of a new man and a new world. But nothing of this ever hardened into a cut-and-dried programme. These men did not, as everywhere else in the history of cooperative settlements, bring a plan with them."[49]

One chapter of *Paths in Utopia* addressed Landauer, whom Buber credited with fathoming the communal basis of utopia. Landauer aimed not for the creation of a new state, or even a new political organization, but the renewal of human relations. Buber quotes Landauer that the task is "to loosen the hardening of hearts so that what lies buried may rise to the surface: so that what truly lives yet now seems dead may emerge and grow into the light." What is required is a "true spirit of community." While Landauer saw future possibilities in the "socialist village," he wanted to avoid all fixed solutions. Buber paraphrased Landauer: "Rigidity threatens all realization, what lives and glows today may be crusted over tomorrow."[50]

Buber's 1900 "new society" lecture had referred to Landauer's talk "Durch Absonderung zur Gemeinschaft" (Through isolation to community), which was held before the same group and struck similar notes. In that lecture Landauer drew upon German mystics and called for the establishment of a "new" life. Individuals should delve into themselves and discover not isolation but true community. "Let us begin! Let us create a social life; let us create centers for a new life; let us free ourselves from the unspeakable crudeness of our environment. . . . 'Through isolation to community,' that is to say: we risk the whole to live as a whole."[51]

In life, literature, and spirit Landauer incarnated modern Jewish utopianism. Karl Mannheim's 1929 classic *Ideology and Utopia* holds him up as an exemplar of extreme utopianism.[52] His writings, his gentle personality, his violent death, and Buber's commitment to him have all kept Landauer's ideas alive—but not very successfully. One biographer complains that despite the efforts of Buber, who has become a world-famous philosopher, "Landauer's memory has sunk into an undeserved oblivion."[53]

Landauer drank from the well of Jewish messianism and utopianism.[54] Fritz Kahn in his 1921 *Die Juden als Rasse und Kulturvolk* placed Landauer in the tradition of Moses and Marx, a Jewish redeemer and prophet. The idea to lead mankind from contemporary slavery to "beauty, love and dignity" consumed Landauer.[55] Yet he is difficult to categorize. A modern editor puts it well: Landauer was an anarchist, "who had no choice than to make common cause with doctrinaire socialists and party regulars; a pacifist who recognized that the other side of revolution was the terror; a mystic . . . who did not believe in God; a Jew who did not adhere to Judaism; and a Zionist sympathizer who despised nationalism."[56] He was also an iconoclastic utopian—a utopian who distrusted utopias plans.

For some years the paths of Landauer and Buber crossed so often that it is difficult to apportion who influenced whom.[57] Both were studying German mysticism but from slightly different angles, Landauer as a radical and Buber as a Jew. If Buber first followed Landauer, later Landauer followed Buber. Buber's interpretation of Hasidism, mainly his *Legend of the Baal-Shem*, caused Landauer to redirect his utopianism and reassert his Judaism. Landauer wrote a booklet in 1907 titled *Revolution*, which resounded with mystical politics, for a series edited by Buber.[58] He called the revolution a "microcosm." "In an unbelievably short time, in a fantastic rush of events, the spirit of mankind, which was suppressed, springs up, and the possibilities of the world are brought to realization—like a flaming torch. In a revolution everything goes so incredibly fast, like a dream of a sleeper who is freed from worldly weight. "[59]

In other essays around this time Landauer wrestled with the issues of Jews and Germans, and Jews and radicalism; he drew upon Buber and sought to introduce "culture" or "*Geist*" into politics.[60] In a 1913 address called "Are these Heretical Thoughts?" for the same Prague Zionist group which Buber had addressed, Landauer took up Jewish renewal. For Landauer, Jewish renewal or Jewish nationalism required a general renaissance, not a cramped fixation on Jewish issues. "The emphatic stress on one's own nationality, even if it avoids degeneration into chauvinism, is a weakness." Landauer called for Jews to tap into their own tradition in order to revitalize the larger community. The more Jews reach into themselves, the more that they sense their deep traditions lead to "revolution and regeneration of mankind." From the depths of being comes a voice to say "that the Jew can only be redeemed together with mankind and that is one and the same thing: to wait in banishment and exile for the messiah and to be the messiah of the people."[61]

Landauer's approach to radicalism roughly paralleled Buber's to Zionism; both criticized the purely technocratic method. In a talk on Jewry and socialism, Landauer argued that for many adherents socialism signaled the "praxis" of party politics, but for others, including himself, socialism meant a unity of "praxis and *Geist*." Landauer's socialism places "a regulating *Geist* [*verbindenden Geist*]," not a new state in the place of rents, money, and corruption of capitalist society. He believed that "something Jewish" inhered in this idea to bring "*Geist*" to bear on the life of men.[62]

"*Geist*" and "culture" pervaded the intellectual atmosphere of these years, and Landauer and Buber joined several groups that sought to revamp the world by rediscovering or reinvigorating "*Geist.*" While it is easy to lampoon the loose romanticism of these intellectuals, Landauer, at least, retained a hard and material edge. He protested the conceptual looseness of the New Society group; he thought its leader, Julius Hart, covered everything with flabby labels such as "transformation." Contradictions and bodily pain vanished into chatter of spiritual change. Landauer caricatured Hart: "If a sheep is devoured by a lion, both sheep and men would be wrong to call that a death and bemoan it; the life of the sheep has been transformed into the life of the lion." The sheep has not even disappeared. "It lives as a spiritual entity in the memory of all that knew it." Landauer broke with a lazy romanticism that conflated "being," "material" and "*Geist.*"[63]

In the same way, Landauer distanced himself later from the classic work of Jewish utopianism, *The Spirit of Utopia*, by Ernst Bloch, which appeared in 1918 and reveled in "*Geist.*" Bloch tapped Christian mystical sources, as did Landauer. Both men brewed a heady mix of mysticism, Judaism, and revolution, but cloudy vapors envelop *The Spirit of Utopia*. "So we at least long to voyage into color. The settled life is over, and what juice is still in it has become increasingly sluggish. But deep within us something else wants to ferment, and we seek the grain that would not grow here."[64] Bloch's book closed with a section "Karl Marx, Death, and the Apocalypse." He wrote that Jews have always been motivated by "the myth of utopia;" he characterizes the Israelites as "anxious worshipers of an unseen God," suspicious of the "theology of a definite, pictorial factuality [*fertigen, bildhaften Unterwegs*]."[65]

Yet there is Jewish mystical utopianism and Jewish mystical utopianism. Landauer found murky the writings of Julius Hart; he also found insupportable Bloch's *Spirit of Utopia*. He thought the book contained nothing new; it was rather a word salad of "shameless charlatanry." Bloch was not writing in the tradition of Spinoza but in that of fakers like Rudolf Steiner and Mme.

Blavatsky. The "swindle of all mystification" consists of the inability to distinguish words and reality.[66] When Landauer penned these words, reality in the form of the German revolution beckoned him.

Landauer's efforts to transform reality—to politicize "*Geist*"—extended over his whole life. Some years after he and Buber departed from the New Society, they joined the Forte Circle, a group motivated by utopian and political aspirations.[67] A loose collection of writers, poets and visionaries, the Forte Circle sought to establish a "*Bund*," or association, to arrest or at least transcend the intensifying political crises of pre–World War I Europe. Its members wanted to create a privileged zone of talk and community in the almost mystical hope that the truths they uncovered would radiate outward and transform society. As war erupted, Landauer and Buber called upon the group to assemble with the goal of creating a community "that would have significance for the development of the world."[68]

Prior to the meeting, Buber had circulated to the group theses that resounded with unearthly utopianism. He believed a "true union" of like-minded souls could alter the course of the world. He alluded to a "minyan," the quorum of ten men required by Judaism for communal prayers and reading of the Torah. "When ten men want one thing and unite to achieve it, the diaspora will be over. When everyone pushes for something different, the spiritual planet will not budge an inch. However, ten individuals can pull it out of its paths into their direction."[69] Alas, since the group did not obtain a minyan—only eight came to its spring 1914 meeting—the planet did not move. At least, World War I soon ensued. Their lack of success continues to disappoint. A recent Buber biographer regrets that "the circle failed to accomplish its goal of bringing the unity of mankind to authoritative expression at that decisive hour."[70]

Gershom Scholem, who knew many of its participants, including Landauer and Buber, recalls in his memoirs the notion that motivated these individuals seems today "almost incredible." Scholem appears well apprized of circle's mission, since his characterization of it sixty years afterward alludes to the metaphor of planetary orbits that shows up in Buber's theses. Scholem describes the association as follows: "A small group of people would set up a community devoted to intellectual and spiritual activity for a certain period of time to engage without any reservation in a creative exchange of ideas; in doing so they might manage to shake the world off its hinges."[71]

Landauer shared this hope. His own road to utopia passed through mysticism and anarchism. He took from the anarchists a protest against an idea of revolution as just a new state or economic order; he borrowed from the mystics an idea of reality that went beyond the here and now; and he added romantic notions about community and "spirit" or "*Geist*."[72] Indeed, "*Geist*" infused Landauer's key work, the utopian *For Socialism* (*Aufruf zum Sozialismus*), which appeared in 1911. We need, Landauer wrote, "a cohesive spirit [*Geist*] " for our age. "Yes, yes," he admitted, "the word spirit [*Geist*] does occur often in this book."[73]

Landauer's heated denunciation of Marxism turned on this: it lacked spirit. It was "unspirit" or, at best, no more than "the paper blossom on the beloved thornbush of capitalism." Marxism consisted of wheels, springs, and levers. "The Marxists have, in their declarations and views, excluded the spirit for a very natural, indeed almost excellent material reason: namely, because they have no spirit." For Landauer, Marxism smacked of dead technologies and cold plans. "The boundless reverence of the adulators of progress for technology is the key to understanding the origin of Marxism. The father of Marxism is neither the study of history, nor Hegel. . . . The father of Marxism is steam," he sneered. Compared to the Marxists, "we are poets," not "cold, hollow, spiritless" activists. We anarchist utopians want "poetic vision," creativity, enthusiasm, harmony, and solidarity.

Despite his unswerving utopianism, Landauer eschewed blueprints. As with Buber, not "communal kitchens," but "*Geist*" and "*Gemeinschaft*" defined his utopianism. Landauer rhapsodized about the warmth and beauty of human contact. Inasmuch as he honored the cultural rapport among individuals, his utopian plans remained vague, a fact he trumpeted. "I will not say, as some may well expect, how the new reality we desire should be constituted as a whole. I offer no depiction of an ideal, no description of utopia." He reiterated this. The utopian Landauer wrote, "no depiction of an ideal, no description of a Utopia is given here."[74]

Landauer's resistance to depicting the future extended to doubting language, inevitably the means of conceiving utopia. Utopia, he felt, escaped the confines of the written language. Words imperfectly conveyed human desires and thoughts; they could hardly express utopian impulses. The written language belongs to the world of domination and control. For this reason, Landauer considered music the best "human language," a "wordless language" that transcends prose and pictures.[75] A perfect utopia existed only as a linguistic construction—in the domain of "contradictions and solid reification [*Gegensaetzlichkeit und runde Dinglichkeit*]." "What I call socialism is not perfection. I do not believe in such perfection."[76]

Landauer's mistrust of language did not diminish his mysticism or utopianism. Rather, Landauer's utopian esprit, linguistic skepticism, and mysticism went hand in hand. In his suspicion of the written language and in his reticence about the future, Landauer exemplified a Jewish iconoclastic utopianism stamped by loyalty to the biblical commandment forbidding graven images. From Marx to Landauer and Max Horkheimer, this commandment hovers over Jewish utopianism. For much of their history, the taboo on graven images barred Jews from depicting the absolute and, by inference, the future, which could at best be sought and felt abstractly. Inasmuch as language derives from images and pictures, the taboo also challenged the written word. The pious Jew could not write or say the name of God.

"If the heathen of the old story, who wished to learn the whole *Torah* standing on one leg" wrote Ahad Ha'am, "had come to me, I should have told him: 'Thou shalt not make unto thee any graven image or any likeness' —that is the whole *Torah*, and the rest is commentary." Ahad Ha'am explained that this "essential characteristic of Judaism" rendered "religious and moral consciousness independent of any definite human form." The "abstract ideal which has 'no likeness' " marks Judaism; this devotion to an imageless idea is carried over to the notion of future salvation that "has no defined concrete form."[77] Implicitly and explicitly, this commandment shaped Jewish utopianism, including Landauer's. The Jewish iconoclasts offered an abstract and imageless utopia—a utopia without blueprints and details.

Landauer imbibed the consequences of the Second Commandment from other Jewish thinkers. If his Jewish spiritualism and abstract utopianism came by way of Buber, another close acquaintance spurred his linguistic skepticism. Landauer adopted linguistic mistrust from Fritz Mauthner, who today figures only in accounts of fin de siècle central European intellectual life. To those who value his work, "even more than Landauer himself," he has been forgotten.[78]

Mauthner, a Czech Jew, became a successful journalist in Berlin specializing in satirical sketches. Yet his heart lay in a more serious scholarly endeavor, the study of language. In this, of course, he was hardly alone; he can be situated within a broad circle of fin de siècle central Europeans such as Karl Kraus, Ludwig Wittgenstein, and the Vienna Circle philosophers who, all examined the limits of language. As George Steiner put it, "Starting with Genesis 11:11 and continuing to Wittgenstein's *Investigations* or Noam Chomsky's earliest, unpublished paper on morphophonemics in Hebrew, Jewish thought has played a pronounced role in linguistic mystique, scholarship, and philosophy."[79]

In 1901 Mauthner published the first of a multivolume critique of language. "What disturbed Mauthner," write Allan Janik and Stephen Toulmin in *Wittgenstein's Vienna*, was people's tendency to "attribute reality to abstract and general terms," which led not only to intellectual confusion but to practical injustice and evil. Mauthner reacted to the "political witchcraft he saw being exercised all around him by the use of such grandiose abstract terms as *Volk* and *Geist*."[80] He adopted a radical nominalism that put into question the truth and efficacy of language. Like Wittgenstein, he concluded that what was truly important could not be uttered. Mauthner quoted with approval Maeterlinck, "As soon as we really have something to say we are forced to be silent."[81]

Mauthner traced his doubts about language to growing up as a Jew in Bohemia. Equally at ease or ill at ease in several languages, he believed he possessed no "real Muttersprache." He wondered how a Jew "born in the Slavonic region of the Austrian-Hungarian Empire could not be drawn to the study of language," since he or she had to learn three languages at once: German, the language of officialdom and education; Czech, the language of peasants, servants, and larger Bohemia; and Hebrew, the language of the bible and the basis of Jewish-German jargon [*Mauscheldeutsch*]. The mixing of three "dissimilar languages," he recalled in his memoirs, made a child attentive to language and its deceits. From an early age, he marveled that objects were called one thing in Czech and another in German.[82]

Mauthner wrote a series of stories, novels, and treatises puncturing the claims of language.[83] In the opening story of a fairy tale collection, Dark Yearning (Sehnsucht) overcomes obstacles of mountains, seas, and storms in the search for her sister, Bright Truth (Wahrheit). When Yearning locates her sister, she greets and questions her in every known language, but Truth does not understand; she speaks an unknown tongue. The saddened Yearning presents her cherished child, Belief, to her sister to have her teach Belief the mysteries of her language. Truth carries Belief about, but returns the infant to Yearning with a book of fairy tales which the child is too young to understand. When Belief grows up, however, she accompanies Yearning through life, espying in nature and life "the fairy tale of truth" ("*das Märchenbuch der Wahrheit*").[84]

In his short and long works alike Mauthner hammered away at the inadequacies of language—indeed, at the concept of truth, which he considered a dogmatic invention. He consistently pursued what he called his "inborn disgust with all pseudo concepts [*Scheinbegriffen*]," including the concept of God.[85] Language, he said, is an illusion. He wanted to free mankind from its "tyranny."[86] Of course, he realized this was a quixotic or impossible task: to use language to demonstrate the hopelessness of language. Would the demonstration sink the critique itself? At the beginning of his three-volume *Kritik der Sprache* (*Critique of Language*), Mauthner tells the story of a pope plagued by bedbugs. Nothing worked to get rid of the bugs, until one day the pope obtained a powder billed as infallible. "He scattered the powder about and lay down. In the morning all the bugs were dead, but so was the pope. What killed the bugs killed the pope." Mauthner was prepared to run the risk.[87]

Separated by twenty years, Landauer and Mauthner approached the world very differently. They disagreed about Judaism, and their contrary responses to World War I almost led to a rupture. Yet intellectually they felt profoundly drawn together. They exchanged over 600 letters and wrote a series of works honoring each other. Landauer helped edit the first volume of Mauthner's *Critique of Language*. Mauthner's 1906 *Die Sprache* (*Language*), published in Buber's collection, was dedicated to Landauer, who in turn wrote several articles and one small book, *Skepsis und Mystik* (*Skepticism and Mysticism*), about his friend.[88] When Landauer read *Language* he was completing his own book for Buber, and he wrote to Mauthner,

I have now finished reading your book with great sympathy. . . . This book . . . often seems to speak to me directly. . . . Once you have read my book you will realize how much we have in common, but you will also learn at the same time how different are our views of the world. My first aim always is a practical one, to change society. This is most important to me, although . . . I often wonder how much I will be able to achieve. I hope that you will always realize how close our views are, that you are part of me, and that I am with you in spirit.[89]

After Landauer's death, Mauthner planned to write a book about him that would signal his "nobility."[90]

What bound them so closely together? a suspicion of language, a visceral anarchism, a challenge to conventional truths, and a mystical urge. For Mauthner, the religious and philosophical dogmatists claimed perfect truth. "It was always the free spirits, the heretics in religion and philosophy, who extended the idea that all human knowledge was relative to the highest level, to truth itself."[91] Mauthner pursued this insight logically and ruthlessly. Indeed, he pursued it till the door to mysticism opened. While skepticism and mysticism might seem incompatible, for Mauthner and Landauer, they fed each other. Mauthner judged himself "a godless mystic" and wrote, at the end of his life, a three-volume study of atheism in Western society.[92] A profound skepticism about fixed truths and language allowed them glimpses of another dimension. Something about the world escapes language. In his atheism study, Mauthner put it this way: "The critique of language is my first and last word. Looking backwards the critique of language is all destructive skepticism; looking forward, playing with illusions, it is a longing for oneness; it is mysticism."[93]

Landauer gave these ideas a more political and social twist. "You go your way, and I go mine," he wrote to Mauthner, and they would glory in their friendship. However, for Landauer, "the critique of language belongs inseparably to what I call anarchism and socialism, and I don't know how it could be otherwise."[94] He followed Mauthner in the belief that language could not capture a world rich "in its wordlessness and inexpressibility [*in ihrer Sprachlosigkeit und Unaussprechbarkeit*]." For Landauer life precedes and supercedes language. "The world is without language." Words are at best a poor means to access life and its feelings. Landauer's *Skepticism and Mysticism*, which is devoted to Mauthner, opens with a long and complex parable on the insufficiencies of language.

> In a dream a man proceeds along a road and does not know he is dreaming. He comes to a high, hard, bronze mountain that blocks his way and that is so shiny that he is reflected in it. He looks at himself in the dark light and says startled, "This is a mirror. I see nothing. I see myself—nothing." A voice calls out, "Have you left the world behind you?" "Yes," the man whispers. "It is done." "Then look into me. Behind your reflection you will see the world." The man stares in the dark reflection and says slowly, "I see the world, but I see nothing." And he sinks into gloomy reflections about himself and the world.

The parable continues as the man awakens and departs, troubled but happy. To Landauer, Mauthner proved that linguistic chains enslave man. "Doesn't everyone who has tried to put dreams into words know that the best is dissolved and destroyed when they are cast into a language?" Yet Mauthner's achievement— his demonstration that language dominates and distorts—does not suffice. "What would this great accomplishment be worth, if all the absolutes were killed and every truth destroyed?" asks Landauer. The critical enterprise should open the way to joy and the "play of life." In breaking the chains of language, should we not become "dreamers? flyers? artists? free?" For Landauer, Mauthner's critique of linguistic deficiency not only "opens the door" to mysticism, but to "action," beauty, and life.[95]

Like Buber and Landauer, Mauthner drew upon mysticism, but unlike them, he did not see himself as Jewish. Landauer proclaimed he was both Jewish and German. "I feel my Judaism in my gestures, my expressions, in my deportment, my appearance," and in everything "I begin and I am." But, Landauer continued, insofar as he was Jewish, he was German. Both identities were essential; neither was secondary.[96] Mauthner dissented from this religious proclamation: "I feel myself only a German."[97] Mauthner's atheism was closely linked to his philosophical and linguistic skepticism, at least autobiographically. "Just as a Jew in a dual language country I had no real mother tongue, so as a son of a completely irreligious Jewish family, I had no mother religion [*Mutterreligion*]." This statement comes from a chapter in his autobiography entitled "Without Language and Without Religion."[98]

Mauthner's distance from a "mother" language and religion may have informed his thoughts about correct German and Yiddish-inflected German, which was sometimes derogatorily called "*Mauscheldeutsch*." Like many assimilated German Jews, who spurned the religion, mores, and habits of the Eastern European Jews, Mauthner's father despised "*Mauscheldeutsch*" as a crude idiom. Mauthner recalled that his father "pitilessly fought any hint" of Czech or Jewish jargon; he "struggled inadequately to teach us a pure, exaggerated high German language."[99] The son inherited this scorn. Linguistic and religious identity were inextricably connected. If the Jews in Germany, wrote Mauthner, "would pay more attention to themselves, then they must recognize that they will continue to form a tribe as long as they continue, more or less, to speak a jargon, which is incomprehensible to non-Jewish Germans. The Jew will only become a full German when *Mauschel*-expressions become a foreign language" to him.

In *Jewish Self-Hatred*, Sander L. Gilman cites this sentence and clumps Mauthner with Karl Kraus, Herzl, and even Hitler, all of whom saw the Jews as the polluters of German culture. Gilman compares the Jewish critics of language with anti-Semites who attack Jews for contaminating the press. The Jews "sedulously avoid any outward crude forms," declared Hitler, but "amid a *Gezeires* of fine sounds and phrases" they "pour their poison into the hearts of the reader."[100] Hitler was referring to the Jewish liberal press, and Gilman finds in Hitler echoes of the great critic of the press, Kraus. Gilman believes "the Jewish critics" of *Mauschel*, like Mauthner and Kraus, "are not that far apart" from Hitler. [101] Both saw the Jewish idiom as corrupting German.

Gilman may be overstating the case, yet he is signaling a central irony of contradiction in the Jewish tradition: the simultaneous distrust and fetish of the word. Mauthner can be exhibit A. If his linguistic skepticism drew upon his Jewish experience, he nonetheless indicted the Jews as the worst sinners because they idolized words.[102] The religious Jew may not be allowed to utter the name of God, he wrote, but he has also developed the "corresponding opposite" fetish of words. Judaism become a "religion of words [*Wortreligion*]," a preoccupation with the word of God in the Talmud and bible. "The 'learned' in the Polish orthodox Jewish communities confine themselves to the holy texts of the bible. 'Learning' means in Yiddish sometimes praying and reading from the bible, sometimes theological disputations, meaning applying logic to the sacred text."[103]

The Jews "know the exact terms and melody for addressing the Jewish God," writes Gilman, "but they also recognize the uniqueness of the superstition of the word, by which they dare not speak the name of God for fear of punishment."[104] This fetish or taboo marks the great critics of language like Mauthner, an obsession with words and a total rejection of them. Mauthner's *Critique of Language* opens biblically: " 'In the beginning there was the word,' " and continues: "With this word, humanity stands at the beginning of knowledge and stops if it remains with the word. Whoever wants to step further—and even the smallest step requires the intellectual work of an entire life—must try to free himself of words and superstition of words; he must try to redeem the world from the tyranny of language."[105]

Landauer concurred, but for him redemption required more than intellectual work. During World War I he participated in pacifist and antiwar activities. As disillusion with the war mounted, Landauer found a new audience. "It is not my fault," he noted in December 1917, that before the war his writings almost seemed like "private publications." He had stood up a "a little too early." Now almost fifty years old, he had been rediscovered, and he intended to republish and rework many of his essays.[106] As the war ended in 1918, the old regime tottered and revolutionary outbreaks flared across Germany. An acquaintance, Kurt Eisner, called upon Landauer to join him in revolutionary Munich. Eisner hoped that through speeches and discussions Landauer could help in the "transformation of souls." Landauer could not resist and prepared to travel to Munich. He wrote to Buber the day after he heard from Eisner that the revolution must bring forth "a new spirit out of new conditions." He asked Buber to join him. "There is," he said, "enough work to do."[107]

Over the following months, reform, revolution, and counterrevolution fought cheek-to-jowl in Germany. Landauer played the role of orator, deputy, and commissioner in Munich. A revolution never had much of a chance in conservative Bavaria, but Munich continued to lurch to the left. By spring, a "council republic" came into being and chose Landauer as its commissar of "Public Instruction." The day was April 7, 1919, Landauer's forty-ninth birthday. He wrote to Mauthner, "Give me a few weeks, and I hope to accomplish something; but it is very possible, that I will only have a few days, and then it was a dream."[108]

Landauer sought to reform education, but, of course, he was

right; it was a dream.[109] Within one week, an attempted putsch by a rightist Munich garrison against the "council republic" led to another turn of the screw, the coming to power of a Red council republic, consisting of new and tougher leaders such as the communist Max Levien. The American writer Ben Hecht worked as reporter in those years and found himself in Munich, where he interviewed key players. He recalled that Landauer mainly wanted to talk about Walt Whitman, whom he had translated into German during the war. " 'Every Bavarian child at the age of ten is going to know Walt Whitman by heart,' Landauer told me. 'That is the cornerstone of my new educational program.' " But the new guard, including Levien, had other ideas. Hecht records a speech in which the Bolshevik-saluting Levien "barked and threatened" in his Russian tunic. At the end, "Levien announced sharply, 'There will be no more poetry!' "[110]

Landauer withdrew from the government, protesting the communist style of revolution. "I have understood struggle to mean making the conditions that will allow every man to partake of the goods and culture of the earth." Your ideas, he wrote to the new communist leadership, are "somewhat different." I have seen "your education," "your sort of struggle," and how reality appears to you. Landauer recognized that rejection, for him and the communists, was "mutual." He deeply regretted that only the smallest part of his contribution to "warmth and improvement, culture and renaissance" remained.[111]

This was Landauer's last letter. He planned to resume his literary life, but within two weeks, Munich fell before White troops sent from Berlin to extinguish the revolution. On May 1 he was arrested at Kurt Eisner's house. The next day, he was sent to Stadelheim prison near Munich, where jeering soldiers first bludgeoned and then shot him. The *New York Times* reported that "Gustav Landauer, Minister of Enlightenment" was "murdered by a mob" after being imprisoned by government troops.[112] Landauer's last words, as conveyed to Buber, were, "Yes, beat me to death! To think you are human beings!"[113] Ernst Niekisch, a writer and political activist, whom the Nazis later incarcerated, was also in Munich at the time. He described Landauer's end in his memoirs, and added that the murder "showed the extent of bestiality that resides in the German soul, and it already announced the later horrors of the Third Reich."[114]

Several months earlier Landauer had written a new preface to *For Socialism* that seemed to anticipate the trajectory of this utopian experiment. Dated "January 1919 Munich," the preface closed, "We will die soon, we all die. . . . Nothing lives but what we make of ourselves, what we do with ourselves. . . . Nothing lives but the action of honest hands and the governance of a pure, genuine, spirit [*reinen wahrhaften Geistes*]."[115] This might be a fitting epitaph; only spirit remains. As if to confirm it, Landauer's grave was dedicated some years later. Buber describes the monument as a "simple but powerful obelisk" that stands among trees and bears Landauer's name and a quotation from *For Socialism*. Forty-five years later, a biographer of Landauer made his way to the cemetery and observed, "the monument is no longer to be found. A man named Dr. Morsbach now lies in the grave."[116]

In *For Socialism*, Landauer had ridiculed the Marxist idea of utopia as a "gigantic goiter" on the neck of capitalism; he denounced Marxism for worshiping steam and technology. Landauer believed in spirit and brotherhood. "We are poets," he said. We "want to create from the heart." Nor would he depict the future. "I will not say . . . how the new reality we desire should be constituted as a whole. I offer no depiction of an ideal, no description of a utopia."[117] In his simultaneous hope for the future and refusal to depict it Landauer placed himself in the mainstream of a side road—he placed himself among the Jewish iconoclastic utopians.

4. *A Longing That Cannot Be Uttered*

And God spake all these words, saying,
I am the Lord thy God, which have brought thee out of the
land of Egypt, out of the house of bondage.
Thou shalt have no other gods before me.
Thou shalt not make unto thee any graven image, or any
likeness of any thing that is in heaven above, or that is in
the earth beneath, or that is in the water under the earth.
—EXODUS 20:1—4

THE PROHIBITION AGAINST "GRAVEN IMAGES" FOUND IN
the Old Testament shows up often and allows little latitude:

Ye shall make you no idols nor graven image, neither rear
you up a standing image, neither shall ye set up any image
of stone in your land, to bow down unto it: for I am the
Lord your God. *(Lev. 26:1)*

Take heed unto yourselves, lest ye forget the covenant of
the Lord your God, which he made with you, and make
you a graven image, or the likeness of any thing, which the
Lord thy God hath forbidden thee. *(Deut. 4:23)*

Cursed be the man that maketh any graven or molten image, an abomination unto the Lord, the work of the hands of the craftsman, and putteth it in a secret place. And all the people shall answer and say, Amen.

(Deut. 27:15)

Cautionary tales and the temptations to transgress abound, most notably in the story of the golden calf. The people of Israel, impatient at the absence of Moses, call upon Aaron "to make us gods." Aaron proceeded to collect gold jewelry, to cast a golden calf and to construct an altar to celebrate it. He proclaimed a feast day, and people assembled and made offerings to the golden calf. "Moses returned unto Jehovah, and said, Oh, this people have sinned a great sin, and have made them gods of gold" (Exod. 32:31). The Lord waxed hot with anger at the transgression and slaughtered the people.

What was the commandment against graven images, and what were its consequences? "The Second Commandment," writes one study, " was an innovation, revolutionary in character, which was to lift the Mosaic faith above the hitherto common sensuous conceptions of the deity."[1] The prohibition had virtually no precedent among ancient peoples; it distinguished the Jews from other religions.[2] Believers also paid a price. Throughout the millennia Jews have interpreted, reinterpreted, and ignored this commandment. Especially in regard to art, rabbis and scholars have pondered how this commandment applied. What artistic practices does it allow? "Is there such a thing as Jewish art?" asks an art scholar.[3] Has the commandment crippled the development of Jewish painting?

The full entry under "painting" in the twelve-volume *Jewish Encyclopedia*, published early in the twentieth century, ran to eighty words—compared, for instance, to that under "poetry," which clocked in at eight thousand. It reads:

The art least developed among the Hebrews. If it is borne in mind that painting was affected by the Mosaic interdiction against images, it is not surprising that this art is hardly mentioned in the Old Testament. Decorations on walls include only carvings in relief, as in the Temple, and drawings traced by means of a sharp point, the outlines of which were colored (comp. Ezek. viii. 10, xxiii. 14). The decorations on earthenware also were only colored outline-drawings.[4]

A classic German-Jewish encyclopedia of the 1930s stated "Jewish art" did not exist. The reason? As a diasporic people Jews lacked the requisite stability, and as an "anti-Hellenic" people they remained loyal to the prohibition of the Second Commandment. The Jews valued ethical conduct more than harmonious art forms.[5] Such sentiments can be traced backward and forward. For some commentators (and Jews) the prohibition kept Jews spiritually pure by restricting the visual arts. A nineteenth-century German rabbi proposed that as long as it "battled" paganism, Judaism must treat the plastic arts (*Plastik*) as its "severe foe" and "find its own symbols only in the sphere of the spiritual." Judaism allows poetry, "but no plastic art form should awaken thoughts of God, no sculptured statues represent Him." Judaism, this rabbi asserted, "is hostile to the plastic arts."[6]

The impact of the taboo against graven images on Jewish culture remains a contested topic. Virtually all recent discussions of the prohibition champion Jewish art against both friendly insiders—Jews who question it—and hostile outsiders—sometimes anti-Semites—who deny its existence. Doubting whether Jews have produced art, remarks the Israeli scholar Yaacov Shavit, may come as a "surprise" to anyone familiar with the "corpus of literary and artistic work created by Jews, which encompasses works . . . of all types." In the nineteenth century, however, he tells us that the notion that Jews lacked art and imagination reigned supreme. Shavit identified Ernest Renan, the French historian, as the most influential exponent of this idea. Inasmuch as they were people of an arid desert and sterile monotheism, the Jews lacked creativity, according to Renan.[7] "This theory," writes Shavit, "permeated endless texts, and resurfaced as an irrefutable truth in works of scientific nature, as well as in ideological tracts."[8]

Katman P. Bland, a professor of religion, who cites the nineteenth-century German rabbi calling upon Jews to resist visual paganism, traces the attitude not to the commandments but to a German-Jewish denigration of the pictorial dimension. The biblical injunction itself "cannot explain why Jewish aniconism, denying the existence of Jewish art, became the established conventional wisdom in modern secular scholarship. It cannot explain why the idea of Jewish aniconism has persisted throughout the twentieth century despite the apparent evidence to the contrary amassed by a host of archaeologists, ethnographers, archivists, and art historians." For Bland, assimilationist pressures and anti-Semitism fuel this prevalent misunderstanding. Some German intellectuals, following the lead of Kant and Herder, devalued Jewish visual achievement; at the same time, anti-Semites like Richard Wagner asserted that Jews lacked visual talent and imagination.[9]

To establish the reality of a Jewish visual arts, defenders usually begin with an appreciation of temple architecture, ornamental crafts, and illuminated manuscripts, which can be traced over the centuries. This is the approach of Gabrielle Sed-Rajna, a French expert on Jewish art, who argues that the impact of the Second Commandment has been "exaggerated" and that, with some exceptions, Jews have encouraged the visual arts.[10] In the modern period, the emergence of identifiable and self-identified Jewish artists has made the issue more urgent as the artists themselves began to inquire about Jewish achievement. In a slightly longer entry under "pictorial art," the old *Jewish Encyclopedia* notes that "during the last 150 years a certain number of Jews" have taken up painting. Moreover, the rise of cubism and postcubist art has led to a twist. Inasmuch as abstract art fragments the human form, observant Jews find it more acceptable. Something of the old prohibition on graven images haunts abstract art, declared T. W. Adorno.[11]

Is this true? Evidence for an elective affinity between Jews and abstract art may exist. At least, numerous abstract artists were Jewish by origin. In 1916 the Jewish Ethnographic Society of Russia financed two young artists, El Lissitzky and Issachar Ryback, in their exploration of the art of wooden synagogues along the Dnieper River in southern Russia. Several years later Ryback coauthored an article-manifesto, "The Paths of Jewish Painting," that began with a motto: "Long live the abstract form." Its authors attacked Russian and Jewish realism and proclaimed that "only through the principle of abstract painting . . . can one achieve the expression of one's own national form. . . . Abstraction, which is an autonomous form of painting, does not allow for any other form . . . than the pure painterly . . . its pure essence." The art historian Avram Kampf guesses that the Second Commandment is "never evoked as a supporting reason" in this manifesto because in the new Soviet Union the mood ran sharply against religious arguments.[12]

In their travels Lissitzky and Rybeck happened with great excitement upon the murals and painting of the Mohilev synagogue, all attributed to Haim, the son of Isaac Segal from Sluzk. "I felt like a child," recalled Lissitzky, "opening his eyes upon awakening and being startled by the sunflies and butterflies glittering in the rays of the sun."[13] Using folk and Jewish motifs, Segal had painted the walls with great simplicity, skill, and imagination—foxes, bears, the Tree of Life, twinkling stars turning into flowers, fish hunted by birds, and all intertwined with blooming acanthus.[14] Two contemporary critics remarked that since Jewish art "permitted decoration but not illustration," the Jewish artist infused the decorative with imagination. "For instance, the synagogue of Mohilev contains twelve figures of the zodiac, various birds, serpents, cities, trees, etc. Without the possibility of presenting the human figure, the artist carried the human into beasts and birds. These are really not beasts but symbols of Jewish life."[15] These observers could have been describing some work of Marc Chagall, who in fact later "adopted" as his fictitious grandfather Segal, the artisan of Mohilev.[16]

Art and utopianism spring from the same soil and confront or circumvent the same taboo.[17] It is hardly by chance that Ernst Bloch's *Spirit of Utopia* opens with a discussion of ornaments and art. Yet the issue here is more utopianism than art. What were the consequences of the prohibition on graven images for the utopian tradition in general or Jewish utopianism in particular? This question has hardly been asked, much less pursued. A recent collection that surveys utopianism is typically titled *Visions of Utopia*.[18] Undoubtedly, visual markers define almost all utopias. Many set out in precise detail what the future should be. "It is neither an idle dream, nor useless vanity," stated an early-nineteenth-century American utopian, J. A. Etzler, "to draw the picture in full of what is easily attainable for us."

In his effort to show how a community can attain "the possible greatest sum of enjoyments, comforts and pleasures," Etzler in *The Paradise Within the Reach of All Men* (1833) provided exact dimensions of the future: "Every adult member of either sex is to have an apartment for exclusive use, consisting of several rooms. . . . Every such private apartment communicates . . . with the outside . . . by a door to a gallery around the whole building." The building will be one hundred feet wide, and each person will have two spaces, twenty-four feet long and forty feet wide, divided by a corridor, for his or her exclusive use. If the building were one thousand feet long, one hundred feet wide, and ten stories high, it would house four hundred apartments.

4 such edifices joined together in right angles, so as to form a square of 1000 feet between them, could in the above manner lodge 1600 persons, leaving yet at each of the 4 corners a square of 100 feet, which, in the 10 stories, contain 40 rooms each of 100 square feet: these may be used for dormitories of children.

Etlzer also describes how the kitchens would work and how each would be outfitted with "movable boxes," which enclose "one kind of victuals for one meal of the community."[19]

With a few exceptions, Jewish utopianism lacked these sort of details and blueprints. Without the visual markers, the Jewish utopians are easy to miss. Two representative anthologies of utopian writings, *The Quest for Utopia* and *The Utopia Reader*, published almost fifty years apart, include no writings by them.[20] Is there a utopianism without blueprints? How did the prohibition on graven images affect Jewish utopianism? Is there a utopianism that listens for, but does not look into the future? That pines for the future, but does not map it out? An iconoclastic, not blueprint utopianism?

Scholars often adduce pragmatic reasons for the prohibition on graven images; it preserved the uniqueness of the Jews amid competing religions. The God of the Old Testament announces his jealousy frequently. On the heels of the graven image prohibition, God states, "Thou shalt not bow down thyself to them, nor serve them: for I the Lord thy God am a jealous God" (Exod. 20:5). This is regularly repeated. "Take heed unto yourselves, lest ye forget the covenant of the Lord your God, which he made with you, and make you a graven image, or the likeness of any thing, which the Lord thy God hath forbidden thee. For the Lord thy God is a consuming fire, even a jealous God" (Deut. 4:23–24).

To some specialists the prohibition reflected the "early Israelite bias" against kingship.[21] For others it served as a tactical measure of a desert people surrounded by tribes with cult practices. The invisible God gave the exiled and powerless Jews purpose and consolation, argues Hermann Vorländer, a professor of Old Testament studies.[22] "The proscription against making graven images," writes the scholar Joseph Gutmann, "must therefore be understood within the context of a semi-nomadic experience. . . . The purpose of the law . . . seems to have been to assure loyalty to the invisible Yahweh and to keep the [Jewish] nomads from creating idols or adopting the idols of the many sedentary cultures with which they came in contact."[23] In *The Forbidden Image*, the French scholar Alain Besançon links the prohibition to the "laws of purity" or efforts to keep Israelites untainted by foreign religions.[24]

Faced with a polytheistic world of Egyptians gods with cat heads and Greek deities wielding tridents, the Jewish prophets commanded monotheism and prohibited worshiping graven images.[25] "You foolish people," states the partly Jewish *Sibylline Oracles* about the Egyptians, "who worship snakes, dogs, cats and honor birds and animals that crawl on the ground, stone images, statues made by human hand, roadside cairns—these are your gods, these and many other foolish and unmentionable things."[26]

The practical explanation for the prohibition has its limits; many other strategies might have been pursued to preserve autonomy from other tribes. Yet the taboo encapsulated a series of interlocking notions about monotheism, representation, and language.[27] For starters, it entailed a radical disenchantment of the world. Max Weber, the great German sociologist, glimpsed a "rational" religious ethic in Judaism. The prophets promoted a puritanical, anti-idolatrous and antimagical devoutness.[28] The invisible God could not be wooed by offerings to an icon or by attendance to astrology. The prohibitions undercut witchcraft and astrology.

Flavius Josephus, the first-century Jewish historian, present-ed evidence of this rational ethic. He recounted the story of a Jewish archer, Mosollam, the most skilled in the army, who ac-companied Alexander's forces till they came to a stop because a seer was taking readings from the movements of a bird. The augur counseled that if the bird failed to fly away, the army should stop; if the bird flew forward, the army should advance, but if the bird flew backward, the army should retire.

> Mosollam made no reply, but drew his bow and shot at the bird, and hit him, and killed him; and as the augur and some others were very angry . . . he answered them thus-ly—Why are you so mad as to take this most unhappy bird into your hands? For how can this bird give us any true in-formation concerning our march, which could not foresee how to save himself? For had he been able to foreknow what was the future, he would not have come to this place, but would have been afraid lest Mosollam the Jew would shoot at him and kill him.[29]

"The principal purpose of the whole Law," declared the twelfth-century Moses Maimonides in his *Guide for the Per-plexed*, "was the removal and utter destruction of idolatry, and all that is connected therewith, even its name, and everything that might lead to any such practices, e.g. acting as a consulter with familiar spirits, or a wizard, passing children through the fire, divining, observing the clouds, enchanting, charming, or inquiring of the dead."[30]

Inasmuch as it taps images and pictures, language itself for Maimonides suffers from idolatry. Yet the prophets themselves used language that suggested God was a human entity with a fin-ger or lips or voice. Was this a transgression? These linguistic formulations can be accepted as a rhetorical device, according to Maimonides, but in truth we can only describe God negatively—

by what he is not. Graphic language misses the essence of God. "We cannot describe the Creator by any means except by negative attributes."[31] Maimonides approaches a conclusion that would mark Jewish philosophy about language in general—and utopianism in particular. The impossibility of depicting God commends silence. The concreteness of written language signifies a failure to reach the absolute, which an ineffable communication might escape.

Maimonides recounts the story from the Talmud of Rabbi Haninah, who overheard a prayer that included "God, the great, the valiant, and the tremendous, the powerful, the strong, and the mighty." The pious rabbi protested, "Have you finished all the praises of your Master?" The rabbi himself told a parable of a wealthy king who possessed millions of gold coins. "He was praised for owning millions of silver coin; was this not really dispraise of him?" Maimonides considers this parable and the foolish people who think they can praise God. He concludes this discussion by stating that the "glorification of God does not consist in *uttering* that which is not to be uttered, but in *reflecting* on that on which man should reflect."[32]

Six centuries later another Moses, Mendelssohn, pondered the prohibition. "We have seen how difficult it is to preserve the abstract ideas of religion. . . . Images and hieroglyphics lead to superstition and idolatry." Humanity had succumbed to base practices.

Man, animals, plants, the most hideous and despicable things in nature were worshiped and revered as deities. . . . In the most magnificent temples, constructed and decorated according to all the rules of art, one looked, to the shame of reason, as Plutarch put it, for the deity worshiped there, and one found on the altar a hideous, long-tailed monkey; and to this monster blooming youths and

maidens were slaughtered. So deeply had idolatry debased human nature![33]

For Mendelssohn the ceremonial laws of Israel induced men to "speculative knowledge of religion and teachings of morality." This search for truth was "utterly removed from all imagery; for this was the main purpose and fundamental law of the constitution."

A century later, Hermann Cohen, the German-Jewish philosopher, addressed the prohibition. Cohen, whom Leo Strauss called "the master" for a generation of philosophically minded Jews, folded monotheism and the ban on graven images into each other.[34] "One has not acquired a true understanding of monotheism," stated Cohen, "if one has not understood the destruction of idolatry as a relentless necessity." The opposition between the unique God and the many gods is that between "the unseen *idea* and a perceptible *image*." In his posthumous *Religion of Reason* Cohen returned often to this idea: "Monotheism teaches that God absolutely cannot be an object that can be thought of through the instruction of an image . . . *it is the proof of the true God that there can be no image of Him*."[35]

The flight from idols might include the flight from language, which could be fetishized as readily as visual art forms. Mendelssohn had feared that the written language itself might be worshiped—and it would be. Some Jews believed that words or numbers could unlock the mysteries of the universe.[36] Deity was "concealed in these numbers; one ascribed miraculous powers to them." These philosophers had succumbed to idolatry. "For this reason," Mendelssohn indicates, "there were but few written laws, and even these were not entirely comprehensible without oral instructions and tradition. . . . The unwritten laws, the oral tradition, the living instructions from man to man, from

mouth to heart, were to explain, enlarge, limit, and define more precisely what . . . remained undetermined in the written law."[37]

The people of the book also feared the book; at least, its words could bewitch. The prohibition on graven images might encompass the written language. "The very words that men used contained both image and likeness," offers Leo Baeck, "and men had to strive to reach words that were full of life and yet free of myth. The image in the words must not be really an image, but only a hint, a parable." Baeck refers to the exchange in Exodus where Moses asks God his name. God answers enigmatically, "I am that I am" (Exod. 3:13). Baeck explains, "that means He for Whom no word or name is sufficient. The fight for language here becomes the fight *against* language."[38]

These contrary passions—a simultaneous love and repudiation of words—surfaced even more sharply in mystical and Kabbalistic Judaism. For mystical Jews, every single word or letter of the Torah is crucial. For some Kabbalists, wrote Scholem, "the Torah contains not so much as one superfluous letter or point." The whole is a flawless document. Scholem cites from a commentary: "To omit so much as one letter or point from the Torah is like removing some part of a perfect edifice." A second-century sage recalled that when he was a student, he visited an elder Rabbi: " 'He asked me: My son, what is your occupation? I answered: I am a scribe [of the Torah.] And he said to me: My son, be careful in your work, for it is the work of God; if you omit a single letter, or write a letter too many, you will destroy the whole world.' "[39]

An obsessive literalism coexisted with, and sometimes yielded its opposite, a mystical belief in the non-literal or invisible. The written word recedes before the oral. The letter is dead without the spirit. A twelfth-century Kabbalist offered an elaborate metaphor of the Torah as composed of white and black fire. The white fire comprised the written Torah's scroll before the letters appeared; the black fire or oral Torah constituted the ink.

"And so the written Torah can take on corporeal form only through the power of the oral Torah, that is to say: without the oral Torah, it cannot be completely understood." "A far-reaching idea!" Scholem comments, inasmuch as "strictly speaking, there is no written Torah." Instead only the invisible "black light" of the oral laws renders the Torah palpable. Oddly, Scholem does not comment about this Kabbalist's name, "Isaac the Blind."[40]

The inclination to treasure the oral does not simply crop up in the Kabbalah or in mystical Judaism but informs the whole Jewish tradition. The ear trumps the eye. Alone, the written word may mislead; it is too graphic. For Kabbalists and non-Kabbalists alike this applies to the name of God, which should not be written—or should not be spoken as written; many Kabbalists considered "God's Torah" not simply an emanation of God, but a reworking of God's name. "The whole Torah is a fabric of appellatives . . . of God," writes a thirteenth-century Spanish Kabbalist. "These holy names are connected with the tetragrammaton YHVH and dependent upon it. Thus the entire Torah is ultimately woven from the tetragrammaton."[41]

For the Jews the four-letter Hebrew word, or tetragrammaton, for God, YHVH (usually rendered "the Lord" in English translations) was too sacred to use.[42] As Scholem puts it in a (German) word play, "One can approach, but not pronounce the name of God." ["Der Name Gottes ist *an*sprechbar, aber nicht *aus*sprechbar."][43] The prohibition on using or pronouncing the true name of the Lord can claim a long history. The favorite biblical reference again is Exodus where Moses asks God his name. "And God said unto Moses, 'I am that I am' " (Exod. 3:13–14). God is strictly nameless. In Jewish practice, Louis Jacobs explains, "this name [YHVH] was never pronounced as it is written but as *Adonai*, 'the Lord.' In printed texts the vowels of *Adonai* were placed under the letters of the Tetragrammaton." (Christian scholars later erroneously conflated these vowels with YHVH to derive Jehovah as the name of God.)[44] For Judah Halevi, the eleventh-century poet and sage, Adonai "points to something which stands as such an immeasurable altitude that a real designation is impossible."[45]

How does one name the unnameable? Arguments over the proper name or synonym for God caused "bitter struggle" lasting centuries, states Arthur Marmorstein in his study on the name and attributes of God. For the pious, the name of God was heard only on the holiest days from the high priest in the temple—and perhaps not even then. Marmorstein reports that in the Temple the High Priest muffled the name of God, as if it were too sacred to be heard. "Even in the Temple the pronunciation was not distinct. The High Priest tried to utter the Name in such a way that the people listening to the blessing should not hear the same distinctly." A Greek source tells the story of Moses, who enters the royal palace and awakens the king. The terrified king demands that Moses *"name the God who sent him,"* but Moses only whispers the name in the King's ear. Marmorstein explains, "The king asked for *God's Name*. Moses whispers, but does not pronounce the same."[46] From the Mishnah, the digest of the oral teachings, comes the edict that among the doomed is "the man who utters the name [of God] as it is spelled."[47]

Names smack of domination, an effort to control or limit. The superior creature names the inferior. Adam names the animals. "Whatsoever Adam call every living creature, that was the name thereof. And Adam gave names to all cattle, and to the fowl of the air, and to every beast of the field" (Gen. 2:19–20). Some rabbinical texts suggest the real name of God cannot be employed till the era of redemption. "The Tetragrammaton is read as Adonai but in the Messianic age the name will once again be pronounced as it is written," summarizes one scholar.[48] In the same vein, a Kabbalist pronounced that in the age of the Messiah "the image and its object can no longer be related." Not only will man no longer quarrel with his fellow man, but the world, according to Scholem, " will be a world without images . . . a new mode of being will emerge which cannot be pictorially represented."[49]

These ideas would resonate in those who might be called the Weimar utopian Jews—intellectuals such as Ernst Bloch, Gershom Scholem, T. W. Adorno, and Walter Benjamin.[50] They all rejected—to crudely generalize—scientific ideas of language as a tool or set of signs used to communicate; they all advanced what might be called messianic ideas about language. Until redemption, language miscommunicates; it is less a vehicle of truth than an obstacle to it. This meant that like Maimonides' negative theology, language may pause in the effort to grasp the absolute. An ethos of silence permeates the oeuvre of the Weimar utopians. Benjamin's dense and difficult *Origin of German Tragic Drama* draws on Franz Rosenzweig: "The tragic hero has only one language which completely corresponds to him: precisely keeping silent."[51] The same notion crops up in Scholem. "The 'true' language," he writes in "Ten Unhistorical Aphorisms on Kabbalah," "cannot be spoken."[52] Leo Strauss concurred. In his reflections on the "good society" Strauss wrote that rabbinic Judaism "always held that the written Torah must be understood in the light of the oral or unwritten Torah, and the most profound reason for this is that the most profound truth cannot be written and not even said."[53]

Adorno's statement that to write poetry after Auschwitz is barbaric has elicited much comment, but the idea is part and parcel of his own reworking of the taboo on graven images.[54] The absolute—here absolute violence—cannot be comprehended; it requires diffidence, perhaps silence. The refusal to name the absolute preserved the possibility of redemption.[55] Conversely, language seduces by the illusion that it captures the truth. What Adorno called the "liberal fiction of the universal communicability of each and every thought" must be resisted.[56] We must retain awareness of the distance and gaps, the inability to visualize the absolute. "The materialist longing to grasp the thing," Adorno wrote in *Negative Dialectics*, aims at the opposite of idealism. "It is only in the absence of images that the full object could be conceived. Such absence concurs with the theological ban on images."[57] For Adorno "the true speech of art is speechlessness."[58]

The ban on images informed the "critical theory" of the Frankfurt School as a whole. From their early to their late writings, references abound to utopian redemption and the taboo on graven images. "The Jewish religion," wrote Max Horkheimer (with Adorno) in the *Dialectic of Enlightenment*, "associated hope only with the prohibition against calling on what is false as God, against invoking the finite as the infinite. . . . The guarantee of salvation lies in the rejection of any belief that would replace it: it is knowledge obtained in the denunciation of illusion."[59] After Adorno died, a troubled acquaintance asked Horkheimer why Judaism found no place in the funeral. Horkheimer tried to explain. He wondered himself if Adorno had lived longer and planned for his demise, things would have been done otherwise; he referred to Adorno's statement about poetry and Auschwitz as demonstrating his identification with the persecuted Jews. He pointed out Adorno's mother was Catholic. "On the other hand, I must say that the critical theory, which we both developed, has its roots in Judaism. It originates from the thought: You should make no image of God."[60]

Even twentieth-century philosophical Jews distant from Judaism gravitated to the idea of silence in the face of the absolute.[61] Mauthner's entire work led to silence and mysticism. A section of his three volume critique of language is titled "silence." When he favorably cited Maeterlinck on the need for silence, he anticipates the famous last line of Wittgenstein's *Tractatus*: "What we cannot speak about we must pass over in silence."[62] Wittgenstein himself has conventionally been interpreted as a positivist who wanted to break with philosophy as a literary endeavor. While his work gave support to hard-nosed philosophers committed to purging philosophy of muddy language, the opposite view of him as a neo-Jewish mystic may be more illuminating.

To be sure, everything about Wittgenstein remains clouded, including his religious and sexual identity. As the philosopher G. H. von Wright put it, the man who claimed that ' "everything that can be said can be said clearly,' was himself an enigma."[63] Wittgenstein was a complex and conflicted soul; he came from a family riven with emotional strife; to wit, three of his brothers committed suicide. Three of his grandparents also converted to Christianity, and the nominally Christian Wittgenstein mulled over his Jewishness or lack of it sporadically over the years.[64] Ray Monk, Wittgenstein's biographer, views him as haunted by Otto Weininger, the anti-Semitic and misogynist Jew who famously committed suicide in Vienna at the age of twenty-three, shortly after the publication of his book, *Sex and Character*.[65] Weininger, who himself converted to Protestantism, obviously fascinated Wittgenstein. In 1938 the Christian Wittgenstein and his siblings suddenly and unhappily discovered they were Jews in the eyes of the state. With the *Anschluss*, the incorporation of Austria into Nazi Germany, the Viennese Wittgensteins became subject to the so-called Nuremberg Laws that defined pure Jews as those with three Jewish grandparents. The Wittgenstein children passed the test.

Paul Engelmann, Wittgenstein's friend, who sought refuge in Israel, wrote a memoir in 1967 that challenges the prevailing interpretation of Wittgenstein as a positivist seeking to reduce all knowledge to verifiable propositions.[66] Allan Janik and Stephen Toulmin's 1973 *Wittgenstein's Vienna* followed Engelmann and persuasively argued that ethical and mystical concerns drove Wittgenstein's philosophical analysis.[67] Engelmann highlighted the ethos of silence that permeated Wittgenstein's work and that sought to protect, not deny, the ineffable.

In 1917 Engelmann had sent a poem to the young Wittgenstein by a virtually forgotten nineteenth-century German poet.[68] The poem had stirred the budding philosopher who found it "magnificent." He added: "And this is how it is: if only you do not try to utter what is unutterable then *nothing* gets lost. But the unutterable will be—unutterably—*contained* in what has been uttered!"[69] Drawing on this and other comments, Engelmann declared,

> A whole generation of disciples was able to take Wittgenstein for a positivist because he had something of enormous importance in common with the positivists: he draws the line between what we can speak about and what we must be silent about just as they do. The difference is . . . positivism holds—and this is its essence—that what we can speak about is all that matters in life. *Whereas Wittgenstein passionately believes that all that really matters in human life is precisely what, in his view, we must be silent about.*[70]

In a letter about the *Tractatus* to his editor and publisher Ludwig Ficker, Wittgenstein seems to lend support to Engelmann's argument. He explains that his purpose is "ethical":

> I once meant to include in the preface a sentence which is not in fact there but which I will write out for you. What I meant to write, then, was this: My work consists of two parts: the one presented here plus all that I have *not* written. And *it is precisely this second part that is the important one.*[71]

The idea that what is most important is what is unwritten would be congenial to believing and nonbelieving Jews from

Maimonides to Mauthner. Indeed, Wittgenstein goes further. Not only is the essential part of his book missing, but the reference to its absence is absent as well.

From the prohibition on naming God ensued manifold consequences, which go far beyond the scope of this chapter. The prohibition gave support to an oral, ineffable, and mystical Judaism as the way to avoid idolatry of the written language. Sacred texts possessed dual meanings, the outward and the inward. The truths of the written text could only be disclosed by attention to the oral tradition. Indeed, a text's overt and real meaning might be completely opposed. The surface could misrepresent the interior. Obviously, this state of affairs leads to dense commentary. How could one know whether what is written is false or true? It requires discussion; it calls for tapping into the history of oral commentary.

Maimonides believed in the superiority of oral teachings and distrusted the written text. To follow Leo Strauss, he betrayed this principle by writing the *Guide to the Perplexed*. He put in print truths reserved for oral transmission. Nonetheless, he heeded the Jewish reluctance to express the inexpressible by writing in a veiled and contradictory manner. Only the initiated could understand. Maimonides teaches the truth "not plainly, but secretly." In this way he remained loyal to the ban on naming God. Strauss pursued this logic to its paradoxical conclusion. To write the opposite of what one believes preserves the truth! "There probably is no better way of hiding the truth than to contradict it."[72] To understand a text, then, requires the most careful sifting of words and phrases. The real meaning may contradict the explicit meaning.

Strauss's defense of the veiled truth in the Jewish tradition was not simply an apology for a past or idiosyncratic practice; he advanced almost the same notion in his essay on "persecution and the art of writing." Truth must be concealed, if only because it is dangerous. Authors must mask their points "in such a way that only a very careful reader can detect the meaning." In this essay, composed during World War II, Strauss argued that independent thought needs to be protected from oppressive authorities and some-times from oppressive nonphilosophical readers. Philosophical authors must present their argument not on the line but "between the lines." They should give clues in the text or "limit themselves to oral instruction of a carefully selected group."[73] To get at their truths requires careful study.

Scholem offered a dialectical twist on Strauss's paradoxical idea that the best way to protect a truth is to contradict it. In Scholem's version truths are preserved by revealing them to the uncomprehending reader. They are not contradicted overtly but are safeguarded by stating them overtly—perhaps in the same way a shoplifter escapes attention by wearing, not hiding, the filched garment. Exposing the truth hides it. In his ten aphorisms on the Kabbalah, Scholem wrote that "the public nature [*Öffentlichkeit*] of the main works of the old Kabbalistic literature is the strongest guarantee of their secrets." He explained that even after opening a Kabbalistic tome it remains, as it were, a closed book. Scholem ponders this, and asks, "Don't we have here again the mystical-anarchistic politics in which secrets are better protected through expression than through silence?"[74]

If Strauss provided a traditionalist account of veiled writing and Scholem an anarchist version, perhaps Max Horkheimer gave the Marxist slant. The same year that Strauss produced "Persecution and the Art of Writing," Horkheimer published "Art and Mass Culture." More explicitly than Strauss, Horkheimer situated his thoughts as between Nazism on one side and the Anglo-American democracies on the other. Where people are frightened by the authoritarian state in Europe and mesmerized by market capitalism in America, he wondered how art can communicate. Indeed, to define art—and philosophy—as communication damns them to reinforce conventional responses. "Men as they are today understand each other. . . . To the extent that the last works of art still communicate, they denounce the prevailing forms of communication." What does this mean for artists and philosophers? It may require formulating truths that cannot be communicated. "The only hope remaining is the deaf ears in Europe imply an opposition to the lies that are being hammered at men from all sides." Hence, Horkheimer concluded, "it may not be entirely senseless to continue speaking a language that is not easily understood."[75]

Rabbinic wisdom, of course, was not necessary mystical, anarchistic, or, obviously, Marxist, but it privileged the oral transmission of knowledge, without which the text remained closed.[76] Even the Hebrew of the Torah required interpretation in as much as it lacked vowels; to read it entailed supplying sounds and meaning. Barry Sander explains that Hebrew "presents this special burden of responsibility for the reader," who must scan each root, adding vowels. The reader "must at the same time interpret it for all possible meanings, making certain that the word created will make sense in the context of the entire narration." Small variations in vowels can produce "very disparate meanings from the same root."[77]

José Faur, a Maimonides scholar, put it this way: "The Torah embodies two textual levels: at the written level, the text consists only of consonants, therefore it is categorically unreadable; the vocalized text must be transmitted orally and may not be put down in writing." The oral "reading" supplies vowels and gives meaning to the text.[78] Spinoza used a famous metaphor to illuminate the distinction. Hebrew letters are "bodies without souls." The vowels are the "souls of letters." "To make the difference between letters and vowels more clearly intelligible, it is possible to explain it suitably by the example of a flute touched by fingers for playing. The vowels are the musical sound of the flute, the letters are the openings touched by the fingers."[79]

To ferret out the truth from a text requires oral communication and teachings—it requires playing and hearing the flute.[80] We cannot see the written truth. At best we must listen to other scholars and students who direct us toward it. In the same way we cannot see God, but we can hear him: "Hear O Israel!" The god of the Old Testament is the God of words, but he cannot be seen. The Lord tells Moses, "Thou canst not see my face: for there shall no man see me, and live" (Exod. 33:20). Rather the Lord speaks, listens, and commands. "There is a striking contrast," writes Besançon, "between the overwhelming and imprecise majesty of theophanies and the unequivocal familiarity of the word. . . . Discussions with God fill the lives of Abraham, Moses, and the prophets. God is endlessly consulted and endlessly replies."[81]

The issue of the Jewish relationship to the visual and auditory arts resurfaces. Painting beguiles, but spoken poetry instructs. The eye misleads; the ear leads. Hermann Cohen calls it "striking" that the sources of Judaism are literary and those of polytheism visual. "The form of poetry, the original language of literature . . . can make thought more spiritually inward than plastic art."[82] Franz Rosenszweig, the twentieth-century German-Jewish philosopher, who both followed and differed from Cohen, believed that the Jews were drawn to poetry. Jews never responded to the visual arts "without some misgivings." However, "no such misgivings apply to poetry." For Rosenzweig, poetry "supplies structure as well as discourse." Poetry is "the most alive, the most vital art." Indeed, Rosenszweig states that while it is possible to be a "complete human being" without painting or music, "one cannot become human" without—at least for a moment—"composing poetry."[83] It is hardly surprising that Rosenszweig translated Judah Halevi's poetry and that he felt affinities with its religious pathos and fire.[84]

Heinrich Gratz, the great nineteenth-century historian of

Judaism, presented what he considered the essence of the religion. Like Mendelssohn he emphasized the oral tradition. The people of the book were the people of the ear. "Judaism began as a negation, a negation of paganism." The pagan conceives of God as "coextensive with nature" and therefore worships nature. For the Jews, however, God precedes and transcends nature.

> The pagan perceives the Divine in nature through the medium of the eye, and he becomes conscious of it as something to be looked at. On the other hand, to the Jew, who conceives God as being outside of nature and prior to it, the Divine manifests itself through the will and through the medium of the ear. He becomes conscious of it as something to be heeded and listened to. The pagan beholds his god; the Jew hears Him.[85]

Vision, writes Martin Jay, is the "master sense of the modern era." Yet the Jewish tradition challenges the familiar idea of vision or the "light" of the Enlightenment as defining truth. (Indeed, if there is an "antiocular impulse" to French postmodern thought, it may derive from the impact of French Jewish scholars like Emmanuel Levinas.)[86] The color and vividness of the image arrests thought. The Jewish utopian screen is almost blank; it is ready to be filled in—but is not yet. It is defined by imageless longing. "Someone who is deeply moved," wrote Bloch in *The Spirit of Utopia*, "must close his eyes."[87]

In everyday life the visual seems matter-of-fact—"you get what you see"—but hearing requires interpretation and understanding. Seeing is immediate, hearing mediates. "The rustling of an animal in the leaves, the footsteps of men, the noise of a passing car," writes Hans Jonas, "betray the presence of those things by something they do." When I hear a dog barking, "I can say I hear a dog, but what I hear is his bark." To know a dog is present requires inference and interpretation; it is not obvious. Moreover, unlike sight, sound is "dynamic"; it intrudes upon the "passive subject." Ears cannot wander nor can they close, like eyes; they do not rotate or pivot. Ears are always ready to hear. "The deepest reason for this," writes Jonas in "The Nobility of Sight," "is the fact that [hearing] is related to event and not to existence, to becoming and not to being."[88]

Numerous Jewish thinkers developed, or seconded, this idea.[89] Jews listen, and hearing exists in a temporal continuum. By their ears, as it were, Jews are wedded to history. One hears the ticking clock of history. "Time, by its very nature," wrote Israel Eldad, a twentieth-century messianic thinker, is "unidimensional. That is not true of place. What you looked at a moment ago, you can look at a second and third time. But when something is heard . . . you cannot hear again what you heard a moment ago." From this emerges "a responsibility for every deed" and moment.[90]

"On what grounds then," asks Lionel Kochan in his study *Beyond the Graven Image*, "does the ear acquires its superior status" for Jews? He answers: "By the virtue of the ear's capacity to receive and apprehend a verbal message. . . . The eye is limited in its power of apprehension to no more than the surface appearance of the object, its patterning, color, shape and so on. When apprehended in this way, the object's identity may not be apparent." Not only can the ear receive a message, but it registers the sequence of time; sounds require duration. "It is necessary to await the moment when a sound (or series of sounds) is completed before its import can be evaluated."[91]

This may be crucial. Sound includes time—and time implies history. Sight is spatial and static, writes Jacques Ellul, in his defense of a modern iconoclasm. "I need not wait in order to grasp the meaning of what I see." Sounds "form a sequence of impressions." They are temporal, and insert us "within a duration rather than an expanse." To understand the spoken word requires us to wait to the end of the sequence. "The beginning of the sentence has already been pronounced, and has already faded away; the end has not yet been spoken, and it will give meaning to what was said at the beginning." With sounds and spoken words, we wonder, "What next?"[92]

Is this a link to Jewish iconoclastic utopianism? Jews keep their ears, not their eyes, on the future. To depict the future is sacrilegious, but it can be heard and longed for. Sound encapsulates unpredictable change. We don't know what will follow but can ponder and hope about the next chord or note. "The Jews were prohibited from investigating the future," wrote Walter Benjamin in his final writings. The Torah "stripped the future of its magic" by instructing its readers in remembrance. "This does not imply, however, that for the Jews the future turned into homogenous, empty time. For every second of time was the strait gate through which the Messiah might enter."[93]

Eighty years earlier, Moses Hess, the one-time comrade of Karl Marx, reflected in *Rome and Jerusalem* on the "irrepressible longing" for the "hour of redemption" by suffering Jews. He recalled that his pious grandfather spurned descriptions of the future society. "Whenever they spoke to him of plans for the future, he always objected to making such plans, remarking that we Jews, being in exile, have no right to plan for the future, as the Messiah may suddenly arrive."[94]

The question of a Jewish orientation towards the ear or eye alludes to an old debate associated with the terms "Hellene" and "Hebrew." Matthew Arnold in *Culture and Anarchy* expounded upon a distinction between what he called two rival "forces" in civilization, Hellenism and Hebraism. He did not invent these categories; he took them from Heine, but they predate the German poet by several millennia. Tertullian, the third-century Roman theologian, had already asked, "What then has Athens to do with Jerusalem?"[95] For Heine, "all men are either Jews or Hellenes," and like Arnold after him, he opts for the Greeks, who reveled in life. The Jews, in contrast, were "image-hating" moralists (*"mit asketischen, bildfeindlichen, vergeistigungssüchtigen Trieben"*).[96] To be sure, Heine, born Jewish, was baptized in the Lutheran church, mainly—it seems—to help his job prospects. He famously remarked, "the baptismal certificate is the entry ticket to European culture."[97]

Toward the end of his life Heine moderated his portrayal of the Hebrew temperament. Perhaps the terminal illness that kept him bedridden for many years prompted him to alter his views. He recalled his last visit to the Louvre to bid adieu to the Venus de Milo, but the lovely Greek goddess failed him.[98] He explained that his earlier "Hellenic temperament" had been repelled by "Jewish asceticism." He had not appreciated Moses because he could not forgive his "hatred of all images and sculpture [*seinen Hass gegen alle Bildlichkeit, gegen die Plastik*]," but he now understood that Moses himself was an artist who did not fashion his works from bricks and granite, as did the Egyptians, but created "a people . . . Israel." Heine realized that "the Greeks were only beautiful youths, but that the Jews were always men, mighty, unyielding men, not only in the past, but to this very day."[99]

While Arnold himself later tilted more towards Hebraism, in *Culture and Anarchy* he resolutely declared that contemporary England suffered "the long exclusive predominance of Hebraism," a life-denying asceticism or inflexible moralism.[100] Hebraism focused narrowly on conduct and ethics; it spoke the language of rigid conscience. Arnold associated the Hellenic temperament with his vaunted "sweetness and light." Hellenism "sees" things "in their true nature as they really are." It prizes harmony and gives rise to Greek art.[101]

Is there any truth to this opposition between the visual and auditory dimensions? Does Greek culture see and Jewish culture hear?[102] The topic is fraught with stereotypes and oversimplification, yet some clues may be found that illuminate two cultural approaches. Even language, it has been argued, registers such differences. To follow Walter J. Ong's *Orality and Literacy*, Greek marked an advance over Semitic writing inasmuch as it included vowels. The reader of the Semitic language had to rely on external cues—mainly other individuals—to supply the appropriate sounds. "Semitic writing was still very much immersed in the non-textual human life world." Greek marked a shift from "sound to sight." The Greek alphabet was "more remote" from the nontextual world "as Plato's ideas were to be." It "analyzed sound more abstractly into purely spatial components."[103]

The relationship of poetry to Greek and Hebrew might also be offered as evidence of two opposing traditions. Plato, who excluded the poets from his "well-governed state," is a case in point. We can "admit no poetry into our city," he decreed. For if we admit "the honey Muse in lyric or epic," law will be dethroned. [104] For many commentators Plato's hostility to the poetic mode derives from his desire to break with the Homeric and oral traditions. Plato challenged the dominant oral tradition, according to Eric A. Heavelock, which was the means of cultural transmission up to that time. The oral tradition relied on memory, recital, and a vigilant community. In championing an "abstract intellectualism," Plato undermined "a whole way of life." He asks men that they reexamine the communal experience, instead of merely expressing it.[105]

In contrast, the Jewish tradition opens more to oral and poetic modes. Here, again, thinkers such as Franz Rosenzweig, who enthused over poetry, come to mind. Rosenzweig himself was probably following Herder, who in 1782, published *The Spirit of Hebrew Poetry*. In a typically romantic vein, Herder praised the Jews for their lyricism, which he believed was virtually a product of their primitivism. They were close to the childhood of civilization; this explained their poetic power; their spontaneous expression of emotion had not suffered the ravages of time.[106] The Hebrew "tongue strives to express itself, and falls upon strong expressions, because its language is not become weak and facile from a multiplicity of empty sounds and stale metaphorical expressions."[107]

In *Hebrew Thought Compared with Greek*, a Norwegian theologian accentuated the differences between the two cultural styles, especially in regards to history. While his 1960 book has been sharply criticized, the issues raised by Thorleif Boman continue to resonate. He judges Greek thinking static, peaceful, and moderate, and Hebrew dynamic, vigorous, and passionate.[108] For the Greeks the most important sense was seeing; for the Jews hearing. Impressions received by hearing are "constantly changing." Those received by sight "are static in principle because the eye acts as a camera." Boman summarizes the differences by outlining two characteristic figures, "the thinking Socrates and the praying Orthodox Jew."

> When Socrates was seized by a problem, he remained immobile for an interminable period of time in deep thought; when Holy Scripture is read aloud in the synagogue, the Orthodox Jew moves his whole body ceaselessly in deep devotion and adoration. The Greek most acutely experiences the world and existence while he stands and reflects, but the Israelite reaches his zenith in ceaseless movement. Rest, harmony, composure, and self-control—this is the Greek way; movement, life, deep emotion, and power— this is the Hebrew way.[109]

Arnold might almost agree. At least when he wrote an essay on Heine himself, he altered the valence of the Greek and Hebrew terms. Hebrew does not simply imply an inflexible moralism, he says in this essay, but an inexhaustible energy and longing. "No account of Heine," Arnold stated, "is complete which does not notice the Jewish element in him." He rehearses the difference between the Greek and Jewish mentality, and concludes. "By his perfection of literary forms, by his love of clearness, by his love of beauty, Heine is Greek; by his intensity, by his untameableness, by his 'longing which cannot be uttered,' he is Hebrew."[110]

The Jewish iconoclastic utopians longed for the future but verged on mysticism and silence about it. Nevertheless, pieces and phrases emerge from their writings that hint of harmony and joy.[111] Utopian traces even appear in the legalistic Babylonian Talmud. "Three things are a reflex of the world to come," it states, "Sabbath, sunshine, and *tashmish*. *Tashmish* of what? Shall I say of the bed?" A modern editor explains that *tashmish* of the bed refers to lovemaking.[112] One finds here no elaborate pictures of the future, only allusions to rest, sun, and love.

This visual asceticism of the Jewish utopians does not entail a renunciation of life and its possibilities. Rather, their pictorial reserve about the future coexisted with attentiveness to the present. "I offer no depiction of an ideal, no description of a utopia," wrote Landauer.[113] Yet Landauer believed that life today shapes life tomorrow. Not brassy proclamations and floor plans but love and solidarity determine the future. Herein lies an essential element of the iconoclastic utopianism: its regard for the here and now. It yearns for the future and values the present.

Heine himself exemplifies this ethos. By virtue of his "untameable longing," Arnold calls him a Hebrew. Arnold follows this judgment, however, with an extract from *Pictures of Travel* that he thinks reveals a contrasting side of the poet. He juxtaposes to the "longing" Heine, a "comic" Heine who depicts Jews rejoicing in the pedestrian pleasures of the day. Yet these were less opposing than complementary attitudes. Heine's passage ran:

> There lives in Hamburg . . . a man named Moses Lump—
> the folks call him Lumpy for short,—and he runs around
> the whole week, in wind and rain, with his pack on his
> back, to earn a few marks. Well, when Friday evening
> comes round, he goes home, and finds the seven-branched
> lamp all lighted, a clean white cloth on the table, and puts
> off his pack and all his sorrows, and sits down with his
> crooked wife and his crooked daughter, and eats with
> them fish which has been cooked in nice garlic sauce, and
> sings the finest songs of King David, and rejoices with all
> his heart. . . . He feels glad, too, that all the malefactors
> who did bad things to the children of Israel died at last;
> that King Phaoraoh, Nebuchadnezzar, Haman, Antiochus,
> Titus and such like, are all dead, but that Lumpy is still
> alive, and eats fish with his wife and child. And, tell you
> what, Doctor, the fish are delicate, and the man is
> happy. . . . And I can tell you that if the lamps should hap-
> pen to burn dim, and if the woman, who ought to clean
> them, isn't at hand, and if Rothschild the Great should
> happen to come in with all the brokers, discounters, for-
> warders, and head clerks . . . and if he should say, "Moses
> Lump, ask what thou wilt, it shall be given thee," Doctor,
> I believe that Moses would say, quiet and easy, "Clean the
> lamps, then!"[114]

This comedy is no joke. The utopian commitment to the future
coexists with an embrace of the here and now. One savors the
sweets of the present and yearns for a future still sweeter. Both.
Almost to illustrate this attitude, elsewhere in *Pictures of Travel*
Heine reflects on the morning greetings of his traveling companion: "It will be a fine day."

"Yes—it will be a fine day," slowly reechoed my praying heart, as it trembled with grief and joy. Yes, it will be a beautiful day, the sun of freedom will warm the world with a more thrilling joy than that which comes from cold aristocratic stars;—there will spring up a new race, begotten in the embraces of free choice and not in the bed of compulsion and under the control of clerical tax gatherers; and with free birth there will arise in mankind free thoughts and free feelings of which we—poor born serfs—have no conception.[115]

While cherishing today, the iconoclastic utopians harbor keen hopes for the morrow, hopes for a world of freer lives and passions. Clues, fragments, and whispers—not blueprints—sustain that hope.

Forty years ago, Kurt Wilhelm, a rabbi and scholar, distilled from Jewish writings an idea of a future humanity living in peace and harmony. He cited the words of Isaiah that nations "shall beat their swords into plowshares, and their spears into pruninghooks: nation shall not lift up sword against nation, neither shall they learn war any more" (Isaiah 2:4). He added, "thus can Isaiah, the contemporary of kings whose faithlessness evoked disillusionment after disillusionment, portray the future of mankind."[116] Yet today disillusionment drains that impulse. Not only manmade deaths but manmade prosperity sap utopian speculation. Distant and not-so-distant suffering, on the one hand, and an anxious affluence, on the other, poison its source. Many, of course, believe that the eclipse of utopian iconoclasts signals a great advance. For these observers, the demise of utopianism frees the world from a curse. But a world without utopian longings is forlorn. For society as well as for the individual, it means to journey without a compass.

Utopianism does not require blueprints. On this score, the protest of anti-utopian liberals like Karl Popper and Isaiah

Berlin may be on the mark. The blueprinters have had their day. But if they constitute the bulk of the utopian tradition, they do not exhaust it. A smaller school of Jewish iconoclastic utopians resisted providing precise dimensions for the future. In the well-managed house, they opened a window to let in the breeze. In the rustling of the objects and the cooling of the brow, the breeze can be heard and felt, but not seen. But the unseen is neither unreal nor inessential. On the contrary. If the name of God is unpronounceable and the portrait of God unpaintable, a future of peace and happpiness—a world without anxiety—may not be describable. We hear of it in parables and hints. It speaks to us, perhaps more urgently than ever.

Epilogue

"WHEN I STARTED TO EXPLORE THE HISTORIC UTOPIAS," explained Lewis Mumford almost fifty years ago in his new preface to *The Story of Utopias*, "I was seeking to discover what was missing, and to define what was still possible."[1] These sentiments infuse my efforts in this book: to signal what is missing and to suggest what is possible. The "and" must be underlined, otherwise the project to trace what is lost becomes antiquarianism, collecting postcards from the past for its own sake. While this activity may satisfy and instruct, it is not my goal—or not my only goal.

To indicate what is possible requires entering the terrain of political options. Almost by definition, however, utopian thought keeps a distance from the daily to-and-fro of political life. It does not take up the issues of the day, be they elections, national health care, or war and peace in the middle East. If it did, it would forfeit its own commitment to a realm beyond the immediate choices. Which plan solves urban traffic gridlock? Endemic unemployment? World pollution? Civil war in the horn of Africa? To the extent that utopian thought directly speaks to these crises, it betrays its heart and soul.

Yet, paradoxically, the opposite is also true. To the extent that utopian thought remains transcendental, it betrays its heart and soul. Utopian thinking consists of more than daydreams and doodles. It emerges out of and returns to contemporary political realities. As I see it, this contradiction defines the utopian project: it partakes at once of the limited choices of the day and the unlimited possibilities of the morrow. It straddles two time zones: the one we inhabit now and the one that might exist in the future. Nor is this unusual in the history of utopianism. At least since More's *Utopia*, contemporary crises motivate the utopian author who dreams of another world.

More's *Utopia* was written in two parts. Book 1 boldly addresses poverty, capital punishment, and economic inequalities of sixteenth-century England. "Revive agriculture and the wool industry," counsels the visitor from Utopia, "so there's plenty of honest, useful work for the great army of unemployed. . . . Until you put these things right, you're not entitled to boast of the justice meted out to thieves," who have no choice but to rob in order to eat.[2] Only in book 2 does More sketch out his utopian society. Significantly, More wrote the second book before the first. The utopian idea precedes the political program. The relationship between books 1 and 2 in More bespeaks the tension in utopian thought between "the critique of what is and the representation of what should be."[3]

The problem today is how to connect utopian thinking with everyday politics. How can dreams of "what should be" link to "what is"? The end of the Cold War hardly brought the global peace and prosperity that was promised. What is now called the "post-9/11" world appears dark, bloody, and unstable. Is there space for a utopian politics or even for utopian dreaming? To be sure, the temptation of historical narcissism should be resisted—the temptation to think this historical moment is unique in its grimness. Mumford's *Story of Utopias* may have originated during confident years before World War I, but Mumford himself soldiered on through bright and black decades both. By the end of his life in 1990, he was warning of nuclear annihilation and technological imperialism. Yet a utopian vision spurred his practical criticism and politics—indeed, spurred his pessimism.[4]

The difficulty of spelling out a contemporary politics is especially knotty for the iconoclastic utopians whom I have foregrounded. They eschew the positive program; they specialize in negatives. "Insofar as we are not allowed to cast the picture of utopia," Adorno writes, "insofar as we do not know what the correct thing would be, we know exactly . . . what the false thing is." And this means "that the true thing determines itself via the false thing."[5] While it may appear esoteric, this Hegelian logic is practical, intuitive, and political. It is the reason that many political slogans are framed negatively: "Stop the War Now!" or "End Racism!" What comes after the end of the war or the end of racism? This is not clear, but it is also less important than the elimination of the evil. The "negation" of the false—here war or racism—allows the true to unfold.

Without a concrete condition to negate, utopian impulses seem vague. Without a specific political context they seem insubstantial. Can one long for world peace without dismantling the contemporary war machine? Can one desire global prosperity without ending savage economic inequalities? Toward the conclusion of his three-volume work *The Principle of Hope*, Ernst Bloch comments that "man desires and wishes throughout his life, but if he has to say what he wants absolutely . . . he is at a loss for an answer." Many fairytales, Bloch notes, reflect this truth. In Hebel's "The Little Treasure Chest," a fairy grants a poor couple three wishes. As they bask in their future happiness, the wife cooks potatoes and remarks, "If only we had a fried sausage with it." The finest sausage instantly appears. The waste of a wish enrages her husband, who wishes the sausage be stuck to his wife's nose. Of course, the third wish is used to unglue the sausage.[6] For cynics or skeptics the conclusion is at hand. People do not know what they want or else what they want is specific and banal; they desire this plate of food or that pair of shoes. Utopia expires on impoverished wishes.

Yet another conclusion is possible: utopian wishes need to be situated against something. A perfect school must be positioned, for instance, against the failed schools of this society. Moreover—and this is decisive—utopianism demands boldness and audacity in dreaming. This is an aptitude that does not automatically emerge in an individual. Rather, utopian dreaming is a fragile plant, which is prey to the prevailing weather. It needs protection, cultivation and warmth. Today the winds blow hard, the frost comes early. The post-9/11 world—replete as it is with real and imagined threats, bellicose statesmanship, precious affluence, brutal poverty, and civil wars—saps the utopian impulse.

Once students dreamt of healing the ills of society; now—based on the students I have—they dream of going to good law schools. I am not the only one to notice, and lament, that in the wake of 9/11 the United States missed a historical opportunity. Instead of tapping into the latent idealism of the young and calling for a new peace corps or some comparable commitment, the top guns only wanted to nail the bad guys. We were instructed to keep on shopping and to watch for suspicious packages. The American response to shoot first and figure it out later redoubles an inclination to hunker down, to trade utopian dreams for home security systems. Elsewhere the same mindset dominates. Who can believe that an armored bulldozer flattening Palestinian homes helps bring about a harmonious Middle East? A single performance by the West-Eastern Divan Orchestra, cofounded by Daniel Barenboim and the late Edward Said for young Palestinian and Israeli musicians, does more for peace than a hundred "antiterrorist" forays; it emits a spark of utopianism.

To connect a utopian passion with practical politics is an art and a necessity. As the political alternatives narrow, it may be more difficult than ever. Yet I believe it can and should be done. Without a utopian impulse, politics turns pallid, mechanical, and often Sisyphean; it plugs leaks one by one, while the bulkheads give way and the ship founders. To be sure, the leaks must be stanched. Yet, we may need a new vessel, an idea easily forgotten as the waters rise and the crew and passengers panic.

A utopian-inflected politics need not confine itself to demands such as "End the War Now!" or "Stop the Killing!"—as salient as these are. The world suffers not simply from wanton wars but from a degraded environment, limited medical services, unemployment, and the list goes on. Today these crises appear unsolvable, but that is a political not a technical observation. We have the wherewithal to engineer precision automobiles with luxurious fittings; and we can place a high-tech vehicle on Mars that moves on cue; but we cannot muster the will or resources to fix a defective social order. The human consequences of this failure—too many left behind and too many damaged—cause the lucky to retreat behind higher gates. This is not the only path. It is possible, even necessary, to join the pressing issues of the day while keeping an ear, if not an eye, on the future, when, as Fourier might have said, the whole earth will be "brought under the wing" of a butterfly.[7]

Notes

Unless noted otherwise, all translations from the German are my own.

Preface

1. Lewis Mumford, *The Story of Utopias* (1922; rev. ed., New York: Viking Press, 1962), pp. 307, 1.

2. Ovid, *The Metamorphoses*, trans. Horace Gregory (New York: Signet, 2001), p. 33.

3. L. Frank Baum, *The Emerald City* (1910; reprint, New York: Dover Publications, 1988), pp. 30–31.

4. Alfred Rosenberg, *The Myth of the Twentieth Century* (1930; reprint, Newport Beach, Calif.: Noontide Press, 1982), p. 333.

5. "Remarks by Undersecretary of Defense for Policy Douglas Feith to the Council on Foreign Relations," Federal News Service, 13 November 2003.

6. See generally Roxanne L. Euben, *Enemy in the Mirror: Islamic Fundamentalism and the Limits of Modern Rationalism* (Princeton, N.J.: Princeton University Press, 1999), pp. 53–92.

7. Qutb, quoted in Paul Berman, *Terror and Liberalism* (New York: Norton, 2003), p. 86.

8. Malise Ruthven, *A Fury for God: The Islamist Attack on America* (New York: Granta Books 2002) pp. 90–91

9. Sayyid Qutb, *Social Justice in Islam* (Oneonta, N.Y.: Islamic Publications International, 2000), pp. 90–91.

10. See the discussion of the document in Ruthven, *A Fury for God*,

p. 37. The complete text has been posted variously on the internet, such as http://abcnews.go.com/sections/world/DailyNews/attaletter_1.html.

11. Max Horkheimer and T. W. Adorno, *Dialectic of Enlightenment*, trans. John Cumming (New York: Herder and Herder, 1972), p. 64.

12. Jacques Ellul, *The Humiliation of the Word* (Grand Rapids, Mich.: William B. Eerdmans, 1985), pp. 115, 94.

13. Darly Hepting, "What's a Picture Really Worth?" http://www2.cs.uregina.ca/~hepting/proverbial.

14. Hugo Bergmann, "Die Heiligung des Namens," in *Vom Judentum: Ein Sammelbuch*, ed. the Verein jüdischer Hochschüler Bar Kochba in Prag (Leipzig: Kurt Wolff Verlag, 1913), pp. 32–43. The collection also includes an essay by Landauer.

15. John Felstiner, *Paul Celan: Poet, Survivor, Jew* (New Haven, Conn.: Yale University Press, 2001), p. 153. Celan said that he "grew up" with the writings of Landauer (and Peter Kropotkin); see his speech, "The Meridian," in *Selected Poems and Prose of Paul Celan*, ed. J. Felstiner (New York: Norton, 2001), p. 403.

1. An Anarchic Breeze

1. "South Africa Confronts Landless Poor, and a Court Sends Them Packing," *New York Times*, 12 July 2001.

2. See generally Everett W. MacNair, *Edward Bellamy and the Nationalist Movement, 1889 to 1894* (Milwaukee: Fitzgerald Co., 1957).

3. Edward Bellamy, "Looking Forward," *The Nationalist* 2, no. 1 (December, 1889): 4; "Chicago's Advance," *Nationalist*, 3, no. 2 (February, 1890): 98; "A $4,000,000 Lesson" (about a Boston electrical outage and fire) *Nationalist*, 2, no. 1 (December, 1889): 69. See Arthur Lipow, *Authoritarian Socialism in America: Edward Bellamy and the Nationalist Movement* (Berkeley: University of California Press, 1991).

4. Condorcet, *Tableau historique des progès de l'esprit humain* (Paris: G. Steinheil, 1900), p. 189. On Condorcet, see Frank E. Manuel and Fritzie P. Manuel, *Utopian Thought in the Western World* (Cambridge: Harvard, 1979), pp. 487–518.

5. See Daniel P. Resnick, "The Societe des Amis des Noirs and the Abolition of Slavery," *French Historical Studies* 7, no. 4. (Autumn 1972): 558–69.

6. See Léon Cahen, "La Société des Amis des Noirs et Condorcet," *La Révolution française* 50 (January–June 1906): 480–511; and J. Salwyn Schapiro, *Condorcet and the Rise of Liberalism* (New York: Harcourt, Brace and Co., 1934), pp. 148–152.

7. Condorcet, "Rules for the *Society of the Friends of Negroes*" (1788), in *Condorcet: Foundations of Social Choice and Political Theory*, ed. I. McLean, F. Hewitt (Hants, U.K.: Edward Elgar, 1994), p. 343. "The practical bent of French abolitionism received more disinterested expression in the writings of Condorcet . . . the most eminent intellectual sponsor of the *Amis*": Robin Blackburn, *The Overthrow of Colonial Slavery, 1776–1848* (London: Verso, 1988), pp. 170–71.

8. Zachary Karabell, *Parting the Desert: The Creation of the Suez Canal* (New York: Knopf, 2003), pp. 28–37.

9. Thomas More, *Utopia*, intro. P. Turner (1516; New York: Penguin Books, 1965), p. 44.

10. Victor Considerant, *The Great West* (1854), in Considerant, *Au Texas*, ed. R. V. Davidson (Philadephia: Porcupine Press, 1975), pp. 54–58.

11. Nathaniel Hawthorne, *The Blithedale Romance* (1852; New York: Dell, 1962), p. 41.

12. John Humphrey Noyes, *History of American Socialisms*, intro. Mark Holloway (1870; reprint, New York: Dover Publications, 1966), p. 21.

13. Fredcrick Law Olmsted to Charles Loring Brace, 26 July 1852, in *The Papers of Frederick Law Olmsted: Volume I: The Formative Years, 1822–1852*, ed. C. C. McLaughlin (Baltimore, Md.: Johns Hopkins University Press, 1977), pp. 375–387. The North American Phalanx that Olmsted visited was in fact one of the more successful communities, lasting twelve years. See George Kirchmann, "Why Did They Stay: Commmunal Life at the North American Phalanx," in *Planned and Utopian Experiments: Four New Jersey Towns*, ed. P. A. Stellhorn (Trenton: New Jersey Historical Commission, 1980), pp. 11–27 .

14. See my *Dialectic of Defeat: Contours of Western Marxism* (New York: Cambridge University Press, 1981).

15. Bernard le Bovier de Fontenelle, *Conversations on the Plurality of Worlds*, ed. N. G. Gelbart (1686; Berkeley: University of California Press, 1990), pp. 33–34.

16. More, *Utopia*, p. 68.

17. According to Alexandra Aldridge he did so "incorrectly" or at least applied it incorrectly; see her opinionated work, *The Scientific World View in Dystopia* (Ann Arbor: UMI Research Press, 1984), p. 11; and for some criticism of Aldridge's definition, see David W. Sisk, *Transformations of Language in Modern Dystopias* (Westport, Conn.: Greenwood, 1997), pp. 6–9.

18. Glenn Negley and J. Max Patrick, *The Quest for Utopia: An Anthology of Imaginary Societies* (New York: Henry Schuman, 1952), p. 298. To be exact, it is not accurate to credit Patrick with "dystopia"; he reinvented or rediscovered it. To John Stuart Mill belongs the honor of first using the term *dystopia*. In a parliamentary debate about Ireland, Mill objected with characteristic vigor to the conservative government's proposal not to disestablish the Catholic Church but to establish a Protestant one as well; he pointed out that this was not only a bad idea, it would be rejected by all parties. He stated, "I may be permitted, as one who, in common with many of my betters, have been subjected to the charge of being Utopian, to congratulate the Government on having joined that goodly company. It is, perhaps, too complimentary to call them Utopians, they ought rather to be called dys-topians, or cacotopians. What is commonly called Utopian is something too good to be practicable; but what they appear to favour is too bad to be practicable." *Hansard's Parliamentary Debates*, third series, vol. 190, 1867–68 (London: Cornelius Buck, 1868), p. 1517.

19. William Morris, "News from Nowhere," in *Stories in Prose*, ed. G. D. H. Colse (London: Nonesuch Press, 1948), p. 5.

20. George Orwell, *1984* (New York: Signet/New American Library, 1950), p. 5.

21. My quotation of Berdyaev begins before that cited by Huxley; Nicholas Berdyaev, *The End of Our Time* (New York: Seed and Ward, 1933), p. 187.

22. Aldous Huxley, *Island* (New York: Harper and Row, 1962), p. 103.

23. For a discussion of the impact of Wells on Zamyatin, Huxley, and Orwell, see Mark R. Hillegas, *The Future as Nightmare: H. G. Wells and the Anti-Utopians* (New York: Oxford University Press, 1967).

24. Huxley, *Island*, p. 167.

25. Aldous Huxley, *Brave New World and Brave New World Revisited*, intro. M. Green (New York: Harper and Row, 1965), p. 93.

26. Huxley, *Brave New World Revisited*, p. 2.

27. See George Woodcock, *Dawn and the Darkest Hour: A Study of Aldous Huxley* (London: Faber and Faber, 1972), pp. 173–78.

28. See Alex Zwerdling, *Orwell and the Left* (New Haven, Conn.: Yale University Press, 1974).

29. Orwell, "Why I Write," in *The Collected Essays, Journalism, and Letters of George Orwell*, ed. S. Orwell and I. Angus, vol. 1 (Middlesex, U.K.: Penguin Books, 1970), p. 28.

30. Orwell, "Author's Preface to the Ukranian Edition of *Animal Farm*," in *The Collected Essays, Journalism, and Letters of George Orwell*, ed. S. Orwell and I. Angus, vol. 3 (Middlesex, U.K.: Penguin Books, 1970), p. 458.

31. See Fredric Warburg, *All Authors Are Equal* (New York: St. Martin's Press, 1973), pp. 106–19.

32. Orwell, statement dictated to Warburg, cited in Bernard Crick, *George Orwell: A Life* (Boston: Little, Brown and Co., 1980), p. 395.

33. Orwell, "Letter to Francis A. Henson (extract)" in *The Collected Essays, Journalism, and Letters of George Orwell*, ed. S. Orwell and I. Angus, vol. 4 (Middlesex, U.K.: Penguin Books, 1970), p. 502.

34. Isaac Deutscher, "*1984*—the Mysticism of Cruelty," in his *Russia in Transition* (New York: Grove Press, 1960), p. 258.

35. George Orwell, *1984* (New York: Signet Books, 1950), pp. 199–203.

36. To what degree? For some aspects of the argument, see Alex M. Shane, *The Life and Works of Evgenij Zamjatin* (Berkeley: University of California Press, 1968), p. 140. For a discussion of Huxley, Zamyatin, and Orwell, see Peter E. Firchow, *The End of Utopia: A Study of Aldous Huxley's Brave New World* (London: Bucknell University Press, 1984), pp. 121–28.

37. Alexander Voronsky, "Evgeny Zamyatin" (1922), in *Zamyatin's We: A Collection of Critical Essays*, ed. G. Kern (Ann Arbor, Mich.: Ardis, 1988), pp. 44, 47.

38. Yevgeny Zamyatin, *We*, trans. and intro. Mirra Ginsburg (New York: Avon Books, 1999), p. 174.

39. Zamyatin, "H. G. Wells," in *Soviet Heretic: Essays by Yevgeny Zamyatin*, ed. and trans. M. Ginsburg (Chicago: University of Chicago

Press, 1970), p. 286. To be sure, Zamyatin did not use "utopian" consistently. In an essay from the following year, he protested that an increasingly conformist Soviet literature juxtaposed "useful" and "harmful" works. Even if revolutionary commissars approved "useful" literature, it remained conservative. Harmful liteature, on the other hand, challenged "calification, sclerosis, crust, moss, quiescence." For Zamyatin, literature should be at once "utopian" and "absurd": Zamyatin, "On Literature, Revolution, Entropy and Other Matters," in *Soviet Heretic: Essays by Yevgeny Zamyatin*, ed. and trans. by M. Ginsburg (Chicago: University of Chicago Press, 1970), p. 109.

40. See Clarence Brown, introduction to *We*, by Yevgeny Zamyatin (New York: Penguin Books, 1993), p. xxi.

41. Evgeny Zamyatin, *The Islanders* (Ann Arbor: Trilogy Publishers, 1978), p. 2.

42. Orwell, "Review," in *The Collected Essays, Journalism, and Letters of George Orwell*, ed. S. Orwell and I. Angus, vol. 4 (Middlesex, U.K.: Penguin Books, 1970), pp. 74–75.

43. Raphael Lemkin, *Axis Rule in Occupied Europe* (Washington, D.C.: Carnegie Endowment for International Peace, 1944), p. 79.

44. As an admirer put it, "He died, almost penniless, of a heart attack in 1959, in shabby one-room apartment . . . in Manhattan . . . mourned by very, very few." Steven L. Jacobs, "The Papers of Raphael Lemkin: A First Look," *Journal of Genocide Research* 1, no. 1 (1999): 106.

45. On Lemkin, see Samantha Power, *"A Problem from Hell": America and the Age of Genocide* (New York: HarperCollins, 2003), pp. 17–60.

46. Ralf Dahrendorf, *Reflections on the Revolution in Europe* (New York: Times Books, 1990), pp. 61–62.

47. Virtually nothing, but something. Obviously all ideas about the future and future society share something, but the question is how decisively the visions converge. Hence some critics have argued that More and Hitler hold kindred ideas. See, for instance, Henner Löffler, *Macht und Konsens in den klassischen Staatsutopien: Eine Studie zur Ideengeschichte des Totalitarismus* (Cologne: Carl Heymanns, 1972). Löffler limits himself to utopias that sketch out a state—nothing here about Fourier or William Morris. He also includes Orwell, Huxley, and Zamyatin as utopians, which makes a hopeless muddle of his argument that utopians are totalitarians.

He makes some good points but generally remains on a formal level. For instance, he writes that utopian states seek to educate their citizens from the earliest ages. Guess what? "Hitler demanded something similar" (p. 86). Conclusion? Utopians equal totalitarians.

48. More, *Utopia*, pp. 128, 109, 1200; I am using here, as preferable to the Turner edition, some sentences from Robert M. Adams's translation, *Utopia*, ed. And trans. R. M. Adams (1516; New York: Norton, 1992), pp. 82, 66, 74.

49. Adolf Hitler, *Mein Kampf*, trans. R. Manheim (1925–1926; Boston: Houghton Mifflin, 1971), pp. 561–62, 679, 300, 296.

50. Hitler, January 1939, cited in Saul Friedländer, *Nazi Germany and the Jews*, vol. 1 (New York: HarperCollins, 1997), p. 310.

51. Hanns Ludwig Rosegger, *Der Golfstrom* (1913), cited in Jost Hermand, *Old Dreams of a New Reich: Volkish Utopias and National Socialism* (Bloomington: Indiana University Press, 1992), pp. 37–38.

52. Hans Mommsen, "The Realization of the Unthinkable: The 'Final Solution of the Jewish Question' in the Third Reich," in *From Weimar to Auschwitz*, trans. Alan Kramer and Louise Willmot (Princeton, N.J.: Princeton University Press, 1991), p. 251.

53. Hans Mommsen, "Die Realisierung des Utopischen: Die 'Endlösung der Judenfrage' im Dritten Reich," *Geschichte und Gesellschaft* 9 (1983); 381–420; and "The Realization of the Unthinkable," pp. 224–253.

54. Frank-Lothar Kroll, *Utopie als Ideologie: Geschichtsdenken und politisches Handeln im Dritten Reich* (Paderborn: Ferdinand Schöningh, 1998), is perhaps the most serious effort to use utopia as framework for considering Nazism. Kroll resolutely rejects confining the term utopianism to the Marxist tradition, which is fine. Yet his effort to dub the Nazi's ideas as utopian do not wash. Try as he may, he does not really find utopian themes in Nazi thought. For instance, he writes that Hitler's "living room" concept has the "theoretical character" of a utopian principle because it has a goal beyond day-to-day politics. The content of that goal is "struggle" driven by "blood" and "soil" (pp. 62–63). Only in the most formal way does this make Hitler a "utopian." Yet his final conclusion turns on this formal definition. The problem is that Kroll uses "utopia" in a very restricted sense, partly because he follows Mannheim at his most sociologi-

cal. "Utopia" constitutes a break or transcendence—no matter what it is—of the existing social order. Hence the plans of a maniac to blow up the world in order to end all human life would be termed utopian. With his formalistic approach, Kroll states that efforts to oppress and dispossess are every as bit as utopian as efforts to emancipate. The "inhuman character" of such a project does not "diminish its utopian potential" (pp. 310–311). Rainer Rotermundt's study, *Verkehrete Utopien: Nationalsozialismus, Neonazismus, Neue Barbarei* (Frankfurt: Verlag Neue Kritik, 1980), might also be noted, but this is smaller potatoes. Essentially, he considers Nazi ideas on "Volksgemeinschaft," where German differences are subsumed in nationalist community as the inversion of the Marxist utopian ideas of a classless society.

55. Frédéric Rouvillois, "Utopia and Totalitarianism," in *Utopia: The Search for the Ideal Society in the Western World*, ed. Roland Schaer, Gregory Claeys, and Lyman Tower Sargent (New York: New York Public Library/Oxford University Press, 2000), p. 316.

56. Charles Fourier, *The Theory of the Four Movements*, ed. G. S. Jones (New York: Cambridge University Press, 1996), p. 167.

57. Eric D. Weitz, *A Century of Genocide: Utopias of Race and Nation* (Princeton, N.J.: Princeton University Press, 2003), p. 190.

58. Weitz, *Century of Genocide*, pp. 195, 199, 110, 114. Some of these sentences are taken from my review of Weitz in the *Los Angeles Times Book Review*, 15 June 2003, p. 11.

59. G. W. F. Hegel, introduction to *The Philosophy of History* (New York: Dover, 1956), p. 21.

60. David Henige, *Numbers from Nowhere: The American Indian Contact Population Debate* (Norman: University of Oklahoma Press, 1998), pp. 23, 315.

61. David E. Stannard, *American Holocaust: Columbus and the Conquest of the New World* (Oxford: Oxford University Press, 1992), p. x, 151. As the historian David White put it in a review, "Stannard's desire to establish a very large population in 1492 is tied to his intention to show a campaign of calculated genocide greater than any other in human history (including that of the Nazis). The more people alive in 1492, the greater the population decline, and the greater the genocide." See his incisive review of *American Holocaust* in *The New Republic* 208, no. 3 (18 January 1993): 33–37.

62. Peter Martry D'Anghera, "De Orbe Novo," in *The Gold of Ophir: Travels, Myths, and Legends in the New World*, ed. E. Dahlberg (New York: Dutton, 1972), p. 73.

63. Hoxie Neale Fairchild, *The Noble Savage: A Study in Romantic Naturalism* (New York: Columbia University Press, 1928), pp. 10. See Christian Marouby, *Utopie et primitivisme* (Paris: Seuil, 1990).

64. Stannard, *American Holocaust*, p. 221.

65. Bartolomé de las Casas, *The Devastation of the Indies* (1552), intro. B. M. Donovan (Baltimore, Md.: Johns Hopkins University Press, 1992), p. 31.

66. Gil Elliot, *Twentieth Century Book of the Dead* (New York: Charles Scribner's Sons, 1972), pp. 1, 215.

67. Stéphane Courtois, "Introduction: The Crimes of Communism" and "Why?" in *The Black Book of Communism*, ed. S. Courtois et al. (Cambridge, Mass.: Harvard University Press, 1999), pp. 9–15, 737. *The Black Book of Communism* has provoked much discussion. For two very able critiques, see J. Arch Getty, "The Future Did Not Work," *The Atlantic Monthly*, March 2000, p. 113 ff., and John Torpey, "What Future for the Future? Reflections on *The Black Book of Communism*," *Human Rights Review* 2, no. 2 (January 2001): 135 ff.

68. Enzo Traverso, *The Origins of Nazi Violence* (New York: The New Press, 2003), pp. 77–85.

69. François Furet, *The Passing of an Illusion* (Chicago: University of Chicago Press, 1999), pp. 19–20.

70. Weitz, *Century of Genocide*, p. 230.

71. "Wars and Deaths, 1700–1987," in *World Military and Social Expenditures, 1987–88*, ed. Ruth Leger Sivard (Washington, D.C.: World Priorities, 1987), p. 28.

72. All figures from Milton Leitenberg, "Deaths in Wars and Conflicts Between 1945 and 2000," paper prepared for Conference on Data Collection in Armed Conflict, Uppsala, Sweden, 8–9 June 2002, p. 9.

73. See R. J. Rummel, *China's Bloody Century: Genocide and Mass Murder Since 1900* (New Brunswick, N.J.: Transaction Publishers, 1991), pp. 103–36.

74. CIA Research Study, *Indonesia—1965: The Coup That Backfired* (Washington, D.C.: Central Intelligence Agency, 1968), pp. 70–71.

75. Samantha Power, *"A Problem from Hell,"* p. 303.

76. Leitenberg, "Deaths in Wars," p. 3.

77. Philip Gourevitch, *We Wish to Inform You That Tomorrow We Will Be Killed with Our Families* (New York: Picador USA, 1998), p. 94.

78. Zamyatin, *We*, pp. 179–80.

79. To be sure, an increasing number of historical studies deal with "imagined communities" or the "imperial imagination," but imagination in these usages is a form of ideology or is distant from imagination as utopian fantasy in the individual.

80. Eva T. H. Brann, *The World of the Imagination: Sum and Substance* (Lanham, Md.: Roman and Littlefield, 1991). J. M. Cocking's, *Imagination: A Study in the History of Ideas* (London: Routledge, 1991) uses a historical approach but is only concerned with the idea of imagination among philosophers—and is really not historical, to boot; that is, he offers no explanation for the shift in ideas.

81. See Judith Plotz, "The Perpetual Messiah: Romanticism, Childhood, and the Paradoxes of Human Development," in *Regulated Children/ Liberated Children*, ed. B. Finkelstein (New York: Psychohistory Press, 1979), pp. 63–95.

82. Harry Hendrick, "Construction and Reconstruction of British Childhood: An Interpretative Survey, 1800 to the Present," in *Constructing and Reconstructing Childhood*, ed. A. James and A. Prout (London: Falmer Press, 1997), p. 38.

83. For a good overview, see Colin M. Heywood, *A History of Childhood* (Cambridge: Polity Press, 2001).

84. Nicholas Orme, *Medieval Children* (New Haven, Conn.: Yale University Press, 2001), p. 10. See also Linda A. Pollock, *Forgotten Children: Parent-Child Relations from 1500 to 1900* (Cambridge: Cambridge University Press, 1983): "The results of this study . . . demonstrate that the main arguments put forward by many historians are incorrect. . . . Contrary to the belief of such authors as Ariès, there was a concept of childhood in the 16th century" (p. 267).

85. Keith Thomas, "Children in Early Modern England," in *Children and Their Books: A Celebration of the Work of Iona and Peter Opie*, ed. G. Avery and J. Briggs (Oxford: Clarendon Press, 1990), p. 70. For a recent critique that challenges Ariès's numbers and conclusions, see Robert

Woods, "Did Montaigne Love His Children? Demography and the Hypothesis of Parental Indifference," *Journal of Interdisciplinary History* 33, no. 3 (2003): 421–42.

86. For a good survey of nineteenth-century England, see Thomas E. Jordan, *Victorian Childhood: Themes and Variations* (Albany: State University of New York Press, 1987).

87. See Katherine A. Lynch, *Family, Class, and Ideology in Early Industrial France: Social Policy and the Working-Class Family, 1825–1848* (Madison: University of Wisconsin Press, 1988), pp. 168–241.

88. "By 1930, most children [in the United States] under fourteen were out of the labor market and into schools." Viviana A. Zelizer, *Pricing the Priceless Child: The Changing Social Value of Children* (New York: Basic Books, 1985), p. 97.

89. Harry Hendrick, *Children, Childhood, and English Society, 1880–1990* (Cambridge: Cambridge University Press, 1990), p. 18.

90. Max Horkheimer, "Art and Mass Culture," in *Selected Essays* (New York: Seabury Press, 1972), p. 277.

91. David Buckingham, *After the Death of Childhood: Growing Up in the Age of Electronic Media* (Cambridge: Polity Press, 2000), p. 32.

92. Buckingham, *After the Death of Childhood*, pp. 70–71.

93. Neil Postman, *The Disappearance of Childhood* (New York: Delacorte Press, 1982), p. 129.

94. Marie Winn, *The Plug-In Drug* (1985; revised ed., New York: Penguin Books, 2002), p. 4.

95. See Julie B. Schor, "The Commodification of Childhood: Tales from the Advertising Front Lines," *Hedgehog Review* 5, no. 2 (Summer 2003): 7–23. This is drawn from her forthcoming *Born to Buy: Marketing and Transformation of Childhood and Culture*.

96. Stephen Kline, *Out of the Garden: Toys, TV, and Children's Culture in the Age of Marketing* (London: Verso, 1993) p. 146.

97. Robert Abelman and David Atkin, "Evaluating the Impact of Affilia-tion Change on Children's TV Viewership and Perceptions of Network Branding," in *Advertising to Children: Concepts and Controversies*, ed. M. C. Macklin and L. Carlson (Thousand Oaks, Calif.: Sage Publications, 1999), p. 49.

98. Walter Benjamin, "The Storyteller," in *Illuminations*, trans. Harry

Zohn (New York: Harcourt, Brace and World, 1968), p. 91. See Barry Sanders, *A is for Ox: Violence, Electronic Media, and the Silencing of the Written Word* (New York: Pantheon Books, 1994), pp. 42–43.

99. Peter Burke, "The Invention of Leisure in Early Modern Europe," *Past and Present*, no. 146 (February 1995): 136–51.

100. See generally Ian Irvine, "Acedia, Tristitia, and Sloth: Early Christian Forerunners to Chronic Ennui," *Humanitas* 12, no. 1 (Spring 1999): 89 ff.

101. See Reinhard Kuhn, *The Demon of Noontime: Ennui in Western Literature* (Princeton, N.J.: Princeton University Press, 1976). Kuhn is anxious to distinguish ennui from boredom, which he dismisses as a psychological disorder, dependent "entirely on external circumstances" (pp. 6–7). Unfortunately, in his learned survey, he comes to no conclusion except that the forms of ennui have changed. See also George Steiner, "The Great Ennui," in *In Bluebeard's Castle* (New Haven, Conn.: Yale University Press, 1971), pp. 1–26. Steiner dates ennui from after the French Revolution, the collapse of hopes and change.

102. Patricia M. Spacks, *Boredom: The Literary History of a State of Mind* (Chicago: University of Chicago Press, 1995), p. 9.

103. Mrs. Humphry Ward, "A Country Dinner-Party," (1842) cited in Spacks, *Boredom*, p. 203.

104. Peter N. Stearns, *Anxious Parents: A History of Modern Childrearing in America* (New York: New York University Press, 2003), p. 196.

105. Robert Paul Smith, *"Where Did You Go?" "Out" "What Did You Do?" "Nothing"* (New York: Norton, 1957), pp. 98–99.

106. "Robert Paul Smith Dead at 61," *New York Times*, 31 January 1977.

107. Peter N. Stearns, *Anxious Parents*, pp. 199, 170–71, 196.

108. Stephen Kline, *Out of the Garden*, p. 321.

109. M. C. Macklin and L. Carlson, introduction to *Advertising to Children: Concepts and Controversies*, ed. Macklin and Carlson (Thousand Oaks, Calif.: Sage Publications, 1999), p. 11.

110. John Holt, *How Children Learn*, cited in Kline, p. 335.

111. Gary Cross, *Kids' Stuff: Toys and the Changing World of American Childhood* (Cambridge, Mass.: Harvard University Press, 1997), p. 187. To

be sure, Cross himself in this study gives a very upbeat account, which might be called an old-fashioned historicism: things just change over time. To complain about video games or violent toys marketed by vast corporations is to be an old fogy. He also seems to believe that the imagination of children is a static entity, just waiting to be tapped by media giants. Television, he writes, "made possible a constantly changing culture of play that appealed directly to the imaginations of children. Over time this led to the predominance of fantasy-fad toys stimulated and sustained by the media celebrities" (p. 162). Cross's empiricism gets the better of him. The notion, which he regularly repeats, that mass media directly responds to children, forgets that it also molds them.

112. Iona Opie and Peter Opie, *Children's Games in Street and Playground* (London: Oxford University Press, 1969), p. 14. A historian of Catalonia has made a similar argument, although focused on leisure and play in general. "People play draughts in New York's Bryant Park just as they played them on the square in Baga in the thirteenth century." Hence the moral: "The historian of leisure, like the historian of sex, should always bear in mind an old Catalan saying: *sempre han tingut bec les oques* (geese have always had beaks)." Yes, but now their beaks are propped open and mechanically force-fed to produce foie gras. If geese could write history, they might not just quack-quack but register and regret some significant changes in the tending of fowls. Indeed, we need a good history from the point of view of a goose. Nonetheless, this is an informative article. See Joan-Lluis Marfany, "The Invention of Leisure in Early Modern Europe," *Past and Present*, no. 156 (August 1997): 174–98.

113. Opie and Opie, *Children's Games*, p. 15.

114. Only for a moment. Their later *Children's Game with Things* (Oxford: Oxford University Press, 1997) is even more sanguine, although again they qualify that busier roads and smaller families may undermine games (p. 11–12).

115. Smith, *"Where Did You Go?"* pp. 7–18.

116. For a general critique of Scholem's interpretations, see Moshe Idel, *Messianic Mystics* (New Haven: London, 1998).

117. Scholem, "Toward an Understanding of the Messianic Idea in Judaism," in *The Messianic Idea in Judaism*, trans. Michael A. Meyer (New York: Schocken Books, 1971), p. 21.

118. Tommaso Campanella, *The City of the Sun: A Poetical Dialogue*, trans. D. J. Donno (Berkeley: University of California Press, 1981), p. 51.

119. Lewis Mumford, preface to *The Story of Utopias* (1922; second edition, New York: Viking Press, 1962), pp. 4–5.

120. Mumford, *Story*, p. 5.

121. Hans Kohn, *Living in a World Revolution: My Encounters with History* (New York: Trident Press, 1964), p. 61.

122. See Paul Mendes-Flohr, *From Mysticism to Dialogue: Martin Buber's Transformation of German Social Thought* (Detroit: Wayne State University Press, 1989), pp. 54–57.

123. Heinrich Heine, "Concerning the History of Religion and Philosophy," in Heine, *The Romantic School and Other Essays*, ed. J. Hermand, R. C. Holub, trans. Helen Mustard (New York: Continuum, 1985), pp. 180–81.

124. T. W. Adorno, *Notes to Literature*, vol. 1, ed. R. Tiedemann, trans. Sherry Weber Nicholsen (New York: Columbia University Press, 1991), p. 81.

125. Ernst Bloch, afterword to *The Spirit of Utopia*, trans. Anthony A. Nasser (1963; reprint, Stanford, Calif.: Stanford University Press, 2000), p. 279. Perhaps something more should be said of Bloch, who will make several appearances in this book. From *The Spirit of Utopia* to the three-volume *The Principle of Hope*, trans. Neville Plaice, Stephen Plaice, and Paul Knight (English ed., Cambridge, Mass.: MIT Press, 1986), no one is more identified with iconoclastic utopianism than Bloch. Yet for a chapter of his long life, he was an orthodox Marxist, a Stalinist, a defender of the Moscow Trials, and a champion of the DDR (East Germany). To complicate matters, in republishing earlier essays and books, Bloch regularly altered and excised passages; for instance, the first and second edition of the *Spirit of Utopia* differ significantly, which Bloch only alludes to. This habit seems less innocent with his political writings. He drops phrases and whole essays in republishing collections of political essays; for instance, he variously substitutes "Lenin" for "Stalin."

The evidence is clear that Bloch defended the Moscow Trials and, for some years, DDR practices. In 1937 he argued that the Soviet Union needed "to rid itself" of many enemies. "In today's situation it should be clearly evident that anti-bolshevik statements serve only the devil himself . . .

there can be no struggle, there can be nothing good without Russia": Ernst Bloch, "A Jubilee for Renegades [1937]" *New German Critique* 4 (Winter 1975): 18, 24. Much has been written about Bloch's complicated relationship to orthodox Marxism; see for instance, Oskar Negt, "Ernst Bloch— the German Philosopher of the October Revolution," *New German Critique* 4 (Winter 1975): 3–16. Essential is the memoir of a student, Ruth Römer, "Erinnerungen an Ernst Bloch," *Bloch-Almanach* 10 (1990): 107–62, which is both very critical and very laudatory; and the biography by Peter Zudeick, *Der Hintern des Teufels: Ernst Bloch–Leben und Werk* (Bühl-Moos: Elster Verlag, 1985), esp. pp. 153–63. See also Edgar Weiss, "Ernst Bloch und das Problem der konkreten Utopie," in *"Ich bin. Aber ich habe mich nicht. Darum werden wir erst." Perspectiven der Philosophie Ernst Blochs*, ed. J. R. Bloch (Frankfurt: Suhrkamp, 1997), pp. 327–43. It was due to his Stalinism that Frankfurt School people such as Horkheimer kept a distance from Bloch.

The question for sympathizers and critics is similar to that provoked by Heidegger: What is the relationship between Bloch's philosophy and explicit political pronouncements? Unlike Heidegger, Bloch at least had the excuse of his life situation; as a refugee with little means and no secure home he looked to the Soviet Union as the bulwark against Nazism. Nor did Bloch's eleven years in the United States prove successful or undermine his rigid Marxism. As his son recalls, "he did not find a helping hand: no university and no institution, no publisher and no foundation": Jan Robert Bloch, "Dreams of a Better Life: Zum Exil Ernst Blochs in den USA," *Bloch-Almanach* 18 (1999): 130. When the DDR offered him a position in 1948, Bloch who barely had learned English, accepted it with great hope and optimism. In his mid-sixties, it was his first academic appointment and first regular salary. During his years in the DDR, he defended its policies, but eventually he and his followers were harassed, arrested, and sidelined. One might say that the Bloch story is roughly similar to the that of his friend, Bertolt Brecht. See Erdmut Wizisla, "Ernst Bloch und Bertold Brecht," *Bloch-Almanach* 10 (1990):87–106. Both expressed orthodox Marxist and Stalinist sentiments. After less than happy experiences in the United States, both settled in the DDR; and with both, it can be argued, the thrust of their contribution undermined their explicit political pronouncements.

In 1961 as the Berlin Wall was being erected, Bloch accepted a position in West Germany, which opened the final chapter of his long life as a very active teacher, writer, and now as a friend of the German New Left. (For an overview in English of Bloch's life, see Vincent Geoghegan, *Ernst Bloch* [New York: Routledge, 1996]). He died in 1977, reconciled with some earlier critics. A 1965 volume in honor of Bloch for his eightieth birthday includes contributions from Adorno, Paul Tillich, and George Steiner. See *Ernst Bloch zu Ehren*, ed. S. Unseld (Frankfurt: Suhrkamp, 1965). For a careful presentation of Adorno's up-and-down relationship with Bloch, see the excellent study by Detlev Claussen, *Theodor W. Adorno: Ein Letztes Genie* (Frankfurt: S. Fischer Verlag, 2003), pp. 320–57. In 1980, Gershom Scholem, a man not easy to please, and a lifelong anti-Stalinist and anti-Marxist, wrote that "my present regard for Bloch, after so many years and much more extensive attention to the entirety of his production, does not correspond to what I impetuously put to paper in the twenties and thirties": Gershom Scholem, preface to *The Correspondence of Walter Benjamin and Gershom Scholem, 1932–1940*, ed. G. Scholem, trans. Gary Smith and Andre Lefevere (New York: Schocken Books, 1989), p. 7. In 1992, Leszek Kolakowsi, a bitter critic of Marxism, accepted the Ernst Bloch Prize.

Nevertheless biography can explain and illuminate, but not justify philosophy. Negt asks the right question, although his answer is a bit too pat: "Is Bloch's behavior *vis-à-vis* the Stalinist trials an expression of the inner nature of his thought or is it a product of the need for identity and reality of a revolutionary intellectual?" His answer: "Just as we cannot stamp Hegel as the philosopher of the Prussian state because he lets the development of the moral idea end in the Prussian state, we cannot reduce Bloch's thought, the philosopher in combat, to statements he made about the Moscow trials, for these statements clearly contradict his entire philosophy" (Negt, "Ernst Bloch," p. 9). I hope so.

126. Michael Löwy, *Redemption and Utopia: Jewish Libertarian Thought in Central Europe* (Stanford, Calif.: Stanford University Press, 1992).

127. Gershom Scholem, "Reflections on Jewish Theology," in *On Jews and Judaism in Crisis: Selected Essays*, ed. and trans. Werner J. Dannhauser (New York: Schocken, 1976), p. 286.

128. Moses Maimonides, *The Guide for the Perplexed*, trans. M. Friedländer (New York: Dover Publications, 1956), p. 85.

129. Walter Benjamin, "Franz Kafa," in *Illuminations*, ed. H. Arendt, trans. Harry Zohn (New York: Harcourt, Brace and World, 1968), p. 139.

130. Gershom Scholem, "Walter Benjamin," in *On Jews and Judaism in Crisis: Selected Essays*, ed. and trans. Werner J. Dannhauser (New York: Schocken, 1976), p. 196.

131. Michael Löwy, " 'Theologia negativa' and 'Utopia negativa': Franz Kafka," in *Redemption and Utopia: Jewish Libertarian Thought in Central Europe* (Stanford, Calif.: Stanford University Press, 1992), pp. 71–94.

2. On Anti-Utopianism

1. To be sure, this is the claim about Plato advanced by Karl Popper (whom I discuss below) in his *Open Society and Its Enemies*, 2 vols., (1945; rev. ed. New York: The Free Press, 1962). Certainly authoritarianism and even militarism saturate Plato's ideal state as presented in the *Republic*. In any event, I am mainly concerned with the literary utopian tradition, where Plato has played a smaller role than might be expected. As Frank E. Manuel and Fritzie P. Manuel point out in their encyclopedic *Utopian Thought in the Western World* (Cambridge, Mass.: Harvard University Press, 1979), in the rediscovery of Greek and Roman thought in the Renaissance, most attention was paid to the satiric utopians. "The jocular so far outstrips the grave that allegiance to Aristophanes submerges any admiration for Plato" (p. 99). To the extent that the *Republic* is utopian, it is strictly in service of how to build the harmonious state or city; it is almost a practical guide for Greek cities and colonies. "And so long as your city is governed soberly in the order just laid down," states Socrates, "it will be the greatest of cities. I do not mean in repute, but in reality, even though it have only a thousand defenders." (*The Republic*, in *Plato: The Complete Dialogues*, ed. E. Hamiliton and H. Cairns [New York: Pantheon/Bollinger, 1963], p. 664). A recent and fair-minded study concludes that "the *Republic* was always rooted in Greek politics. It was always meant to provide a new ideological basis for an aristocratic and oligarchic society. Its most practical political lesson, and the lesson probably of greatest interest to contemporaries, was its defence of hierarchy." (Doyne Dawson, *Cities of the Gods: Communist Utopias in Greek Thought* [New York: Oxford University Press, 1992], p. 93).

2. See H. C. Baldry, "Who Invented the Golden Age," *Classical Quarterly* 2 (1952): 83–92, for a statement that Hesiod originated the idea of the "golden age" for Greek thought; see also Baldry, *Ancient Utopias* (London: Camelot Press/University of Southampton, 1956), p. 9.

3. Hesiod, *Works and Days*, in *Theogony, Works and Days, Shield*, ed. and trans. A. N. Athanassakis (Baltimore, Md.: Johns Hopkins University Press, 1983), pp. 70–72.

4. Hesiod, *Works and Days*, p. 77, lines 410–13.

5. Joseph Fontenrose, "Work, Justice, and Hesiod's Five Ages," *Classical Philology* 49, no. 1 (January 1974): 12. See also A. S. Brown, "From the Golden Age to the Isles of the Blest," *Mnemosyne* 51, no. 4 (1998): 385–410; Juha Sihvola, *Decay, Progress, the Good Life? Hesiod and Protagoras on the Development of Culture* (Helsinki: Finnish Society of Sciences and Letters, 1989).

6. See M. I. Finley, "Utopianism Ancient and Modern," in *The Critical Spirit: Essays in Honor of Herbert Marcuse*, ed. K. H. Wolff and B. Moore Jr. (Boston: Beacon Press, 1967), pp. 3–20.

7. Aristophanes, *The Birds* in *Four Comedies*, ed. and trans. Dudley Fits (New York: Harcourt, Brace and World, 1962), pp. 163–243.

8. See the discussion of this phrase in the annotated text, Nan Dunbar, *Aristophanes, Birds* (Oxford: Claredon Press, 1995), p. 151.

9. Victor Ehrenberg, *The People of Aristophanes: A Sociology of Old Attic Comedy* (Oxford: Basil Blackwell, 1951), p. 57.

10. See Douglas M. MacDowell, *Aristophanes and Athens: An Introduction to the Plays* (Oxford: Oxford University Press, 1995), pp. 199–228.

11. A. M. Bowie, *Aristophanes: Myth, Ritual, and Comedy* (New York: Cambridge University Press, 1993), p. 177.

12. See Friedrich Solmsen, *Intellectual Experiments of the Greek Enlightenment* (Princeton, N.J.: Princeton University Press, 1975), pp. 76–78.

13. Lucian, *The True History*, in *Satirical Sketches*, ed. and trans. P. Turner (Bloomington: Indiana University Press, 1990), pp. 249–94. For a discussion of Aristophanes and Lucian and a full scale commentary on "The True History," see Aristoula Georgiadou and David H. J. Larmour, *Lucian's Science Fiction Novel* True Histories*: Interpretation and Commentary* (Leiden: Brill, 1998).

14. Richard Marius, *Thomas More: A Biography* (New York: Knopf, 1984), p. 83.

15. See David Marsh, *Lucian and the Latins: Humor and Humanism in the Early Renaissance* (Ann Arbor: University of Michigan Press, 1998), pp. 167–76.

16. Erasmus, "Prefatory Letter: Erasmus of Rotterdam to his friend Thomas More," in *Praise of Folly*, ed. A. H. T. Levi, trans. Betty Radice (Penguin Books: New York, 1993), pp. 6–7.

17. See Paul Turner, introduction to his translation of *Utopia*, by Thomas More (New York: Penguin Books, 1965), p. 8.

18. More, *Utopia*, Turner ed., p. 100.

19. Marsh, *Lucian and the Latins*, p. 193. See Christopher Robinson, *Lucian and His Influence in Europe* (London: Duckworth, 1979), pp. 130–33.

20. T. S. Dorsch, "Sir Thomas More and Lucian: An Interpretation of *Utopia*," *Archiv für das Studium der neueren Sprachen und Literaturen* 203 (1966–1967): 350.

21. M. A. Screech, *Rabelais* (London: Duckworth, 1979), p. 8. For the role of Lucian in Rabelais, see generally, Marsh, *Lucian and the Latins*.

22. For a consideration of Rabelais's links to More, see V. L. Saulnier, "L'Utopie en France: Morus et Rabelais," in *Les Utopies à la renaissance*, ed. J. Lameere (Brussels: Presse Universitaires de Bruxelles, 1963): pp. 135–62. Cf. Michaël Baraz, *Rabelais et la joie de la liberté* (Paris: José Cort, 1983), pp. 241–82.

23. François Rabelais, *Gargantua and Pantagruel,*, trans. and intro. J. M. Cohen (New York: Penguin Books, 1955), pp. 150–59.

24. Robert Bolt, *A Man for All Seasons* (1960; reprint, New York: Vintage Books, 1990), p. 160.

25. R. S. Sylvester and G. P. Marc'hadour, eds., *Essential Articles for the Study of Thomas More* (Hamden, Conn.: Archon Books, 1977).

26. J. H. Hexter, *More's Utopia: The Biography of an Idea* (New York: Harper and Row, 1965), p. 3.

27. George Steiner, "The Book," in *Language and Silence* (New York: Atheneum, 1967), pp. 189–90.

28. Brian Moynahan, *If God Spare My Life: William Tyndale, the English Bible, and Sir Thomas More—a Story of Martyrdom and Betrayal* (London: Little, Brown, 2002), pp. 387, 173.

29. Thomas More, *Utopia*, ed. and trans. R. M. Adams (New York: Norton, 1992), p. 74.

30. Thomas More, "More's Epitaph," in *Utopia and Other Essential Writings*, ed. J. J. Greene and J. P. Dolan (New York: New American Library, 1984), p. 285.

31. John Guy, *Thomas More* (New York: Oxford University Press, 2000), p. 106.

32. Russell Ames, *Citizen Thomas More and his Utopia* (Princeton, N.J.: Princeton University Press, 1949), p. 21.

33. Guy, *Thomas More*, p. 121.

34. More, *The Dialogue Concerning Heresies*, in *Utopia and Other Essential Writings*, ed. J. J. Greene and J. P. Dolan (New York: New American Library, 1984), p. 208.

35. More, *Responsio ad Lutherum*, cited in David Daniell, *William Tyndale: A Biography* (New Haven, Conn.: Yale University Press, 1994), pp. 258–59.

36. More, "Confutation of Tyndale's Answer," in *Utopia and Other Essential Writings*, ed. J. J. Greene and J. P. Dolan (New York: New American Library, 1984), p. 223.

37. Guy, *More*, p. 122.

38. Marius, *Thomas More*, p. 406.

39. Jasper Ridley, *The Statesman and the Fanatic: Thomas Wolsey and Thomas More* (London: Constable, 1982), p. 293.

40. Cited in Ridley, *The Statesman and the Fanatic*, p. 238.

41. C. S. Lewis, *English Literature in the Sixteenth Century* (Oxford: Clarendon Press, 1954), pp. 169–70. Lewis's few pages on More are outstanding.

42. Norman Cohn, *The Pursuit of the Millennium: Revolutionary Messianism in Medieval and Reformation Europe and Its Bearing on Modern Totalitarian Movements* (1957; second edition, New York: Harper and Brothers, 1961), pp. xiv, 308–9.

43. See Thomas Nipperdey, *Reformation, Revolution, Utopie: Studien zum 16. Jahrhundert* (Göttingen: Vandenhoeck and Ruprecht, 1975), pp. 38–84.

44. Abraham Friesen, *Reformation and Utopia: The Marxist Interpretation of the Reformation and its Antecedents* (Wiesbaden: Franz Steiner Verlag, 1974), p. 14.

45. On Müntzer and Luther, see generally Abraham Friesen, *Thomas Muentzer, A Destroyer of the Godless: The Making of a Sixteenth-Century Religious Revolutionary* (Berkeley: University of California Press, 1990). On Müntzer and his links to Christian humanism, including Erasmus, see Ulrich Bubenheimer, *Thomas Müntzer: Herkunft und Bildung* (Leiden: E. J. Brill, 1989), pp. 194–229.

46. Biographical information about Norman Cohn derived from personal communication.

47. They also appear when the American government and scholarly community registered a sharp hike in a demand for experts on Germany and Europe. See Alfons Söllner, *Deutsche Politikwissenschaftler in der Emigration: Studien zu ihrer Akkulturation und Wirkungsgeschichte* (Opladen: Westdeutsche Verlag, 1996), p. 250.

48. Elisabeth Young-Bruehl, *Hannah Arendt: For Love of the World* (New Haven, Conn.: Yale University Press, 1982), p. 294.

49. Hannah Arendt, *The Origins of Totalitarianism* (New York: Meridian/World Publishing, 1958), p. vii

50. Karl Popper, *Unended Quest: An Intellectual Autobiography* (La Salle, Ill.: Open Court, 1976), p. 105.

51. See generally Malachi Haim Hacohen, *Karl Popper—the Formative Years, 1902–1945* (New York: Cambridge University Press, 2000).

52. Popper, *Unended Quest*, p. 13.

53. Popper, *Unended Quest*, p. 33.

54. See Karl Popper, "Die 'politische' Biographie," in Herbert Marcuse and Karl Popper, *Revolution oder Reform?* ed. F. Stark (Munich: Kösel-Verlag, 1971), p. 9.

55. Karl Popper, *The Poverty of Historicism* (New York: Basic Books, 1960), pp. 84, 45, 51.

56. Popper, *The Poverty of Historicism*, pp. 66–67, 78–79.

57. Popper, *Open Society*, vol. 1, pp. viii, 22–23

58. Popper, *Open Society*, vol. 1, pp. 159, 165.

59. Popper, "Utopia and Violence," in *Conjectures and Refutations: The Growth of Scientific Knowledge* (New York: Harper and Row, 1968), pp. 355–63.

60. See Talmon's obituary, *New York Times*, 18 June 1980.

61. J. L. Talmon, *The Myth of the Nation and the Vision of Revolution:*

The Origins of Ideological Polarisation in the Twentieth Century (London: Secker and Warburg, 1981), p. 535.

62. J. L. Talmon, *Political Messianism: The Romantic Phase* (New York: Praeger, 1960), p. 30.

63. J. L. Talmon, *The Origins of Totalitarian Democracy* (1951; reprint, New York: Norton, 1970), pp. 2–3, 253.

64. J. L. Talmon, *Utopianism and Politics* (London: Conservative Political Centre, 1957), p. 12.

65. Talmon, *Political Messianism*, pp. 15, viii.

66. "In its eclecticism," writes Irving Louis Horowitz of *The Myth of the Nation*, "it seems less concerned with establishing a thesis than the earlier volumes," Horowitz, "Introduction to the Transaction Edition," in J. L. Talmon, *Myth of the Nation and Vision of Revolution* (New Brunswick, N.J.: Transaction Publishers, 1991), p. xvi.

67. Talmon, *Myth of the Nation*, pp. 535–554.

68. This is George L. Mosse writing in "Political Style and Political Theory—Totalitarian Democracy Revisited," in *Totalitarian Democracy and After: International Colloquium in Memory of Jacob L. Talmon* (Jerusalem: Israel Academy of Sciences and Humanities, 1984), p. 167. It may illustrate Talmon's declining impact that a subsequent volume in his honor only mentions him in passing; see *The Intellectual Revolt against Liberal Democracy, 1870–1945: International Conference in Memory of Jacob L. Talmon*, ed. Z. Sternhell (Jerusalem: Israel Academy of Sciences and Humanities, 1996).

69. David Luban, review of *The Cambridge Companion to Hannah Arendt*, *Ethics* 113, no. 3 (April 2003): 724.

70. Walter Laqueur, "The Arendt Cult," in *Hannah Arendt in Jerusalem*, ed. S. E. Aschheim (Berkeley and Los Angeles: University of California Press, 2001), pp. 47–48.

71. Ian Harris, "Berlin and His Critics," in *Liberty*, ed. H. Hardy (Oxford: Oxford University Press, 2002.), p. 351; Henry Hardy, "The Editor's Tale," in *Liberty*, ed. H. Hardy (Oxford: Oxford University Press, 2002), p. xxviii. Berlin's story is in the same volume, "The Purpose Justifies the Ways," pp. 332–35.

72. Steven Lukes, "Isaiah Berlin in Conversation with Steven Lukes," *Salmagundi*, no. 120 (Fall 1998): 62.

73. Lukes, "Isaiah Berlin in Conversation," p. 76.

74. Hacohen, *Karl Popper*, p. 524

75. Berlin, "The Sense of Reality," in *The Sense of Reality*, ed. H. Hardy (New York: Farrar, Straus and Giroux, 1996), p. 1.

76. Isaiah Berlin, "Political Ideas in the Twentieth Century," *Foreign Affairs* 28 no. 3 (April 1950): 385.

77. A. Arblaster, "Vision and Revision: A Note on the Text of Isaiah Berlin's *Four Essays on Liberty*," *Political Studies* 19, no. 1 (March 1971): 81–86.

78. Isaiah Berlin, *The Crooked Timber of Humanity*, ed. H. Hardy (New York: Vintage Books, 1992).

79. Isaiah Berlin, "Political Ideas," pp. 384–85.

80. Perry Andeson, *A Zone of Engagement* (London: Verso, 1992), pp. 232–35.

81. Manuel and Manuel, *Utopian Thought*, p. 519.

82. Cited by Ted Humphrey in his edition of "Idea for a Universal History," in Immanuel Kant, *Perpetual Peace and Other Essays*, ed. and trans. Ted Humphrey (Indianapolis: Hackett, 1983), p. 40.

83. Kant, "Idea for a Universal History," ed. Humphrey, p. 33; and "Idee zu einer Allgemeinen Geschichte in Weltbürgerlicher Absicht," in I. Kant, *Werke in Zehn Banden*, ed. W. Weischedel, vol. 9, part 1 (Wiesebaden: Insel Verlag, 1964), p. 40.

84. Isaiah Berlin, *Four Essays on Liberty* (Oxford: Oxford University Press, 1969), p. 123,

85. Berlin, *Four Essays*, pp. 131, 144.

86. Isaiah Berlin, *Freedom and its Betrayal: Six Enemies of Human Liberty* (Princeton, N.J.: Princeton University Press, 2002), pp. 52, 54, 70–71.

87. Isaiah Berlin, *Four Essays*, pp. 132, 166.

88. Matthew Arnold, *Culture and Anarchy and Other Writings*, ed. S. Collini (Cambridge: Cambridge University Press, 1993), p. 83.

89. Matthew Arnold, "My Countrymen," in *Selected Prose*, ed. P. J. Keating (Penguin: New York, 1987), pp. 192–93.

90. Berlin, *Freedom and its Betrayal*, p. 103.

91. Berlin, "The Decline of Utopian Ideas in the West," in *The Crooked Timber of Humanity*, ed. H. Hardy (New York: Vintage Books, 1992), pp. 46–47.

92. Berlin, "The Pursuit of the Ideal," in *The Proper Study of Mankind*, ed. H. Hardy (New York: Farrar, Straus and Giroux, 1997), p. 11.

93. Berlin, "The Pursuit of the Ideal," p. 15.

94. Stefan Collini, *English Pasts: Essays in History and Culture* (Oxford: Oxford University Press, 1999), pp. 203–4.

95. Berlin also indicated that Popper's *Open Society and its Enemies* influenced him considerably. (See Lukes, "Isaiah Berlin in Conversation," p. 92.)

96. Of course, there are some minor exceptions; for instance, Berlin reviewed Bertrand Russell's *History of Western Philosophy* at length in *Mind* 56, no. 222 (April 1947): 151–66. The other exceptions are his brief, invariably laudatory memoirs of twentieth-century acquaintances, collected in Berlin, *Personal Impressions*, ed. H. Hardy (New York: Viking, 1980).

97. Berlin, "Philosophy and Government Repression," in *The Sense of Reality*, ed. H. Hardy (New York: Farrar, Straus and Giroux, 1996), p. 64.

98. Christopher Hitchens, "Goodbye to Berlin," in *Unacknowledged Legislation: Writers in the Public Sphere* (London: Verso, 2000), p. 144.

99. Hitchens, "Goodbye to Berlin," p. 151.

100. For a different take on these final remarks, see Avishai Margalit, "The Crooked Timber of Nationalism," in *The Legacy of Isaiah Berlin*, ed. M. Lilla et al. (New York: New York Review Books, 2001). "What was so surprising was not the content of the letter, but the very fact that he wrote it . . . In his last statement he [Berlin] wanted to stand up and be counted" (p. 158).

101. Norman Podhoretz, "A Dissent on Isaiah Berlin," *Commentary* 107, no. 2 (February 1999): 25.

102. Benjamin Constant, "The Spirit of Conquest and Usurpation and Their Relation to European Civilization," in *Political Writings*, ed. B. Fontana (Cambridge: Cambridge University Press, 1988), 104.

103. Constant, "The Liberty of the Ancients Compared with that of the Moderns," in *Political Writings*, ed. B. Fontana (Cambridge: Cambridge University Press, 1988, p. 316.

104. See Constant, "De la Perfectibilité de l'espèce humaine," in *Écrit politiques*, ed. M. Gauchet (Paris: Gallimard, 1997), pp. 700–730.

105. Berlin, *Four Essays*, p. 129.

106. Constant, "The Liberty of the Ancients," pp. 314–16.

107. Constant, "The Liberty of the Ancients," p. 326.

108. B. Constant to Claude Hochet, 5 October 1812, in Benjamin Constant and Madame de Staël, *Lettres à un ami: Cent onze lettres inédites à Claude Hochet*, ed. J. Mistler (Neuchatel: Baconnière, 1949), p. 225.

109. See B. Constant, "Ecrits sur la liberté de la presse," in *Oeuvre completes*, vol. 9, part 1(Tübingen: Max Niemeyer Verlag, 2001), pp. 31–190.

110. See Kurt Kloocke, *Benjamin Constant: Une biographie intellectuelle* (Geneva: Librarie Droz, 1984), p. 235.

111. Stephen Holmes, *Benjamin Constant and the Making of Modern Liberalism* (New Haven, Conn.: Yale University Press, 1984), p. 44.

112. Hannah Arendt, *The Human Condition* (Garden City, N.Y.: Doubleday Anchor, 1959), p. 6.

113. Hannah Arendt, *The Life of the Mind*, 1 vol. (San Diego: Harcourt Brace, 1978).

114. Gershom Scholem, "Letter to Hannah Arendt," in *On Jews and Judaism in Crisis: Selected Essays*, ed. W. J. Dannhauser (New York: Schocken, 1976), p. 302.

115. Of course this has been extensively discussed; see Richard Wolin's *Heidegger's Children: Hannah Arendt, Karl Löwith, Hans Jonas, and Herbert Marcuse* (Princeton, N.J.: Princeton University Press, 2001).

116. Arendt, *Life of the Mind*, p. 1. See Mark Lilla, *The Reckless Mind: Intellectuals in Politics* (New York: NYRB, 2001), pp. 38–39.

117. Hannah Arendt, *Rahel Varnhagen: The Life of a Jewish Woman*, rev. ed. (San Diego: Harcourt Brace Jovanovich, 1974), p. 3. The book was begun in 1930 but not published until 1956.

118. Arendt, *The Jew as Pariah*, ed. R. H. Feldman (New York: Grove Press, 1978), p. 245.

119. In an interview Arendt stated as much: "My mother . . . came out of the Social Democratic movement . . . as did my father." Arendt, " 'What Remains? The Language Remains': A Conversation with Günter Gaus," in *The Portable Hannah Arendt*, ed. P. Baehr (New York: Penguin Books, 2003), p. 8.

120. Elisabeth Young-Bruehl, *Hannah Arendt*, pp. 8–9, 28.

121. Hannah Arendt, *The Origins of Totalitarianism*, 2nd ed. (New York: World Publishing, 1958), pp. 475, 468–69. For instance, out of vast

literature on ideology, see George Lichtheim, *The Concept of Ideology and Other Essays* (New York: Random House, 1967); and Brian William Head, *Ideology and Social Science: Destutt de Tracy and French Liberalism* (Dordrecht: Maartinus Nijhoff, 1985). To be sure, Arendt knew Mannheim's book, since she reviewed it in 1930; see H. Arendt, "Philosophie und Soziologie: Anlässlich Karl Mannheim, Ideologie und Utopie," *Die Gesellschaft* 1 (1930): 163–76.

122. Arendt, *Origins*, 2nd ed., pp. 443, 458.

123. Hannah Arendt, "Approaches to the 'German Problem,' " *Partisan Review* 12 (1945): 95–96.

124. Hannah Arendt, *Origins of Totalitarianism*, 1st ed. (New York: Harcourt, Brace and Company, 1951), pp. 431–32. This conclusion was dropped from later editions.

125. Arendt, *The Origins of Totalitarianism*, 2nd ed., pp. 470–72.

126. See Roy T. Tsao, "The Three Phases of Arendt's Theory of Totalitarianism," *Social Research* 69, no. 2 (Summer 2002): 579–621. For an overview, see Steven E. Aschheim, "Nazism, Culture, and *The Origins of Totalitarianism*: Hannah Arendt and the Discourse of Evil," in *In Times of Crisis: Essays on European Culture, Germans, and Jews* (Madison: University of Wisconsin Press, 2001), pp. 122–36.

127. Arendt, *Origins*, 2nd ed., p. 470.

128. Arendt, *Origins*, 2nd ed., p. 459.

129. Arendt to Jaspers, 4 March 1951, in Hannah Arendt and Karl Jaspers, *Correspondence, 1926–1969*, ed. L. Kohler and H. Saner (New York: Harcourt Brace Jovanovich: New York, 1992), p. 166.

130. Arendt to Scholem, 24 July 1963, in *The Jew as Pariah*, ed. Feldman, p. 250.

131. Arendt to McCarthy, 20 September 1963, in *Between Friends: The Correspondence of Hannah Arendt and Mary McCarthy, 1949–1975*, ed. C. Brightman (New York: Harcourt Brace, 1995), pp. 147–48.

132. Arendt, *The Life of the Mind*, p. 4.

133. Stephen J. Whitfield, *Into the Dark: Hannah Arendt and Totalitarianism* (Philadelphia: Temple University Press, 1980), p. 225. See Barry Sharpe, *Modesty and Arrogance in Judgment: Hannah Arendt's Eichmann in Jerusalem* (Westport, Conn.: Praeger, 1999.)

134. Richard J. Bernstein, "Did Hannah Arendt Change Her Mind? From Radical Evil to the Banality of Evil," in *Hannah Arendt Twenty Years Later*, ed. L. May and J. Kohn (Cambridge, Mass.: MIT Press, 1996), p. 142.

135. Margaret Canovan, *Hannah Arendt: A Reinterpretation of Her Political Thought* (Cambridge: Cambridge University Press, 1992), p. 24. This book is a learned airbrushing of Arendt's thought. Faced with the obscurities, contradictions, and illogic of Arendt, Canovan offers statements like the following: "As so often when reading Arendt, it is easy to underestimate the complexity of her thinking" (p. 171).

136. Dana R. Villa, *Politics, Philosophy, Terror: Essays on the Thought of Hannah Arendt* (Princeton, N.J.: Princeton University Press, 1999), p. 56. Oddly, Villa himself has changed his mind—in this very same volume: "The criticism I make of Arendt here departs from the more sympathetic reading I give of her notion of radical evil in that essay [chapter 1]" (p. 231). Adi Ophir tries to reconcile her notions of evil; see Adi Ophir, "Between Eichmann and Kant: Thinking on Evil After Arendt," in *History and Memory* 8, no. 2 (Fall 1996): 89–136.

137. Ernst Gellner, *Culture, Identity, and Politics* (Cambridge: Cambridge University Press, 1987), pp. 84–85. Also see Raul Hilberg, *The Politics of Memory: The Journey of a Holocaust Historian* (Chicago: Ivan R. Dee, 1996), pp. 147–57.

138. Richard Crossman, introduction to *The God That Failed*, by André Gide et al., (New York: Bantam Books, 1952), p. 10. Crossman is citing Ignazio Silone.

139. See Dan Diner, "Hannah Arendt Reconsidered: Über das Banale and das Böse in ihrer Holocaust-Erzählung," in *Hannah Arendt Revisited: 'Eichmann in Jerusalem' und die Folgen*, ed. G. Smith (Frankfurt: Surhamp, 2000), pp. 131–32; and William David Jones, *The Lost Debate: German Socialist Intellectuals and Totalitarianism* (Urbana: University of Illinois Press, 1999), pp. 202–3.

3. To Shake the World off Its Hinges

1. Isaac Goldberg, *Major Noah: American-Jewish Pioneer* (Philadelphia: Jewish Publication Society of America, 1936), p. 189.

2. Mordecai Noah, "The Ararat Proclamation and Speech," in *The Selected Writings of Mordecai Noah*, ed. M. Schuldiner and D. J. Kleinfeld (Westport, Conn.: Greenwood Press, 1999), p. 114.

3. See Amos Elon, *The Pity of It All: A History of Jews in Germany, 1743–1933* (New York: Henry Holt, 2002), p. 115.

4. Ben Katchor, *The Jew of New York* (New York: Pantheon Books, 1999), p. 11.

5. Almost as the same time, another plan was hatched for a community in Florida; see Jacob Toury, "M. E. Levy's Plan for a Jewish Colony in Florida—1825," *Michael* 3 (1975): 23–33. See generally, on American Jewish utopian ventures, Uri D. Herscher, *Jewish Agricultural Utopias in America, 1880–1910* (Detroit: Wayne State University Press, 1981).

6. See Bernard W. Weinryb, "Noah's Ararat Jewish State in Its Historical Setting," *Publication of the American Jewish Historical Society* 43 (1953–54): 170–91.

7. Jonathan D. Sarna, *Jacksonian Jew: The Two Worlds of Mordecai Noah* (New York: Holmes and Meier, 1981), p. 68.

8. *Journal des Débats*, 18 November 1825, pp. 2–3. The last phrase reads "défendue comme crime de lèse-authorité divine" (p. 3).

9. Robert S. Wistrich, *Revolutionary Jews from Marx to Trotsky* (New York: Harper and Row, 1976), pp. 2–3.

10. Ernest Renan, *Histoire du peuple d'Israël*, in *Oeuvres complètes*, vol. 6, ed. H. Psichari (Paris: Calmann-Lévy, 1953), p. 12.

11. K. Marx, "Postface to the Second Edition," in *Capital*, intro. E. Mandel, vol. 1, (New York: Vintage Books, 1976), p. 99.

12. For a discussion of the utopianism of *The Jewish State*, see David Herman, "Zionism as Utopian Discourse," *Clio* 23, no. 3 (Spring 1994): 235–47.

13. Theodor Herzl, *The Jewish State* (Mineola, N.Y.: Dover Publications, 1988), pp. 69–72, 102, 105.

14. Theodor Herzl, *The Complete Diaries of Theodor Herzl*, ed. R. Patai, vol. 3 (New York: Herzl Press/Thomas Yoseloff, 1960), p. 1071.

15. Theodor Herzl, *Altneuland: Old-New Land*, trans. P. Arnold (Haifa: Haifa Publishing Co., 1960), pp. 62, 70, 114–15.

16. Miriam Eliav-Feldon, " 'If you will it, it is no fairy tale': The First Jewish Utopias," *Jewish Journal of Sociology* 25, no. 2 (December 1983): 85.

17. Max Osterberg-Verakoff, *Das Reiche Judäa im Jahr 6000 (2241 christlicher Zeitrechnung)* (Stuttgart: Foerster and Sie, 1893), pp. 233–34.

18. H. Pereira Mendes, *Looking Ahead: Twentieth-Century Happenings* (1899; reprint, New York: Arno Press, 1971), pp. 374, 377–78, 381,

19. N.A. (Edmund Eisler), *Ein Zukunftsbild. Romantisches Gemälde* (Vienna: J. H. Holzwarth, 1885).

20. For a discussion of the utopianism of *Altneuland*, see Jeremy Stolow, "Utopia and Geopolitics in Theodor Herzl's *Altneuland*," *Utopian Studies* 8, no. 1 (Winter 1997): p. 55; see also David Herman, "Zionism as Utopian Discourse," 235.

21. Herzl, *Altneuland*, p. 192.

22. Herzl, *Altneuland*, p. 64.

23. Muhammad Ali Khalidi, "Utopian Zionism or Zionist Proselytism? A Reading of Herzl's *Altneuland*" *Journal of Palestine Studies* 30, no. 4 (Summer 2001): 55 ff.

24. Ahad Ha'am, "The Jewish State and the Jewish Problem" (1897), in *The Zionist Idea: A Historical Analysis and Reader*, ed. A. Hertzberg (New York: Atheneum, 1977), pp. 262–69.

25. Achad Haam (Ahad Ha'am), "Altneuland," *Ost und West* 3 (1903): 227–43.

26. Ahad Ha-Am (Ahad Ha'am) to M. Levin, cited in Jacque Kornberg, "Ahad Ha-Am and Herzl," in *At the Crossroads: Essays on Ahad Ha-Am*, ed. J. Kornberg (Albany: State University of New York Press, 1983), p. 116.

27. "Nordau's emphatic diatribe [against Ahad Ha'am] was by far the clearest précis of the synthesis between fin-de-siècle cosmopolitanism and Zionism . . . as Herzl . . . conceived it." Michael Stanislawsi, *Zionism and the Fin de Siècle: Cosmopolitanism and Nationalism from Nordau to Jabotinsky* (Berkeley and Los Angeles: University of California Press, 2001), p. 18.

28. Walter Laqueur, *A History of Zionism* (New York: Schocken Books, 1976), p. 133. Also see David Vital, *Zionism: The Formative Years* (Oxford: Clarendon Press, 1982), pp. 348–63.

29. Max Nordau, "Achad-Haam über 'Altneuland,' " *Die Welt* 7, no. 7 (13 March 1903): 1–5.

30. Of course there are many issues. For instance, the Ahad Ha'am,

tradition of Zionism was much more alert to the issues of the indigenous Palestinians. See Hans Kohn, *Living in a World Revolution: My Encounters with History* (New York: Trident, 1964), pp. 50–52.

31. For a critique of Zionism, see Karl Landauer and Herbert Weil, *Die Zionistische Utopie* (Munich: Hugo Schmidt, 1914).

32. Steven J. Zipperstein, *Elusive Prophet: Ahad Ha'am and the Origins of Zionism* (Berkeley: University of California Press, 1993), p. xxii.

33. Martin Buber, "Die Wägende," in *Die jüdische Bewegung. Gesammelte Aufsätze.* Zweite Folge (Berlin: Jüdischer Verlag, 1920), p. 71. This piece was dedicated to Ahad Ha-Am on his sixtieth birthday.

34. See Jehuda Reinharz, *Fatherland or Promised Land: The Dilemma of the German Jew, 1893–1914* (Ann Arbor: University of Michigan Press, 1975), pp. 146–53.

35. Martin Buber, "Herzl and History," in *The First Buber*, ed. G. C. Schmidt (Syracuse, N.Y.: Syracuse University Press, 1999), p. 160. See Maurice Friedman, *Martin Buber's Life and Word: The Early Years, 1878–1923* (London: Search Press, 1982), pp. 65–66.

36. Friedman, *Buber's Life and Work*, pp. 61–62.

37. Kohn, *Living in a World Revolution*, p. 67, 65.

38. Paul Mendes-Flohr, *Divided Passions: Jewish Intellectuals and the Experience of Modernity* (Detroit: Wayne State University Press, 1991), pp. 84–85.

39. Gershom Scholem, "Martin Buber's Conception of Judaism," in *On Jews and Judaism in Crisis: Selected Essays* (New York: Schocken Books, 1976), p. 138.

40. Martin Buber, "Renewal of Judaism," in *On Judaism*, ed. H. N. Glatzer (New York: Schocken Books, 1995), pp. 37–39.

41. See the exemplary discussion in Ritchie Robertson, *Kafka: Judaism, Politics, and Literature* (Oxford: Claredon Press, 1985), pp. 141–84.

42. Scholem, "Martin Buber's Conception of Judaism," pp. 126–27, 169.

43. Paul Mendes-Flohr, *From Mysticism to Dialogue: Martin Buber's Transformation of German Social Thought* (Detroit: Wayne State University Press, 1989).

44. For Landauer's attraction to and break from "Neue Gemeinschaft," see Getrude Cepl-Kaufmann, "Gustav Landauer and the Literary Trends

of his Time," in *Gustav Landauer: Anarchist and Jew*, ed. P. Mendes-Flohr et al. (forthcoming); and Eugene Lunn, *Prophet of Community: The Romantic Socialism of Gustav Landauer* (Berkeley: University of California Press, 1973), pp. 142–54.

45. Hans Kohn, *Martin Buber: Sein Werk und Seine Zeit* (Köln: Joseph Melzer Verlag, 1961), p. 29. See Michael Löwy, "Romantic Prophets of Utopia: Gustav Landauer and Martin Buber," in *Gustav Landauer: Anarchist and Jew*, ed. P. Mendes-Flohr et al. (forthcoming).

46. Martin Buber, "Alte und neue Gemeinschaft: An Unpublished Buber Manuscript," ed. P. R. Flohr and B. Susser, *AJS Review* 1 (1976): 41–56.

47. Martin Buber, "The Holy Way," in *On Judaism*, ed. H. N. Glatzer (New York: Schocken Books, 1995), pp. 140–41.

48. Martin Buber, *Paths in Utopia* (Syracuse, N.Y.: Syracuse University Press, 1996; first English edition: 1949; first Hebrew: 1946), pp. 6, 9, 15, 136.

49. Buber, *Paths*, pp. 142–43. Most accounts agree with Buber that the kibbutzim neither saw themselves nor were seen as utopian communities with blueprints and definite structures. For instance, one earlier study stated that it is "an error" to classify the kibbutzim "in the same category" as utopian communities. "Unlike the Utopian communities," the kibbutzim "did not originate in a deliberate attempt to mold a new form of social organization on the foundations of a preconceived theory . . . what shaped its character was the necessity for adaption to the unusual conditions obtaining in Palestine." Henrik F. Infield, *Cooperative Living in Palestine* (New York: Dryden Press, 1944), p. 25.

50. Buber, *Paths in Utopia*, pp. 46–57.

51. Gustav Landauer, "Durch Absonderung zur Gemeinschaft," in *Zeit und Geist. Kulturkritische Schriften 1890–1919*, ed. R. Kauffeldt and M. Matzigkeit (n.p.: Klaus Voer Verlag, 1997), p. 99.

52. Karl Mannheim, *Ideology and Utopia* (New York: Harcourt, Brace and World, n.d)., pp. 197–98. This American edition fundamentally differs from the first German edition of 1929.

53. Charles B. Maurer, *Call to Revolution: The Mystical Anarchism of Gustav Landauer* (Detroit: Wayne State University Press, 1971), p. 199.

54. See Adam Weisberger, "Gustav Landauers mystischer Messianismus," *Aschkenas* 5 (1995): 425–39; and Lunn, *Prophet of Community*;

Heinz-Joachim Heydorn, foreword to *Aufruf zum Sozialismus*, by G. Landauer, ed. H.-J. Heydorn (Frankfurt: Europäische Verlagsanstalt, 1967), esp. pp. 23–33.

55. Fritz Kahn, *Die Juden als Rasse und Kulturvolk* (Berlin: Welt-Verlag, 1921), pp. 201–3.

56. Arthur A. Cohen, editor's introduction to "The Maturing of Man and the Maturing of the Jew" [on Landauer], by Ernst Simon, in *The Jew: Essays from Martin Buber's Journal, Der Jude, 1916–1928*, ed. A. A. Cohen (Tuscaloosa: University of Alabama Press, 1980), p. 128.

57. See Norbert Altenhofer, "Martin Buber und Gustav Landauer," in *Martin Buber (1878–1965). Internationales Symposium zum 20. Todestag*, ed. W. Licharz and H. Schmidt, vol. 2 (Frankfurt: Haag and Herchen, 1989), pp. 150–77.

58. See generally, Norbert Altenhofer, "Tradition als Revolution: Gustav Landauers 'geworden-werdendes' Judentum,'" in *Jews and Germans from 1860 to 1933: The Problematic Symbiosis*, ed. D. Bronsen (Heidelberg: Carl Winter Universitätsverlag, 1979), esp. pp. 180–85.

59. Gustav Landauer, *Die Revolution* (Frankfurt: Literarische Anstalt Rütten and Loening, 1919), pp. 80–81.

60. See Paul Breines, "The Jew as Revolutionary: The Case of Gustav Landauer," *Leo Baeck Institute Year Book XII* (1967): 75–84.

61. Gustav Landauer, "Sind das Ketzergedanken?" in *Der werdende Mensch* (Telgte-Westbevern: Verlag Büchse der Pandora, 1977), pp. 120–28.

62. Landauer, "Judentum und Sozialismus," in Landauer, *Dichter, Ketzer, Aussenseiter*, ed. H. Delf, *Werkausgabe*, vol. 3 (Berlin: Akademie Verlag, 1997), pp. 160–61.

63. Landauer, *Skepsis und Mystik: Versuche im Anschluss an Mauthners Sprachkritik* (Berlin: Egon Fleischel, 1903), pp. 69–79.

64. Ernst Bloch, *The Spirit of Utopia*, trans. Anthony A. Nasser (1963; reprint, Stanford, Calif.: Stanford University Press, 2000), pp. 7, 168.

65. Ernst Bloch, *Geist der Utopie* (Berlin: Paul Cassirer, 1923), pp. 247–48. Bloch kept revising this work. For instance the section on Jews in the 1923 edition (pp. 287–299) was dropped from later editions.

66. Landauer to Susman, 31 January 1919, in *Gustav Landauer: Sein Lebensgang in Briefen*, ed. M. Buber, vol. 2 (Frankfurt: Rütten und

Loening, 1929), pp. 371–73. See for a discussion of Landauer and Bloch, Bernhard Braun, *Die Utopie des Geistes. Zur Funktion der Utopie in der politischen Theorie Gustav Landauers* (Idstein: Schulz-Kirchner, 1991), pp. 127–140. Scholem concurred in his sharp criticism of Bloch, although he later revised his judgement; see Scholem, *Walter Benjamin: The Story of a Friendship*, trans. Harry Zohn (London: Faber and Faber, 1982), pp. 88–89 and Scholem, preface to *The Correspondence of Walter Benjamin and Gershom Scholem, 1932–1940*, ed. G. Scholem, trans. Gary Smith and Andre Lefevere (New York: Schocken Books, 1989), p.7.

67. See Karin Bruns, "Politische Utopie und ästhetisches Programm. *Die Neue Gemeinschaft*: Vorläufer oder Gegenentwurf zum Forte-Kreis?" in *Der Potsdamer Forte-Kreis*, ed. R. Faber and C. Holste (Würzburg: Königshausen und Newmann, 2001), pp. 69–84; and generally, Christine Holste, *Der Forte-Kreis (1910–1915). Rekonstruktion eines utopischen Versuchs* (Stuttgart: Verlag für Wissenschaft und Forschung, 1992). The name of the group derived from the location of their proposed founding meeting in an Italian fishing port, Forte dei Marmi; plus the name carried the connotation of strong or courageous (Holste, *Der Forte-Kreis*, p. 1).

68. "An den Forte-Kreis Ende November 1914," in *Gustav Landauer. Sein Lebensgang in Briefen*, vol. 2, ed. M. Buber with I. Britschgi-Schimmer (Frankfurt: Rütten und Loening, 1929), p. 15. This appeal to the Forte circle is signed by both Landauer and Buber. On the sad story of Britschgi-Schimmer, who devoted herself to Landauer's letters, see Wolf von Wolzogen, "Ina Britsgi-Schimmer: Co-Editor of Gustav Landauer's Letters," in *Gustav Landauer: Anarchist and Jew*, ed. by Paul Mendes-Flohr et al. (forthcoming).

69. Martin Buber, "Thesen von Martin Buber," reprinted in Holste, *Der Forte-Kreis*, pp. 280–81.

70. Maurice Friedman, *Martin's Buber's Life and Work*, p. 182.

71. Gershom Scholem, *From Berlin to Jerusalem: Memories of my Youth* (New York: Schocken Books, 1980), p. 81.

72. See generally, Christine Holste, " 'Die grausigste Ideenlosigkeit in ihren Dienst zwingen': Gustav Landauers Entwicklung zum utopischen Denken," in *Gustav Landauer (1870–1919)*, ed. L. M. Fiedler (Frankfurt: Capmus Verlag, 1995), pp. 98–117.

73. Gustav Landauer, *For Socialism*, trans. D. J. Parent (1911; St. Louis:

Telos Press, 1978), p. 38; Landauer, *Aufruf zum Sozialismus*, ed. H.-J. Heydorn (Frankfurt: Europäische Verlagsanstalt, 1967), p. 68.

74. Landauer, *For Socialism*, pp. 65, 54, 74.

75. Gustav Landauer, "Der Musik der Welt" (1905), in *Der werdende Mensch: Aufsätze über Leben und Schrifttum* (Telgte-Westbevern: Verlag Büchse der Pandora, 1977), p. 5.

76. Gustav Landauer, "Gott und der Sozialismus" (1911), in *Der werdende Mensch: Aufsätze über Leben und Schrifttum* (Telgte-Westbevern: Verlag Büchse der Pandora, 1977), p. 33.

77. Ahad Ha'am, "Judaism and the Gospels," in *Nationalism and the Jewish Ethic: Basic Writings of Ahad Ha'am*, ed. H. Kohn, trans. Leon Simon (New York: Schocken, 1962), pp. 295–99.

78. Jörg Asseyer, "Nachwort zur Neu-Herausgabe," in Gustav Landauer, *Skepsis und Mystik* (Telgte-Westbevern: Verlag Büchse der Pandora, 1978), p. 86.

79. George Steiner, *After Babel: Aspects of Language and Translation* (New York: Oxford University Press, 1975), p. 60.

80. Allan Janik and Stephen Toulmin, *Wittgenstein's Vienna* (New York: Simon and Schuster, 1973), pp. 122–23.

81. Mauthner, *Beiträge zu einer Kritik der Sprache*, 2nd ed., vol. 1 (Suttgart: J. G. Cotta'sche Buchhandlung, 1906), p. 118. See Elisabeth Leinfellner, "Fritz Mauthner im historischen Kontext der empiristischen, analytischen und sprachkritischen Philosophie," in *Fritz Mauthner: Das Werk eines kritischen Denkers*, ed. E. Leinfellner and H. Schleichert (Vienna: Böhlau Verlag 1995), pp.145–63.

82. Fritz Mauthner, *Erinnerungen. Prager Jugendjahre* (München: Georg Müller, 1918), pp. 32–33.

83. See Elizabeth Bredeck, *Metaphors of Knowledge: Language and Thought in Mauthner's Critique* (Detroit: Wayne State University Press, 1992).

84. Fritz Mauthner, "Aus dem Märchenbuch der Wahrheit," in *Ausgewählte Schriften*, vol. 5 (Stuttgart: Deutsche Verlags-Anstalt, 1919), pp. 123–24. See Katherine Arens, *Empire in Decline: Fritz Mauthner's Critique of Wilhelmian Germany* (New York: Peter Lang, 2001), pp. 1–30.

85. Fritz Mauthner, in *Die Philosophie der Gegenwart in Selbstdarstellungen*, ed. R. Schmidt (Leipzig: Felix Meiner, 1922), pp. 128–29.

86. Fritz Mauthner, *Die Sprache* (Frankfurt: Literarische Anstalt/ Rütten und Loening, n.d.), p.102.

87. Fritz Mauthner, *Beiträge zu einer Kritik der Sprache*, 2nd ed., vol. 1, pp. 2–3.

88. Landauer, *Skepsis und Mystik*. Also see Thomas Regehly, " 'Die Welt is ohne Sprache.' Bemerkungen zur Sprachkritik Gustav Landauers," in *Gustav Landauer (1870–1919) Eine Bestandsaufnahme zur Rezeptions seines Werkes*, ed. L.M. Fielder, R. Heuer, and A. Taeger-Altenhofer (Frankfurt: Campus Verlag, 1995), pp. 220–24.

89. Landauer to Mauthner, 9 July 1907, in *Gustav Landauer–Fritz Mauthner Briefwechsel 1890–1919*, ed. H. Delf (München: Velag C. H. Beck, 1994), pp. 162–63. I'm taking the translation from *Letters to Fritz Mauthner*, trans. Eleanor Alexander, http://www.mauthner-gesellschaft.de/mauthner/fm/land3.html.

90. He never wrote that book. See Hanah Delf, "Einleitung," in *Gustav Landauer–Fritz Mauthner Briefwechsel 1890–1919*, p. xiv.

91. Fritz Mauthner, *Wörterbuch der Philosophie*, 3d ed. (Leipzig 1910–11). Available from www.mauthner-gesellschaft.de/mauthner.

92. Fritz Mauthner, *Der Atheismus und seine Geschichte im Abendlande* (Stuttgart: Deutsch Verlagsanstelt, 1920–23).

93. Cited in and see, Peter Kampits, *Zwischen Schein und Wirklichkeit: Eine kleine Geschichte der österreichischen Philosophie* (Vienna, 1984). Available from: www.mauthner-gesellschaft.de/vereindersprachkritiker. See Bredeck, *Metaphors of Knowledge*, pp.116–17.

94. Landauer to Mauthner, 17 May, 1911, in *Briefwechsel 1890–1919*, p.232.

95. Landauer, *Skepsis und Mystik*, p. 3–4. See generally Uwe Spörl, "Gustav Landauers Wege von der Skepsis zur Mystik," in *Gottlose Mystik in der deutsche Literatur um die Jahrundertwende* (Paderborn: Ferdinand Schöning, 1997).

96. Landauer, "Sind das Ketzergedanken?" p. 126.

97. Mauthner to Landauer, 10 October 1913, *Briefwechsel 1890–1919*, p. 282.

98. Mauthner, *Erinnerungen*, pp.49–53.

99. Mauthner, *Erinnerungen*, p. 33.

100. Adolf Hitler, *Mein Kampf*, trans. Ralph Mannheim (Boston: Houghton Mifflin, 1971), p. 245.

101. Sander L. Gilman, *Jewish Self-Hatred: Anti-Semitism and the Hidden Language of the Jews* (Baltimore, Md.: Johns Hopkins University Press, 1986), pp. 226–43.

102. Mauthner considered himself an atheist; see Gershom Weiler, "Fritz Mauthner: A Study in Jewish Self-Rejection," *Leo Baeck Institute Year Book* 8 (1963): 136–48

103. Fritz Mauthner, *Beiträge zu einer Kritik der Sprache*, 3rd ed., vol.1 (Leipzig: Felix Meiner, 1923), pp.169–70.

104. Gilman, *Jewish Self-Hatred*, p. 231.

105. Fritz Mauthner, *Beiträge zu einer Kritik der Sprache*, vol. 1, p. 1.

106. Landauer to Kesternberg, 13 December 1917, in *Gustav Landauer. Sein Lebensgang in Briefen*, vol. 2, p. 201.

107. Kurt Eisner, cited in footnote of letter to Adolf Otto, 15 November 1918, in *Gustav Landauer. Sein Lebensgang in Briefen*, vol. 2, p. 296; Landauer to Buber, 15 November 1918, in *Gustav Landauer. Sein Lebensgang in Briefen*, vol. 2, p. 298.

108. Landauer to Mauthner, 7 April 1919, in *Gustav Landauer. Sein Lebensgang in Briefen*, vol. 2, pp. 413–14.

109. For Landauer's last months see, Eugen Lunn, *Prophet of Community*, pp. 291–342; and Charles B. Maurer, *Call to Revolution*, pp. 169–200.

110. Ben Hecht, *A Child of the Century* (New York: Simon and Schuster, 1954), pp. 306, 310.

111. Landauer, "An den Aktionsausschuss," in *Gustav Landauer. Sein Lebensgang in Briefen*, vol. 2, p. 420.

112. "Munich Victors Kill Another Red Chief," *New York Times*, 6 May 1919.

113. Landauer, in *Gustav Landauer. Sein Lebensgang in Briefen*, vol. 2, p. 423.

114. Ernst Niekisch, *Erinnerungen eines deutschen Revolutionärs*, vol. 1, *Gewagtes Leben 1889–1945* (Cologne: Verlag Wissenschaft und Politik, 1974), p. 79. In fact, Niekisch himself was a somewhat problematic figure, an extreme rightist and so-called National Bolshevik.

115. Landauer, *For Socialism*, p. 26; *Aufruf*, p. 55.

116. Maurer, *Call to Revolution*, p. 200. In 1933 the Nazis apparently had the monument destroyed and the grave moved. See Braun, *Die Utopie des Geistes*, p. 114.

117. Landauer, *For Socialism*, p. 44.

4. A Longing That Cannot Be Uttered

1. Carmel Konikoff, *The Second Commandment and Its Interpretation in the Art of Ancient Israel* (Geneva: Imprimerie du Journal de Genève, 1973), p. 26.

2. Christoph Dohmen, *Das Bilderverbot. Seine Entstehung und seine Entwicklung im Alten Testament* (Königstein: Peter Hanstein Verlag, 1985), pp. 15–16. See Tryggve Mettinger, "The Veto on Images and the Aniconic God in Ancient Israel," in *Religious Symbols and Their Functions*, ed. H. Biezais (Stockholm: Almqvist and Wiksell, 1979), pp. 15–29.

3. This is the first line of Ernst Cohn-Wiener's *Jewish Art: Its History from the Beginning to the Presesnt Day* (1929; reprint, Northamptonshire, U.K.: Pilkington Press, 2001), p. 7. How the prohibition on graven images played out in the Christian and Muslim traditions is a separate story that is not the issue here.

4. *Jewish Encyclopedia*, vol. 9, s.v. "painting," p. 465 and http://www.jewishencyclopedia.com.

5. *Jüdisches Lexikon*, vol. 3 (Berlin: Jüdischer Verlag, 1929), s.v. "Kunst, Jüdische," pp. 934–35.

6. See Katman P. Bland, "Anti-Semitism and Aniconism: The Germanophone Requiem for Jewish Visual Art," in *Jewish Identity in Modern Art History*, ed. C. M. Soussloff (Berkeley: University of California Press 1999), p. 44.

7. On Renan and his interpretation of Judaism, see David C. J. Lee, *Ernest Renan: In the Shadow of Faith* (London: Duckworth, 1996), pp. 207–33.

8. Yaacov Shavit, "Have Jews Imagination?" in *Athens in Jerusalem: Classical Antiquity and Hellenism in the Making of the Modern Secular Jew* (London: Littman Library, 1997), pp. 220–77.

9. See Bland, "Anti-Semitism and Aniconism," pp. 41–66.

10. Gabrielle Sed-Rajna, *L'Art juif orient et occident* (Paris: Arts and Métiers Graphiques, 1975), pp. 10–11. See also Pierre Prigent, *Le Judaïsme et l'image* (Tübingen: J. C. Mohr/Paul Siebeck, 1990); Gabrielle Sed-Rajna, "L'Argument de l'iconophobie juive," in *Nicée II, 787–1987: Douze*

Siècles D'Images Religeuses, ed. F. Boesflug and N. Lossky (Paris: Les Éditions du Cerf, 1987), pp. 81–88. The more recent study by Sed-Rajna notes that past work on the Jewish art has been "defensive." See the preface to her *Jewish Art*, with essays by A. Amishai-Maisels et al. (New York: Harry N. Abrams, 1997), p. 9. For a summary of an older discussion, see Gavriel D. Rosenfeld, "Defining 'Jewish Art' in Ost and West, 1901–1908," *Leo Baeck Institute Year Book 1994* 39 (1994): 83–110.

11. *Jewish Encyclopedia*, vol. 10, s.v. "Pictorial Art," p. 32. Theodor W. Adorno, *Aesthetic Theory*, ed. and trans. Robert Hallot-Kentor (Minneapolis: University of Minnesota Press, 1997).

12. Avram Kampf, "In the Quest of the Jewish Style in the Era of the Russian Revolution," *Journal of Jewish Art* 5 (1978): 64.

13. El Lissitzky, "The Synagogue of Mohilev, Reminiscences," cited in Avram Kampf, *Chagall to Kitaj: Jewish Experience in Twentieth Century Art* (New York: Praeger, 1990), p. 19.

14. See Rachel Wischnitzer, *The Architecture of the European Synagogue* (Philadelphia: Jewish Publication Society of America, 1964), pp. 141–44; and her "The Wise Men of Worms," *Reconstructionist* 25, no. 9 (June 1959): 10–12.

15. S. Yudovin and M. Malkin, *Yiddischer Folksornament* (1920), cited in Kampf, "In the Quest," p. 55.

16. The temple was later destroyed by the Soviets.

17. Of course, controversy about Jewish art continues. For an argument that Lissitzky's later work owes much to his Judaism, see Alan B. Birnholz, "El Lissitzky and the Jewish Tradition," *Studio International* 186, no. 959 (October, 1973): 130–136. In *Chagall to Kitaj*, Kampf finds a Jewish art in the abstract expressionists of the New York School like Barnett Newman: "Newman worked in the classic 'no graven image' tradition of Judaism not because images are forbidden, but because the absolute cannot be rendered by an image. It is a purely abstract conception, imageless, like the Jewish God" (p. 161). On the other hand, Anthony Julius in his book on Jewish art, *Idolizing Pictures: Idolatry, Iconoclasm, and Jewish Art* (New York: Thames and Hudson, 2001), pp. 42–48, challenges Kampf. Do Jewish motifs constitute Jewish art? According to Julius, the Jewish Abstract Expressionists largely ignored their origins, and their art lacked anything especially Jewish.

18. Edward Rothstein, Herbert Muschamp, and Martin E. Marty, *Visions of Utopia* (New York: Oxford University Press, 2003).

19. J. A. Etzler, *The Paradise within the Reach of All Men, Without Labor, By Power of Nature and Machinery*, 2 parts (Pittsburgh: Etzler and Reinhold, 1833), part 1, pp. 71–74.

20. A partial exception: the more recent anthology includes two pages from Karl Marx, his *Communist Manifesto*—hardly a utopian text. See G. Negley and J. Max Patrick, eds., *The Quest for Utopia: An Anthology of Imaginary Societies* (1952; Garden City, N.Y.: Doubleday/Anchor, 1962); and G. Claeys and L. T. Sargent, eds. *The Utopia Reader* (New York: New York University Press, 1999).

21. See Ronald S. Hendel, "The Social Origins of the Aniconic Tradition in Early Israel," *Catholic Biblical Quarterly* 50, no. 3(July 1988): 365–82.

22. Hermann Vorländer, "Der Monotheismus Israels als Antwort auf die Krise des Exils," in *Der einzige Gott: Die Geburt des biblischen Monotheismus*, ed. B. Land (Munich: Kösel, 1981), pp. 84–113.

23. Joseph Gutmann, "The 'Second Commandment' and the Image of Judaism," in *No Graven Images: Studies in Art and the Hebrew Bible*, ed. J. Gutmann (New York: Ktav Publishing, 1971), p. 3.

24. Alain Besançon, *The Forbidden Image: An Intellectual History of Iconoclasm* (Chicago: University of Chicago Press, 2000), p. 69.

25. For a good discussion of the literature, see Robert Karl Gnuse, *No Other Gods: Emergent Monotheism in Israel* (Sheffield: Sheffield Academic Press, 1997): "The romantic ideas of yore that monotheism should be connected to the desert . . . have been thoroughly discredited. . . . Monotheistic Yahwism more likely arose in the urban centers of Mesopotamia during the Babylonian exile" (p. 131).

26. See a fragment from *Sibylline Oracles* cited in John R. Bartlett, *Jews in the Hellenistic World: Josephus, Aristeas, the Sibylline Oracles, Eupolemus* (Cambridge: Cambridge University Press, 1985), p. 39; and *The Sibylline Oracles*, trans. M. S. Terry (New York: Easton and Mains, 1899), p. 261. See also Erich S. Gruen, *Heritage and Hellenism: The Reinvention of Jewish Tradition* (Berkeley: University of California Press, 1998), pp. 268–91.

27. See generally Moshe Halbertal and Avishai Margalit, *Idolatry* (Cambridge: Harvard University Press, 1992).

28. Max Weber, *Ancient Judaism*, trans. H. H. Gerth, D. Martindale (New York: Free Press, 1967), pp. 222–25.

29. Josephus "Flavius Josephus Against Apion," in *The Works of Josephus*, ed. W. Whiston (Peabody, Mass.: Hendrickson, 1987), p. 786. Erich S. Gruen dubs this tale "a neat illustration of the sardonic humor" of Jewish-Hellenistic writers; see his *Heritage and Hellenism*, p. 205.

30. Moses Maimonides, *The Guide for the Perplexed*, trans. M. Friedländer (New York: Dover Publications, 1956), pp. 317. See Ehud Z. Benor, "Meaning and Reference in Maimonides' Negative Theology" *Harvard Theological Review* 88, no. 3 (July 1995): 339 ff.

31. Maimonides, *Guide for the Perplexed*, p. 81.

32. Maimonides, *Guide for the Perplexed*, p. 87.

33. Moses Mendelssohn, *Jerusalem, or On Religious Power and Judaism*, intro. A. Altmann (Hanover, N.H.: Brandeis University Press, 1983), p. 116.

34. Leo Strauss, "Introductory Essay," in Hermann Cohen, *Religion of Reason Out of the Sources of Judaism*, trans. S. Kaplan, 2nd ed. (Atlanta: Scholar's Press, 1995), p. xxiii.

35. Cohen, *Religion of Reason*, pp. 53–57.

36. For the twentieth century perhaps the most salient exemplar of this was Oskar Goldberg, an acquaintance of both Walter Benjamin and Gershom Scholem, who writes about him in his memoirs and generally dismissed his "extravagant notions." See Manfred Voigts, *Oskar Goldberg. Der mythische Experimentalwissenschaftler. Ein verdrängtes Kapitel jüdischer Geschichte* (Berlin: Agora Verlag, 1992.)

37. Moses Mendelssohn, *Jerusalem*, p. 117–19.

38. Leo Baeck, *God and Man in Judaism* (New York: Union of American Hebrew Congregations, 1958), p. 19.

39. Gershom Scholem, *On the Kabbala and Its Symbolism* (New York: Schocken Books, 1969), pp. 44–45, 39.

40. Scholem, *On the Kabbala*, pp. 49–50.

41. Scholem, *On the Kabbala*, p. 42.

42. See M. Reisel, *The Myserious Name of Y.H.W.H.* (Assen, Netherlands: Van Gorcum, 1957).

43. David Biale, "Gershom Scholem's Ten Unhistorical Aphorisms on Kabbalah: Text and Commentary," *Modern Judaism* 5 (1985): 86. This includes Scholem's text in German with commentary by David Biale.

44. See Louis Jacobs, "Excursus: The Names of God," in *A Jewish Theology* (New York: Behrman House, 1973), pp. 136–51.

45. Judah Halevi, *The Kuzari*, intro. H. Slonimsky (New York: Schocken, 1964), p. 203.

46. A. Marmorstein, *The Old Rabbinic Doctrine of God: I. The Names and Attributes of God* (London: Oxford University Press, 1927), pp. 55, 26. The literature on this topic is vast. See Oskar Grether, *Name und Wort Gottes im Alten Testament* (Giessen: Alfred Töpelmann, 1934).

47. Cited in and see George F. Moore, *Judaism in the First Centuries of the Christian Era*, vol. 1 (Cambridge, Mass.: Harvard University Press, 1950), p. 426.

48. Louis Jacobs, *The Jewish Religion: A Companion* (New York: Oxford University Press, 1995), p. 545. See Reisel, *Mysterious Name*, pp. 66–68.

49. Rabbi Israel of Rizhin, cited in Scholem, *The Messianic Idea in Judaism* (New York: Schocken Books, 1971), p. 34–35.

50. See Anson Rabinbach, "Between Apocalypse and Enlightenment: Benjamin, Bloch, and Modern German-Jewish Messianism," in *In the Shadow of Catastrophe* (Berkeley: University of California Press, 1997), pp. 27–65. For a bracing critique of Benjamin on language, see Robert Alter, *Necessary Angels: Tradition and Modernity in Kafka, Benjamin, and Scholem* (Cambridge, Mass.: Harvard University Press, 1991), pp. 45–46.

51. Franz Rosenzweig, *The Star of Redemption*, trans. William W. Hallo from the 2nd ed. (Boston: Beacon Press, 1972), p. 77. See Benjamin, *The Origin of German Tragic Drama* (London: NLB, 1977), pp. 107–8.

52. David Biale, "Gershom Scholem's Ten Unhistorical Aphorisms," 86.

53. Leo Strauss, *Liberalism Ancient and Modern* (Ithaca, N.Y.: Cornell University Press, 1989), p. 272.

54. See Verenz Lenzen, *Jüdisches Leben und Sterben im Namen Gottes* (Munich: Piper, 1995), pp. 111–29.

55. See generally Elizabeth A. Pritchard, "Bilderverbot Meets Body in Theodor W. Adorno's Inverse Theology" *Harvard Theological Review* 95, no. 3 (July 2002): 291–319; and René Buchholz, *Zwischen Mythos und Bilderverbot. Die Philosophie Adornos als Anstoss zu einer kritischen Fundamentaltheologie im Kontext der späten Moderne* (Frankfurt: Peter Lang, 1991).

56. Theodor Adorno, *Minima Moralia: Reflections from Damaged Life* (London: NLB, 1974), p. 80.

57. T. W Adorno, *Negative Dialectics* (New York: Seabury Press, 1973), p. 207.

58. Cited in and see Buchholz, *Zwischen Mythos*, pp. 112–14.

59. T. W. Adorno and Max Horkheimer, *Dialectic of Enlightenment*, trans. J. Cumming (New York: Herder and Herder, 1972), p. 23.

60. Horkheimer to Otto O. Herz, 1 September 1969, in Detlev Claussen, *Theodor W. Adorno. Ein Leztes Genie* (Frankfurt: Fischer Verlag, 2003), p. 429. This is an outstanding study of Adorno.

61. Of course, the ethic of silence is not exclusively Jewish; see George Steiner, *Language and Silence* (New York: Antheneum, 1967): "This revaluation of silence . . . is one of the most original, characteristic acts of the modern spirit. . . . In much modern poetry silence represents the claims of the ideal; to speak is to say less" (p. 48).

62. Ludwig Wittgenstein, *Tractatus Logico-Philosophicus*, trans. D. F. Pears and B. F. McGuinness (1921; London: Routledge, 1961), p. 74.

63. G. H. von Wright, cited in Allan Janik, *Essays on Wittgenstein and Weininger* (Amsterdam: Rodopi, 1985), p. 64.

64. See David Stern, "Was Wittgenstein a Jew?" and Brian McGuinness, "Wittgenstein and the Idea of Jewishness," both in *Wittgenstein: Biography and Philosophy*, ed. J. C. Klagge (Cambridge: Cambridge University Press, 2001), pp. 221–71.

65. Ray Monk, *Ludwig Wittgenstein: The Duty of a Genius* (New York: Penguin Books, 1991), pp. 19–25, 312–18. See Allan Janik, *Essays on Wittgenstein and Weininger*.

66. On Engelmann, see J. Bakacsy, A. V. Munch, and A.-L. Sommer, eds. *Architecture Language Critique: Around Paul Engelmann* (Amsterdam: Rodopi, 2000).

67. Allan Janik and Stephen Toulmin, *Wittgenstein's Vienna* (New York: Simon and Schuster, 1973). See also Allan Janik, "Paul Engelmann's Role in Wittgenstein's Philosophical Development," in *Architecture Language Critique: Around Paul Engelmann*, ed. J. Bakacsy, A. V. Munch, and A.-L. Sommer (Amsterdam: Rodopi, 2000), pp. 40–58; and Jacques Le Rider, *Modernity and Crises of Identity: Culture and Society in Fin-de-Siècle Vienna* (New York: Continuum, 1993), pp. 52–55.

68. The poet was Ludwig Uhland. A recent book on him opens, "even a knowledgeable reader will not be blamed for asking: Ludwig Who? For a poet who several generations ago was a standard figure of the literary canon Ludwig Uhland has fallen upon hard times." Victor G. Doerksen, *Ludwig Uhland and the Critics* (Columbia, S.C.: Camden House, 1994), p. xi.

69. Wittgenstein to Engelmann, 9 April 1917, in Paul Engelmann, *Letters from Ludwig Wittgenstein with a Memoir* (New York: Horizon Press, 1967), p. 7.

70. Engelmann, *Letters*, p. 97; emphasis in original.

71. Cited in the editor's appendix in Engelmann, *Letters*, p. 143.

72. Leo Strauss, "Literary Character of the *Guide for the Perplexed*" (1941), in *Persecution and the Art of Writing* (Chicago: University of Chicago Press, 1988), p. 73.

73. Leo Strauss, *Persecution and the Art of Writing*, pp. 24–25.

74. David Biale, "Gershom Scholem's Ten Unhistorical Aphorisms," pp. 72–73. Here again in Scholem we find an anarchist note, what David N. Myers has called Scholem's "pervasive religious anarchism." Scholem once stated, "we are perhaps anarchists, but we are opposed to anarchy": Scholem, from the protocol of the Ha-'ol study circle in the Judah Leib Magnes Papers, cited in Paul Mendes-Flohr, *Divided Passions: Jewish Intellectuals and the Experience of Modernity* (Detroit: Wayne State University Press, 1991), p. 400. In this regard it is worth noting (following Myers who is following Barukh Kurzweil) that Scholem in his essay on Buber had identified the philosopher of Hasidism as a religious anarchist. Scholem had a sentence that he dropped from later versions of the Buber essay: "I am an anarchist myself, though not one of Buber's persuasion." See David N. Myers, *Re-Inventing the Jewish Past: European Jewish Intellectuals and the Zionist Return to History* (New York: Oxford University Press, 1995), generally pp. 151–176. David Biale notes that Scholem identified himself as a "theological anarchist." See Biale, *Gershom Scholem: Kabbalah and Counter-History*, 2nd ed. (Cambridge, Mass.: Harvard University Press, 1982), p. 22.

75. Max Horkheimer, "Art and Mass Culture" (1941) in *Selected Essays* (New York: Seabury Press, 1972), pp. 273–90.

76. See Susan A. Handelman, *The Slayers of Moses: The Emergence of*

Rabbinic Interpretation in Modern Literary Theory (Albany: State University of New York Press, 1982), chap. 2, pp. 27–50.

77. Barry Sanders, *A is for Ox* (New York: Pantheon Books, 1994), pp. 56–57.

78. José Faur, *Golden Doves with Silver Dots: Semiotics and Textuality in Rabbinic Tradition* (Bloomington: Indiana University Press, 1986), pp. 9–10. Faur uses these ideas to draw parallels with modern literary theory. See the critical review by Robert Alter, *The New Republic*, 5 January 1987, 27 ff.

79. Baruch Spinoza, *Hebrew Grammar*, ed. M. J. Bloom (1677; New York: Philosophical Library, 1962), p. 7.

80. For an argument that the Rabbinic method informs modern literary criticism, see Susan A. Handelman, *The Slayers of Moses*.

81. Besançon, *The Forbidden Image*, p. 71.

82. Cohen, *Religion of Reason*, p. 37.

83. Franz Rosenzweig, *The Star of Redemption*, trans. W. W. Hallo, from 2nd ed. (Boston: Beacon Press, 1972), pp. 245–46. While Rosenzweig is here defending poetry, he was hardly a critic of the image; see the discussion in Leora Batnitzky, *Idolatry and Representation: The Philosophy of Franz Rosenzweig Reconsidered* (Princeton, N.J.: Princeton University Press, 2000), pp. 83–90.

84. See David N. Myers, *Resisting History: Historicism and is Discontents in German-Jewish Thought* (Princeton, N.J.: Princeton University Press, 2003), p. 74.

85. Heinrich Gratz, "Judaism Can Be Understood Only Through Its History," in *Ideas of Jewish History*, ed. M. A. Meyer (Detroit: Wayne State University Press, 1987), pp. 222–23

86. Martin Jay, *Downcast Eyes: The Denigration of Vision in Twentieth-Century French Thought* (Berkeley: University of California Press, 1993), pp. 543–60.

87. Ernst Bloch, *The Spirit of Utopia*, trans. Anthony A. Nasser (1963; reprint, Stanford, Calif.: Stanford University Press, 2000), p. 144. The category of "*noch nicht*," which he may have borrowed from Landauer, assumes great importance in Bloch's work.

88. Hans Jonas, "The Nobility of Sight," in *The Phenomenon of Life: Towards a Philosophical Biology* (Chicago: University of Chicago Press, 1982), pp. 136–39.

89. For a dissenting interpretation, see the learned and strange book by Elliot R. Wolfson, *Through a Speculum That Shines: Vision and Imagination in Medieval Jewish Mysticism* (Princeton, N.J.: Princeton University Press, 1994). "A distinctive feature of the ocularcentrism in medieval Jewish mysticism is a phallocentrism. . . . The specularized figure that provides the foundational condition for the visionary experience is the disclosure of the phallus . . . it becomes evident . . . the Kabbalist is visually contemplating the divine phallus" (pp. 395–97). A *meshugener*.

90. Israel Eldad, cited in Shavit, *Athens in Jerusalem*, p. 200.

91. Lionel Kochan, *Beyond the Graven Image: A Jewish View* (New York: New York University Press, 1997), pp. 164–65.

92. Jacques Ellul, *The Humiliation of the Word* (Grand Rapids, Mich.: William B. Eerdmans, 1985), pp. 13–14.

93. Walter Benjamin, "Theses on the Philosophy of History," in *Illuminations: Essays and Reflections*, ed. H. Arendt (New York: Harcourt, Brace and World, 1968), p. 266.

94. Moses Hess, *Rome and Jerusalem: A Study in Jewish Nationalism*, intro. M. Waxman (New York: Bloch Publishing, 1943), pp. 108–9.

95. Yaacov Shavit's *Athens in Jerusalem* opens with this quote from Tertullian (p. 1). See Louis H. Feldman, *Studies in Hellenistic Judaism* (Leiden: E. J. Brill, 1996), pp. 487–503.

96. Heinrich Heine, "Ludwig Börne," in *Heinrich Heines Sämtliche Werke*, vol. 8 (Leipzig: Insel-Verlag, 1913), p. 360.

97. Heinrich Heine, cited in Bluma Goldstein, *Reinscribing Moses: Heine, Kafka, Freud, and Schoenberg in a European Wilderness* (Cambridge:, Mass. Harvard University Press, 1992), p. 25.

98. See generally Goldstein, *Reinscribing Moses*, pp. 21–39.

99. Heinrich Heine, "Geständnisse," *Heinrich Heines Sämtliche Werke*, vol. 10 (Leipzig: Insel-Verlag, 1913), pp. 183–84; and Heine, "Moses" (1854), in *The Poetry and Prose of Heinrich Heine*, ed. F. Ewen (New York: Citadel Press, 1948), pp. 661–62.

100. For a good discussion of Arnold's shift, see Donald D. Stone, "Matthew Arnold and the Pragmatics of Hebraism and Hellenism," *Poetics Today* 19, no. 2 (Summer 1998): 179–98.

101. Mathew Arnold, *Culture and Anarchy and Other Writings*, ed. S. Collini (New York: Cambridge University Press, 1993), chaps. 4 and 5.

102. While educing many examples of this polarity, Shavit believes that the notion the Greeks excelled in the visual is "unfounded" (Shavit, *Athens in Jerusalem*, p. 201).

103. Walter J. Ong, *Orality and Literacy: The Technologizing of the Word* (London: Methuen, 1987), pp. 90–91.

104. Plato, *The Republic*, book 10, in *Collected Dialogues*, ed. E. Hamilton and H. Cairns (New York: Bollingen/Pantheon, 1963), p. 832.

105. Eric A. Havelock, *Preface to Plato* (Cambridge, Mass.: Harvard University Press, 1963), pp. 43–47.

106. See generally Eugene H. Reed, "Herder, Primitivism, and the Age of Poetry," *Modern Language Review* 60, no. 4 (October, 1965): 550–67

107. J. G. Herder, *The Spirit of Hebrew Poetry*, vol. 2 (German, 1782; Eng. trans., 1833; Naperville, Ill.: Aleph Press, 1971), p. 10.

108. Thorleif Boman, *Hebrew Thought Compared with Greek* (London: SCM Press, 1960), p. 27.

109. Boman, *Hebrew Thought*, pp. 206, 205.

110. Mathew Arnold, "Heinrich Heine" (1863) in *Essays in Criticism: First Series*, ed. Sister T. M. Hoctor (Chicago: University of Chicago Press, 1968), p. 113. The editors of the University of Michigan Press scholarly edition of Arnold's works (*The Complete Prose Works of Matthew Arnold*, vol. 3, *Lectures and Essays in Criticism*, ed. R. H. Super [Ann Arbor: University of Michigan Press, 1962], p. 439], footnote Romans 8:26 as the sources of Arnold's quotation. "Likewise the Spirit also helpeth our infirmities: for we know not what we should pray for as we ought: but the Spirit itself maketh intercession for us with groanings which cannot be uttered."

111. For a compilation, see Michael Higger, *The Jewish Utopia* (Baltimore, Md.: Lord Baltimore Press, 1932).

112. I. Epstein, ed., *The Babylonian Talmud seder zera'im*, Berakoth 57b, (London: Soncino Press, 1948), part 5, vol. 1, p. 356.

113. Gustav Landauer, *For Socialism*, trans. D. J. Parent (1911; St. Louis: Telos Press, 1978), p. 44.

114. Arnold, "Heinrich Heine," p. 113; Heinrich Heine, *Pictures of Travel*, trans. C. G. Leland (New York: D. Appleton, 1904), p. 301. Translation slightly altered. See Heine, *Reisebilder*, in *Sämtliche Werke*, vol. 2 (Munich: Winkler-Verlag, 1969), pp. 268–69.

115. Heine, *Pictures of Travel*, p. 259.

116. Kurt Wilhelm, "The Idea of Humanity in Judaism," in *Studies in Rationalism, Judaism, and Universalism*, ed. R. Loewe (London: Routledge and Kegan Paul, 1966), p. 297.

Epilogue

1. Lewis Mumford, *The Story of Utopias* (1922; rev. ed., New York: Viking Press, 1962), p. 2.

2. Thomas More, *Utopia*, intro. P. Turner (1516; New York: Penguin Books, 1965), p. 49.

3. Max Horkheimer, "Beginnings of the Bourgeois Philosophy of History," in *Between Philosophy and Social Science: Selected Early Writings*, intro. G. F. Hunter (Cambridge, Mass.: MIT Press, 1993), p. 369.

4. "Ironically," writes Robert Wojtowicz in his study of Mumford, "the root cause of Mumford's later pessimism was 'utopia.' " Robert Wojtowicz, *Lewis Mumford and American Modernism* (Cambridge: Cambridge University Press, 1996), p. 162.

5. T. W. Adorno, in "Something's Missing: A Discussion between Ernst Bloch and Theodor W. Adorno on the Contradictions of Utopian Longing," in Ernst Bloch, *The Utopian Function of Art and Literaturre*, ed. J. Zipes and F. Mecklenburg (Cambridge, Mass.: MIT Press, 1988), p. 11–12. For a comparison of Adorno's and Bloch's ideas on utopia, see Inge Münz-Koenen, *Konstruktion des Nirgendwo. Die Diskursivität des Utopischen bei Bloch, Adorno, Habermas* (Berlin: Akademie Verlag, 1997).

6. Ernst Bloch, *The Principle of Hope*, vol. 3 (Cambridge, Mass.: MIT Press, 1995), p. 1313.

7. I am borrowing this fomulation from Perry Anderson, who draws upon Fourier. See Perry Anderson, "The River of Time," *New Left Review* 26 (March–April 2004): 77.

Index

Kafka, Franz, xvii, 34, 36; anarchism and, 36; Zionism and, 93

Kahn, Fritz, 97

Kampf, Avram, 117

Kant, Immanuel, 74, 75, 116; Berlin on, 64–65, 68

Karabell, Zachary, 3

Katchor, Ben, 83, 84

Kautsky, Karl, 50

Khalidi, Muhammad Ali, 89–90

Khmer Rouge, 16

kibbutzim, 16; utopianism and, 96, 181n49

Kid's Stuff (Cross), 29

King James Bible, 44, 45

Kline, Steven, 29

Kochan, Lionel, 136

Koestler, Arthur, 49

Kohn, Hans, 33, 92–93

Kraus, Karl, 103; critique of, 109

Kritik der Sprache (Mauthner). *See Critique of Language*

Landauer, Gustav, xvii, 34, 96–100; as activist, 110–11; anarchism and, 101; Buber and, 94–95, 96–97, 98–99, 100–101, 108, 111, 112; Celan and, 152n15; execution of, 111–12; German revolution and, 110–11; grave of, 186n116; iconoclastic utopianism and, 101–2, 112; on images/language, 102; Mauthner and, 105–8, 110; mysticism, Christian, and, 99–100; on socialism/Marxism, 101, 111, 112; on utopia, 141; Whitman, Walt, and, 111

language: critique of, 106, 108; fetishism and, 109, 123; identity and, 108; idolatry and, 121–22, 123–28, 190n36; Landauer on, 102;

Mauthner on, 103–5, 109–10; Second Commandment and, 124; Semitic v. Greek, 139

Language (Mauthner), 105

Language and Silence (Steiner), 192n61

Laquer, Walter, 60, 90

Legend of the Baal-Shem (Buber), 97

Leitenberg, Milton, 21

Lemkin, Raphael, 13, 156n44

Leninism, 20

Levien, Max, 111

Levinas, Emmanuel, 135

Leviticus, 113

Lewis, C. S., 49

liberalism, xi

Life and Death of Great American Cities, 30

The Life of the Mind (Arendt), 73, 74, 79, 80–81

Lissitzky, El, 117

Looking Ahead: Twentieth-Century Happenings (Mendes), 88

Looking Backward (Bellamy), xv–xvi, 2, 87–88

Löwy, Michael, 34, 36

Lucian, 40–41; More and, 41, 42

Luther, Martin, xiii

Lutheranism, 52; More and, 46 47, 48–49

Luxemburg, Rosa, 84; Arendt and, 51, 75

Lysistrata (Aristophanes), 40

Machiavelli, Niccolo, 63

Maeterlinck, Maurice, 104, 128

Maimonides, Moses: negative theology of, 35, 121–22, 127; on oral transmission, 131, 133; Wittgenstein and, 130–31

of, 129–30, 131; poetry of Uhland,
Ludwig, and, 130, 193n68
Wittgenstein's Vienna (Janik and
Toulmin), 104, 129
The Woman (Bebel), 88
Wordsworth, William, 23–24
Works and Days (Hesiod), 37–38
The World of Imagination (Brann), 23
World War I, ix, 19, 20, 51, 52, 57–58,
95, 105, 110, 146; Hitler on, 14; po-
litical crisis and, 100
World War II, 19, 20, 21, 27–28, 95,
132; anti-utopianism following, 50

Young-Bruhl, Elisabeth, 75

Zamyatin, Yevgeny, 11–12, 22–23,
155–56n39; as utopian, 156n47
Zeus, 37, 39
Zionism: Arendt and, 74; Buber and,
91–93; cultural v. political, 90–91,
179n27, 179–80n30; Ha'am on,
180n30; Herzl and, 85; Kafka and,
93
Zukunftsbild (Eisler), 88
Zunz, Leopold, 83

———